Preaching the Incarnation

Preaching
the Incarnation

Peter K. Stevenson
Stephen I. Wright

WESTMINSTER
JOHN KNOX PRESS
LOUISVILLE • KENTUCKY

First edition
Published by Westminster John Knox Press
Louisville, Kentucky

10 11 12 13 14 15 16 17 18 19—10 9 8 7 6 5 4 3 2 1

Unless otherwise indicated, Scripture quotations are from the New Revised Standard Version of the Bible, copyright © 1989 by the Division of Christian Education of the National Council of the Churches of Christ in the U.S.A., and are used by permission.

A part of the sermon herein by Anna Carter Florence was originally published in *Lectionary Homiletics* in 2007 and 2008 and is used by permission of the publisher of *Lectionary Homiletics*.

Library of Congress Cataloging-in-Publication Data

Stevenson, Peter K.
  Preaching the incarnation / Peter K. Stevenson, Stephen I. Wright.
      p. cm.
  Includes bibliographical references and indexes.
  ISBN 978-0-664-23280-1 (alk. paper)
  1. Incarnation—Sermons. 2. Incarnation—Sermons—History and criticism.
3. Sermons, English—History and criticism. 4. Incarnation—Biblical teaching.
5. Bible—Homiletical use. 6. Preaching. I. Wright, Stephen I. II. Title.
  BT220.S74 2010
  232'.1—dc22

                                                                     2009033743

PRINTED IN THE UNITED STATES OF AMERICA

∞ The paper used in this publication meets the minimum requirements
of the American National Standard for Information Sciences—
Permanence of Paper for Printed Library Materials, ANSI Z39.48-1992.

Westminster John Knox Press advocates the responsible use of our natural resources. The text paper of this book is made from 30% post-consumer waste.

Contents

Preface   vii

Acknowledgements   ix

Abbreviations   xi

Introduction   xiii

Chapter 1: The involved 'I AM': Exodus 3.1–15   1
Sermon: Thomas G. Long, 'The God of good appearances'

Chapter 2: Embodied Wisdom: Proverbs 8 and John 1.1–14   21
Sermon: William Willimon, 'Personification'

Chapter 3: 'God with us': Matthew 1.1–25 and Luke 1.26–2.21   37
Sermon: Rowan Williams, 'The joy and sorrow of God'

Chapter 4: From infant to adolescent: Luke 2.21–52   55
Sermon: Stephen I. Wright, 'Signs of life and death'

Chapter 5: 'Who do you say that I am?' Luke 9.18–27   71
Sermon: Anna Carter Florence, 'Who do you say that I am?'

Chapter 6: Struggling to obey God: Mark 14.32–42   89
Sermon: Peter K. Stevenson, 'Struggling to obey God'

Chapter 7: In the likeness of sinful flesh: Romans 8.1–8   105
Sermon: Calvin T. Samuel, 'In the likeness of human flesh'

Chapter 8: The self-emptying Christ: Philippians 2.1–11   127
Sermon: Michael J. Quicke, 'Going up? Going down?'

Chapter 9: God's true image: Colossians 1.15–20   149
Sermon: Stephen I. Wright, 'Images and the image of God'

Chapter 10: Able to help: Hebrews 2.5–18   165
Sermon: Peter K. Stevenson, 'Living well . . . in suffering'

Conclusion   187

Bibliography   189

Notes   199

Subject and Name Index   219

Scripture and Ancient Source Index   223

Preface

Like its predecessor, *Preaching the Atonement*, this book is a by-product of our experience of working together in teaching homiletics at Spurgeon's College in London. In it we have tried to unearth insights from the disciplines of biblical studies and systematic theology which we hope will offer resources for *Preaching the Incarnation*.

Preaching is a daunting task, which does not appear to get any easier! Making time to prepare is always a challenge, but we want to encourage preachers to listen carefully to Scripture, engage with the Christian tradition, and be sensitive to the cultural 'signs of the times'.

We are very grateful to a number of people who have generously agreed to contribute sermons: Professor Thomas Long, Bishop Will Willimon, Archbishop Rowan Williams, Professor Anna Carter Florence, Dr Calvin T. Samuel and Professor Michael Quicke. When these sermons arrived, it was encouraging to find, over and over again, how much they complemented and enhanced what we were trying to do in each chapter. Both of us continue to preach regularly, and we have each contributed two of our own sermons.

The chapters move, in biblical order, from the Old Testament, on to the Gospels, finishing up in the Epistles. In reading, some may find it useful to follow that sequence; but since each chapter can stand alone, others may prefer to read the chapters in a different order. Taken as a whole, the book seeks to explore the doctrine of the incarnation from a variety of perspectives. We hope that it will stimulate and provoke you to proclaim the good news of the incarnation.

Stephen has had overall responsibility for Chapters 1–4 and 9, Peter for Chapters 5–8 and 10. However, we are glad once more to add our joint signature to the whole.

Peter Stevenson
Stephen Wright

Acknowledgements

We are grateful to all who have contributed in any way to the preparation of this book.

Our thanks must go especially to the preachers who have contributed sermons: Professor Thomas Long, Bishop William Willimon, Archbishop Rowan Williams, Professor Anna Carter Florence, Professor Michael Quicke and Dr Calvin Samuel.

Spurgeon's College is a community which encourages lively scholarly discussion, and we have gained a great deal from colleagues and students whilst writing this book. It was good to be able to test out some of the material here in the stimulating context of the college's postgraduate seminars.

The late Stephanie Egnotovich of Westminster John Knox Press was very encouraging in the early stages of production, editing chapter 1 with great thoroughness and helpfulness. Along with others, we are sad at her untimely passing, but we are grateful to David Dobson, Dan Braden and other members of the team who have guided us through the final stages of production.

Finally we are deeply thankful to our wives, Susan Stevenson and Linda Wright, and other members of our families for their constant encouragement and support. Writing is not an activity that easily fits into a conventional working day. This places demands on those close to authors, perhaps even more than on authors themselves, who can at least—when things go well—get excitingly engrossed in the task!

Peter Stevenson
Stephen Wright

Abbreviations

AB	Anchor Bible
ABRL	Anchor Bible Reference Library
BibInt	*Biblical Interpretation*
BNTC	Black's New Testament Commentaries
CBQ	*Catholic Biblical Quarterly*
CNTC	Calvin's New Testament Commentaries
CurTM	*Currents in Theology and Mission*
GBS	Grove Biblical Series
IBC	Interpretation: A Bible Commentary for Teaching and Preaching
ICC	International Critical Commentary
IJST	*International Journal of Systematic Theology*
Int	*Interpretation*
JSNTSup	Journal for the Study of the New Testament: Supplement Series
KJV	King James Version
LXX	Septuagint
NIB	*The New Interpreter's Bible*
NICNT	New International Commentary on the New Testament
NIGTC	New International Greek Testament Commentary
NIV	New International Version
NKJV	New King James Version
NRSV	New Revised Standard Version
NT	New Testament
OT	Old Testament
OTL	Old Testament Library
SJT	*Scottish Journal of Theology*

TEV	Today's English Version / Good News Bible
TNIV	Today's New International Version
TNTC	Tyndale New Testament Commentaries
TOTC	Tyndale Old Testament Commentaries
WBC	Word Biblical Commentary

Introduction

A colleague of the authors[1] famously tells those beginning the study of theology that there are really only two questions to ask: What kind of God? So what?

Absolutely central to orthodox Christian faith is the assertion that it is through Jesus of Nazareth that the nature of God is definitively revealed. In Jesus, God became 'incarnate'; that is, he took human flesh. It is a stark claim, shocking to many. If you hold, with Plato, that God 'by definition' is utterly different from us and known only in echoes and shadows, the idea of an 'incarnation' of God will be considered to be a contradiction in terms. Orthodox Muslims, rightly repulsed by the common ancient notion of a divine being consorting sexually with a human, react against the Christian claim of God's incarnation in Jesus, because that is what it sounds like. Yet those who have started out on the journey of *learning from* Jesus as his disciples do not find orthodox belief in the incarnation to be an absurd or degrading fantasy, nor yet a mischievous piece of theological doublespeak. It 'grows on us'. It has what C. S. Lewis memorably called 'the master touch—the rough, male taste of reality, not made by us, or indeed for us, but hitting us in the face.'[2] So, to the question 'What kind of God?' we are glad to give, as a central component of the answer, 'an incarnate God'.

But this leads naturally to an enormous 'so what?' Not, of course, in shrugging indifference, but rather the opposite. What on earth might such a claim *mean*? Within what frameworks of understanding does it make sense? And what are its spiritual, intellectual, ethical and practical implications? It is one thing to declare publicly, as many Christians do in their weekly worship, that Jesus is 'God from God' who 'was incarnate from the Holy Spirit and the Virgin Mary and was made man'.[3] It is quite another to live, love, think, work and serve in the light of this declaration. If the central task of the preacher is to facilitate profound understanding of the claims and call of the gospel, then the task of 'preaching the incarnation' must assume a very prominent place within that.

Should it, in fact, be the *leading* place? It is interesting that whereas the early Christians were in no doubt that the death and resurrection of Jesus were the climax of his work and marked the true turning-point of epochs which they proclaimed, it was the reality of the *incarnation* of God in Christ which soon came to dominate theological reflection.[4] Amid the intense questioning about the nature of the gospel they proclaimed, and both misunderstanding and criticism from inside the church as well as outside it, it was necessary to develop robust formulations of the truth that Jesus was *both* truly God *and* a truly human being. Quite simply, unless both these things were true, the claim of a new epoch inaugurated by his death and resurrection could not stand.

This is not to imply a denigration of other classic orthodox doctrines, for the fundamental teachings of the Church are inextricably interwoven. Nevertheless, it is striking, in the light of much modern debate focusing on the precise way in which God atones for the sins of the world through the *death* of Christ, that in that formative period of Christian doctrine it was not thought necessary to formulate an agreed 'position' or theory on this. The Nicene Creed simply states that God's coming in Jesus was 'for us and for our salvation', and in recounting his death gives the barest of factual statements: 'For our sake he was crucified under Pontius Pilate; he suffered death and was buried.'[5] It is not that the reality of Christ's death for the sins of the world was unimportant to the Church Fathers—far from it! Rather, it was seen as the outflow and culmination of a life that was the life of both Yahweh and a human being. So, having written a book called *Preaching the Atonement*, contributing—we trust in an eirenic manner—to current debate on that subject,[6] it seemed logical to follow it up with a sequel on *Preaching the Incarnation*. It may be that to refocus our gaze on this foundational doctrine, while vital and valuable in its own right, will also help us to see the question of Christ's atoning death in clearer perspective.

This book follows a format similar to *Preaching the Atonement*. In each chapter a theologically-focused study of a key text, drawing on aspects of biblical scholarship and Christian tradition, is followed by a sermon with reflective commentary. We will not repeat here the basic rationale that we set out in the Introduction to the earlier book. It is worthwhile, however, underlying key aspects of what we are *not* aiming to do as well as what we are.

As before, our aim is *reflective integration* between disciplines, rather than *comprehensive coverage* of debates. There is no attempt to offer state-of-the-art summaries of debates about the doctrine of the incarnation,[7] or biblical scholarship on the texts discussed, or the history of their interpretation, or contemporary cultural receptivity (or otherwise) to the idea of incarnation. As practical theologians, we are interested in the way in which preaching—which itself, of course, is a prime expression of practical theology—draws on and brings together elements from all these areas of study (and more) in order to announce and interpret the truth of the Word made flesh for specific occasions and congregations. We therefore want, in a sense, to model that creative process in which all preachers engage, of reading Scripture, drawing from the wells of tradition, and responding to the present.

It could be objected, of course, that this is a somewhat artificial model. As theological teachers we have access to time and resources for studying Scripture, tradition and culture that are less immediately available to most busy ministers in local churches. Some might say the same of the distinguished preachers for whose willing contributions to this book we are so grateful (though the current Archbishop of Canterbury is surely a prime example of how to combine the busiest of pastoral roles with a life of study and prayer). But we would see this, rather, as a question of different kinds (not grades!) of practical theologians working together in partnership. It is those who preach week by week who are at the forefront of the task of practical theology, reflecting on the pastoral and missionary task in the light of Scripture and tradition, and vice versa—all within the living context of worship. The theological teacher is a handmaid for this work. It is a question of similar vocations with different emphases. The authors are ministers of the Word (both continuing to preach on a regular basis), called, for the time being, to concentrate on the task of study and reflection, but no less concerned therefore with pastoral care and mission, nor by any means absolved from the practical outworkings of theology. Those for whom we are writing are, mainly, ministers of the Word who are called, for the time being, to concentrate on the tasks of pastoral care and mission, but are no less concerned therefore with study and reflection, nor by any means absolved from theologizing about their practice.

The integration of disciplines which we seek to achieve consciously in this book, and which preachers are engaged in both consciously and unconsciously week by week, inevitably and refreshingly subverts both the post-Enlightenment quest for scientific (or pseudoscientific) certainty and the fundamentalist quest for religious certainty. Studies of Scripture, theology and culture are evolving all the time, and conversations on these topics have no endpoint. The individual preacher is called, together with others, to tap into these conversations, and to seek from God the Holy

Spirit what he is saying to the Church and the world through them—at *this* time, in *this* place, for *these* people. There is an unpredictability and a randomness about this process. The people we meet, the cultures we inhabit, the books we happen to encounter—or not to encounter—will all shape the way we respond to and articulate the Word of God.

This is not to say that there is no true 'knowledge' to be had. Genuine knowledge is indeed mediated by both science and theology. We are not in a position of radical uncertainty in which we must tremble lest everything we thought we 'knew' be shown up as false the next day. But the honest preacher or scholar must surely recognize how provisional are all our interpretations of reality and formulations of meaning. We must also surely recognize how specialized 'knowledge' has become. No-one can be considered 'expert' in anything but a tiny corner of the limitless field of what there is to 'know'—if that! It is often overlooked that this was the fundamental claim of Jean-François Lyotard, famous for his popularization and definition of the idea of 'postmodernity'. Before advocating any particular philosophy, he highlighted a simple fact: that the days of the polymath who might possibly claim to have a grasp, at least in outline, of all key areas of human knowledge were gone for ever.[8] Investigation of the world in all its dimensions (including, we might say, its spiritual dimensions) had reached a point at which all such grandiose notions must be regarded as illusory. We do each have 'knowledge', but that knowledge is a highly limited and often arbitrary consequence of our social location and personal experiences. Of that, the preacher above all is acutely conscious. How many times has the thrust of our exegesis been controlled, essentially, by the Bible commentaries we happen to have on the shelf? How many times has our interpretation of the world been controlled, essentially, by the dynamics of the community in which we are pastorally immersed? On this basis, a good case can be made for dethroning the monologue sermon: for why should a single person be regarded as 'expert' in the business of discerning the will of God in a complex world?[9] Perhaps more important than the form of the sermon, though, is the humility and openness of the preacher, as one who is ready to engage with the views and expertise of hearers and others on a regular basis.

In that sense, this book may claim to be a genuine model of at least part of the preaching process. True, written sermons are never the same as spoken ones; dispersed readers are never the same as gathered congregations; and those contributing the extended discussions of biblical passages in the following chapters are often not the same people as those contributing the sermons. The authors' present calling may have allowed them more time to engage with particular questions and texts than those caught up in 'frontline' ministry. But our own experiences and encounters shape our work in just as fundamentally mysterious and random a way as any preacher's shapes theirs. These chapters are a snapshot of our experience and encounter with the truth of the incarnation, and a glimpse of how some preachers have preached it. We trust that like any hearers of sermons, our readers will see it as their task to 'complete' what they read here by thinking through how it might connect with their own setting, and thus find inspiration for their own sharing of God's Word. 'Incarnation' is not merely a topic for preaching; it is also a model for the whole process. Only as the Word becomes embodied in particular preachers and hearers does it fulfil the purpose for which God sends it.[10] And our hope for this book is like a preacher's hope for a sermon: that it will be a vehicle of communicating the Word of God, made flesh in Jesus, not because of any knowledge, experience or skill that we may possess, but only through the power of the Spirit of God, who is also the Spirit of Jesus.

A word about our choice of texts. The range selected, from both Old and New Testaments, bears witness to our belief that the doctrine of the incarnation, understood aright, is not a late or strange aberration, but is utterly consistent with Israel's faith in Yahweh, and attested from a variety of angles in earliest Christianity. It will also be clear that we believe the incarnation should be preached at times other than Christmas! The nativity stories, fascinating though they remain, are but one element of the biblical witness to this truth. On the whole the texts will not be surprising to regular preachers and hearers, but the absence of a chapter devoted solely to John 1:1–18 may raise an eyebrow. There are two reasons for this. One, we had a chapter on it in our book *Preaching the Atonement*.[11] Two, we thought it would be interesting and creative to explore how an Old Testament and a New Testament text might be preached in conjunction: Proverbs 8 and John 1 were the chosen pair (chap. 2), and Bishop William Willimon readily and insightfully took up the challenge! It also seemed right to deal with the two nativity stories of Matthew and Luke in a single chapter (3), as precisely in their differences they raise so many shared questions. Another rather different feature in this chapter is the Christmas sermon from Archbishop Rowan Williams. It illustrates well how very familiar biblical truth may be faithfully and imaginatively preached, yet the text coming only in the last sentence, causing the hearer to return to an extremely well-known story with fresh eyes. Though we do not include a sermon that deals in detail with one of the Christmas stories, we trust there is plenty of material in this chapter, and throughout the book, to nourish and refresh preaching at Christmas as well as at other times. And there are other helpful resources available.[12] Often, perhaps, we will find ourselves at Christmas in Archbishop Williams' position of being able to assume fairly widespread knowledge of the stories among our hearers, but much less of their wider significance.

The truth of the incarnation not only stretches the mind but it also fires the imagination. We believe that both are vital for the preacher. We will never communicate effectively that which does not extend and excite us first. We trust that this book may play a small part in that process for those who read it. One deeply at home in the life of the mind and the realms of the imagination, rooted in and transformed by the incarnate Christ, and gifted in the creative communication of this truth to others was C. S. Lewis. Here are some words of his about the act of God in Christ to inspire us as we set out on the journey.

> In the Christian story God descends to re-ascend. He comes down; down from the heights of absolute being into time and space, down into humanity. . . . But He goes down to come up again and bring the whole ruined world up with Him. . . . One may think of a diver, first reducing himself to nakedness, then glancing in mid-air, then gone with a splash, vanished, rushing down through green and warm water into black and cold water, down through increasing pressure into the death-like region of ooze and slime and old decay; then up again, back to colour and light, his lungs almost bursting, till suddenly he breaks surface again, holding in his hand the dripping, precious thing that he went down to recover. He and it are both coloured now that they have come up into the light: down below, where it lay colourless in the dark, he lost his colour too.[13]

1

The involved 'I AM'

EXODUS 3.1–15

God from eternity

Since the incarnation occupies such a pivotal place in our understanding of God, one of the first questions we must ask is this: How are we to conceive of God's relationship to the world before he became incarnate? If it is in the historical occurrence of Jesus' life and death that he is most fully revealed, what are we to make of testimonies to experience of God in earlier times? The chief issue for Christians here is the status of the Old Testament as a record of God's earlier revelations. But we should also note the close analogy with other faiths and their testimony to 'God',[1] whether in pre-Christian or later times.

It was essential to the early Christians' conviction about Jesus that he was not a rival God to the one in whom the Jewish people had always believed, but rather precisely the manifestation of this same God. This was a deeply-contentious claim for Jesus' contemporaries, and in John's account of Jesus' trial, the Jewish authorities insisted to Pilate that according to their law, Jesus must die, 'because he has claimed to be the Son of God' (Jn. 19.7). It's easy to see how high the stakes were. There was no middle ground, no compromise position. If Jesus was indeed the Revealer of God in the unique way his words and actions had directly or indirectly suggested, he required complete allegiance. If he was not that Revealer, then in accordance with their loyalty to their God who was *one* (Deut. 6.4), he must be regarded as a blasphemer and dealt with accordingly. The early Christians staked their lives, not on the premise that Jesus was a 'new God' who had superseded the old one, but on the precise conviction that in Jesus, the God in whom their ancestors had always believed had shown himself in human form.

But who was this God of their ancestors? Again, understanding this is crucial to understanding the force of the claim that in Jesus, 'God' had become incarnate. If this 'God' had been merely a local Jewish deity, a 'god' like those held by most nations to be their protector, the claim that he had become incarnate might still have disturbed Jews, but would hardly have caused much of a stir beyond that. It could readily have been dismissed by the more thoughtful and philosophical types as another example of 'mythology', of the gods appearing in various guises as in the tales of Homer—which had been discredited by Plato. It could also readily have been accepted by those whose worldview allowed the idea of one of the 'gods' taking human form. But the God of the Jews was not a merely local 'god'. He was, unambiguously, the Creator of the whole universe, a living figure of ultimate authority, before whom the gods of the nations were idols or 'nothings'.[2] To say that *this* God had become incarnate was thus both shocking and challenging, not only for Jews but also for pagans.[3]

So, given this, how we are to read and understand the Old Testament witness to God in the light of faith in the incarnation? If it is true that Jesus uniquely embodied the one Creator God known and trusted by Abraham and his descendants, we should expect the record kept by those descendants of their experience of this God to contain both elements which hint at or prefigure Jesus and elements which in certain respects contrast with him. This, I suggest, is exactly what we find in the Old Testament. The fact that it contains features that appear discordant with the way of Jesus—the instructions to the faithful at certain points to exterminate their enemies, for instance—should not be grounds to dismiss it. Nor does it undermine the belief that the Old Testament collection of books as a whole is 'revelation' from God. The mixture of elements is precise testimony, rather, to the very nature of the God we proclaim: that is, that he became an incarnate God at a particular point in history, and all prior, subsequent or separate testimonies to him must be judged in the light of that incarnate manifestation.

The focus of this chapter is Exod. 3.1–15: the story, so important to Israel's history, of God's appearance to Moses in the burning bush and his revelation of his name 'Yahweh', usually rendered in English versions as 'The LORD'. I suggest that this is one of those texts which clearly foreshadows the incarnation, and I hope to demonstrate the vital backward light cast by the coming of Jesus on this earlier event in his people's story. An Old Testament text such as this should not be used merely as an illustration for Jesus, but must be treated seriously in its own right. When we read it as part of a narrative continuous with that of Jesus, it shows us how natural it was for the God who appeared to Moses in the bush eventually to take human flesh himself. In Jesus, *Yahweh* himself walked among us.

Moses' encounter with Yahweh

Yahweh appears to Moses at a low point in the story of the Israelites, when they are groaning under oppression in Egypt (Exod. 2.23). After a privileged upbringing in Pharaoh's household (2.10), Moses had taken the plight of his people to heart, killing an Egyptian (2.11) and trying to sort out an internal Israelite quarrel (2.13). As a result, he was forced to flee from Pharaoh's justice (2.15). As he settles in a nomadic desert community, conscious of his alien status (2.22), there is an expectant pause in the narrative. How will the future of this oppressed people, to whom God has pledged himself in a covenant, be resolved?

Exodus 2 closes with momentous words that herald, summarize and interpret the narrative of liberation that occupies the next thirteen chapters:

> The Israelites groaned under their slavery, and cried out. Out of their slavery their cry for help rose up to God. God heard their groaning, and God remembered his covenant with Abraham, Isaac, and Jacob. God looked upon the Israelites, and God took notice of them. (2.23b–35)

Moses is on his own, safe but helpless in the wilderness. But his enslaved people are not alone. The God in whom their ancestors had trusted is watching over them. As events unfold, God is revealed as a God who hears the cry of the oppressed, who actively 'remembers' promises made in the past and is faithful to them, who looks upon his people and takes their plight to heart.

This language is a vivid example of the anthropomorphic, or humanizing, way in which the Judeo-Christian tradition has regularly spoken of God. The point is often made that such uses of anthropomorphic language bear witness to the inevitable limitations of our human expressive capacities when it comes to speaking of a transcendent being. However, the incarnation highlights the *appropriateness* of such language in speaking of God.[4] In the exodus story, it is true, God has no visible ears or eyes, and to that extent the language of 'hearing', 'looking' and so on is metaphorical. But this kind of language about God—with which the Hebrew Scriptures are thoroughly comfortable—emphasizes that God is close to people, in relationship with them, very much along the lines of their relationships with each other. He is caring and involved, not distant or unknowable. Indeed, he it is who can *truly* speak, see, hear, smell, feel and walk—in contrast to the idols who have human features but no human senses or faculties (Ps. 115.3–8).

The scene is set; and in the first act in the drama of liberation, God meets with the human servant through whom that liberation is to be achieved.

Yahweh meets with Moses (Exod. 3.1–6)

Before we get into any details of the story, notice the striking transition between 2.25 and 3.1, which moves suddenly and without explanation from the image of God looking on his people with concern, to Moses looking after his father-in-law's sheep in the desert. This transition epitomizes the fact that the God of whom Scripture speaks chooses to work out his great purposes through and in concert with human beings. God begins the liberation of a nation not by striking down its oppressors (though there will be a place for that later) but by meeting one individual, an escapee in the wilderness.

Three features of the scene call for comment:

First, the setting. Terence Fretheim notes that this is not a religious setting (such as a shrine or temple) but an everyday one, part of the daily routine of a Near Eastern shepherd. (He further comments on the suggestive parallels with the scene of Jesus' birth in Lk. 2.8–15, where shepherds and angels also figure.)[5] This is a God who appears in the ordinary life of the world and is not confined to 'special' places—something which Jesus' entire life, not only the circumstances of his birth, makes vividly apparent.

The second point is the manner of God's appearing. It is 'the angel of the LORD' who appears to Moses 'in a flame of fire out of a bush' (Exod. 3.2). 'The angel of the LORD' is a figure who regularly appears in the Old Testament narrative. He is, in one way, a shadowy figure, for he is not described. Yet he also expresses precisely the *visibility* of Yahweh, in a variety of forms and at different times. The 'angels' of Gen. 19.1, for example, are clearly two of the three men who visited Abraham and Sarah in Gen. 18.1–15, who were then demanded by the men of Sodom for their sexual pleasure (19.5), and who rescue Lot and his family from the impending destruction (19.10–22). At the same time, the narrator clearly sees them (or one of them?) as a direct spokesperson for Yahweh.[6] It is the Lord who speaks directly to Abraham in 18.13, and the Lord before whom Abraham stands to intercede for Sodom in 18.22–33. (The fact that the men 'turned away and went toward Sodom' in v. 22, leaving Abraham standing before Yahweh, suggests that Yahweh is being identified with the third man, who is no longer there in 19.1.) Whatever different strands of tradition are combined in this account, the narrative in its final form evokes both the mystery and the down-to-earth closeness of an invisible God who none-theless manifests himself in ways accessible to our humanity.

To Moses 'the angel of the LORD' appeared, it seems, not in a human shape (though the text does not explicitly rule this out; for the idea of humans, including one with godlike form, appearing in the midst of a fire, cf. Dan. 3.25), but in, or as,[7] the flames in the bush. As with the Abraham story, the narrator clearly wants us to see this visible sign as forming just a thin veil between Yahweh and Moses; for in Exod. 3.4 it is God himself who calls to Moses from within the bush. Similarly, in the account of God's leading the people when they have set out on their great escape, we read that 'the LORD' goes ahead of them in a pillar of cloud by day and a pillar of fire by night (Exod. 13.21); in 14.19 this is 'the angel of God'. Again the presence and agency of Yahweh himself can either be described directly or by means of an 'angel', and they are discerned in phenomena of the natural world.

Yahweh's appearance to Moses thus exemplifies a truth evident else-where in the Old Testament: it was possible to testify to God's appearance and action in the world by speaking, almost interchangeably, of both his 'angel' and of human or non-human manifestations of him. At the same time, however, these mediating entities have no independent agency, and the narrator repeatedly directs attention away from them and back to Yahweh himself. Given such ways of speaking of God and God's revelation, belief in God's incarnation in Jesus is understandable, and it was not a completely novel development. Gradually—and mostly in retrospect—God came to be recognized in the life and career of a human being, who appeared not in fleeting episodes but for thirty-odd solid years. Highlighting God's direct agency and word in the person of Jesus, as did the Alexandrian theologians of the fourth and fifth centuries, might lead to theoretical problems in accounting for his real humanity, but it is an authentic extension of the mode of Old Testament witness to Yahweh. More colloquially put, wasn't it just like the God who came to visit Abraham by the trees of Mamre, and appeared to Moses in a burning bush, to turn up in a manger in Bethlehem?

The third feature of the scene is the way Yahweh communicates with Moses. He waits until Moses' attention has been fixed by the strangeness of the bush being aflame but not consumed. He does not override Moses' free volition but beckons him via the mystery of a botanical and physical curiosity. John E. Colwell has noted that the doctrine of the incarnation has always been closely connected with the doctrine of creation:[8] the incarnation brings to a climax the movement of outgoing love that always has existed within God himself but was first expressed in the staggering diversity and concreteness of the created universe.[9] Here, the creation is a medium for God's nearness and his gesturing to Moses, as one day it would be the setting for his human life and death. It is the persuasive but not overwhelming initial means of soliciting Moses' cooperation, which is essential at every stage if the plan is to succeed. Although God clearly takes the initiative in the larger narrative of the exodus, just as he is the main actor in the drama of Scripture, 'God's way into the future is . . . not dictated solely by the divine word and will'.[10] This pattern continues throughout Israel's history. God acts and initiates, but he does not compel human co-operation, which anyhow is frequently not forthcoming. In this light it is important to see that when God's purposes were finally achieved in Jesus, it was not because he chose to override free human co-operation, but because he won it, as Hebrews especially emphasizes (e.g. Heb. 5.8–9; 10.5–10).

Once Yahweh has Moses' attention, he speaks to him by name, eliciting the simple response 'Here I am' (Exod. 3.4; cf. the responses of Isaiah and Mary to their respective theophanies: Isa. 6.8; Lk. 1.38). Here again is something so obvious to us, yet so marvellous, that God should encounter and relate to human beings. The incarnation brings the process of God's 'human' self-manifestation to a head but does not usher in anything out of character for God: he has always been like this! But the relationship of Yahweh and Moses is certainly not an 'equal' one. Yahweh calls Moses to remove his sandals, for he is on holy ground (Exod. 3.5). Moses feels awe appropriate to Yahweh's nearness. At this point we note that though Moses foreshadows Jesus, their respective relationships with God are qualitatively different. Though obedient to his Father, Jesus is uniquely close to him. He 'fulfils' *Yahweh's* earlier acts and character, as well as those of his human servants. It is in *Jesus'* presence, after the remarkable catch of fish, that Simon Peter is in awe, as Moses was before Yahweh (Lk. 5.8). Yahweh's physical presence here with Moses—the implication that even if he is visible only occasionally and indirectly, *this* ground is holy, at least for the moment, whereas *that* ground is not holy in the same way—fits with the 'human' manner of Yahweh's response to Israel in 2.23–25, and with the conditions of Jesus' human existence.[11]

Yahweh next identifies himself as the God of Moses' father, of Abraham, Isaac and Jacob. This is important, for up to this point the 'figure' speaking has simply been identified with a strange natural phenomenon. Now, however, he is recognized and defined historically. This is the God of Moses' ancestors, the one who has been known in the twists and turns of their story for generations past, the one who called them to himself and promised that they would be a blessing to the nations of the world.

And when Jesus comes, it is *this* God with whom he is identified. The embodiment of God in a historical person, period and place, though uniquely focused in Jesus, is thus no strange novelty. God, as Israel had come to know him, has always been, precisely, the 'God of the ancestors', the God known in and through their history.

Yahweh promises to rescue his people (Exod. 3.7–10)

Having disclosed who he is, Yahweh now announces to Moses why he has appeared to him. Yahweh's personal involvement with his people is vividly dramatized through first-person speech, echoing the third-person report in 2.24–25. He has, he tells Moses, observed his people's misery, heard their cry and knows their sufferings; and he has come down to rescue them from the Egyptians and bring them to a good and fertile land. The striking new element here is Yahweh's statement 'I have come down' (3.8), language which is typical of the 'human' way in which Yahweh is depicted in the Old Testament. In Gen. 11.5, for example, he is described with irony as 'coming down' to see the city and the tower which people were building to reach to 'the heavens'. Here the phrase expresses the nearness of God, but now as a vigorous and purposeful force, not only a mysterious and sacred presence. The language foreshadows Johannine language about Jesus' 'coming into the world': for example, Jesus' statements in Jn. 6.38, 'I have come down from heaven, not to do my own will, but the will of him who sent me', and Jn. 10.10, 'I came that they may have life, and have it abundantly'.

But although Yahweh himself has come down to save his people, he does not intend to do so single-handedly. His words are actually a commission to Moses to do what *he* must do. 'So come, I will send you to Pharaoh to bring my people, the Israelites, out of Egypt' (Exod. 3.10). To those who have preconceived ideas of God as acting alone and by omnipotent fiat or thunderbolt, these words no doubt suggest a stubborn and puzzling commitment to involve human agents. To those who discern God's action in Jesus, however, his way with Moses and the Israelites is not surprising at all. In Jesus we see the perfect instance of the model first presented in Exodus. Yahweh in compassion 'comes down' to rescue his people, even as that act of rescue involves the obedient co-operation of a human being.

The revelation to Moses of Yahweh's saving intentions is of huge significance. It allows us to see Jesus and his role as Saviour as the ultimate expression of a divine character and purpose that had been known for

generations rather than as a belated expression of divine efforts to sal-
vage something from the wreckage of a broken world. The exodus was
the defining event in Israel's story, uniquely disclosing God's commitment to relationship with Israel and his power to overcome obstacles to
Israel's well-being. And it became one of the dominant reference points
and metaphors by which Jesus and his followers would interpret his own
work as 'redeemer' (see, for instance, Mk. 10.45; Lk. 22.15–20, in which
Jesus clearly understands his forthcoming death as a new 'Passover'; Rom.
3.24).[12] At this point in the story, however, the outcome of God's encounter with Moses remains open—just as the opening chapters of Luke invite
the question 'But how will these great hopes for this child be fulfilled?'[13]
Yahweh lays himself on the line, and the efficacy of his intentions will be
tested by events. Will the Israelites really experience the deliverance here
promised?

Yahweh reveals his name (Exod. 3.11–15)

It immediately becomes clear that Yahweh's path is not going to be
straightforward, as Moses embarks on a series of five objections, or delaying tactics (3.11–4.17; we can deal only with the first two here.)[14] This
demonstrates that Yahweh will not coerce people into his plans. He must
exercise perseverance with Moses— though typically, he is not above getting fed up with Moses (4.14) before Moses eventually accepts the call![15]

His first objection is his self-doubt. 'Who am I that I should go to
Pharaoh, and bring the Israelites out of Egypt?' (3.11). Yahweh's answer is
twofold (v. 12). First, Moses is not alone. 'I will be with you'. Later, in the
New Testament, this real, if mostly unseen, presence of God is recognized
as foundational to Jesus' ministry (see Mt. 3.16; 4.11). Indeed, Jesus is
the culmination of God's promise to be 'with' his people as a whole (Mt.
1.23), and through Jesus that promise is now mediated to all disciples
everywhere (Mt. 28.20). Second, Yahweh says, in reassurance, that once
Moses has led the people out of Egypt, 'You shall worship God on this
mountain', the very mountainside where Moses is now standing (Exod.
3.12). This seems to be not so much a command as the promise of an
awe-inspiring encounter. Yahweh asks to be taken at his word, yet he will
not withhold signs of his presence. And again, Jesus is the fullest and most
wonderful expression of this aspect of Yahweh's character.

Moses' second delaying tactic is a request that God give himself a name
which Moses can use to reassure the Israelites.[16] This is an understandable
request. 'The God of your ancestors' might well seem a distant, shadowy,

even forgotten figure to this enslaved people (v. 13). Moreover, even if this description were to awaken hope or give some preliminary validity to Moses' tale, how would they know that Moses was not simply deluded in his claim to have met this God? So he seeks a more precise token of the identity of the one who has spoken to him. Even given this, he runs the risk of being disbelieved, but a name would give him greater confidence in the message he brought.

God grants his request with the name 'I AM'. The implication is that this will indeed (up to a point) reassure the Israelites, because it is a name by which their God is already known. Thus this passage does not record its first revelation in history, but simply its first appearance in the canon. The name 'I AM' seems to be an interpretative play on the familiar name Yahweh (usually rendered 'The LORD', as in v. 15), which is also derived from the Hebrew verb 'to be'. Before giving Moses this name, Yahweh expands on its significance: 'I am who I am'. This translation has been much debated. Fretheim suggests that the force is simultaneously 'I will be who I am' and 'I am who I will be',[17] drawing attention to the constancy and faithfulness of its bearer.

This mysterious name befits the holiness of its owner (cf. v. 5). On its own, it reveals little of God's nature or character. That, surely, is part of the point: no name can sum him up or encapsulate him. Yet what it does suggest is important. This is a being whose nature is suggested above all *by his very being*. Perhaps the most important thing we need to know about this God is the fact that he *is*. And yet he is not 'being' in the abstract, as some (but not all) medieval theology seems to say.[18] He is 'I AM', forever personal, self-identifying, relating. As the eminent literary critic Harold Bloom observes, 'What we encounter in [Yahweh] . . . is not an abstract becoming or being but an outrageous personality, a person who is more than a person and yet never less than a person'.[19] And his activity on behalf of his people sets the context for knowledge of his identity. 'Israel both understands its history from the name and the name from its history'.[20]

Finally, the very fact that he chooses to identify himself by a name is highly significant. As Fretheim points out, naming entails both availability and vulnerability.[21] People can call on you; people can honour you; people can drag your name in the mud.

The testimony of Christian faith is that Yahweh, the God named 'I AM', chose to make himself available and vulnerable in Jesus of Nazareth. The 'I am' sayings of Jesus in John's Gospel imply a veiled claim of identity with Yahweh. The meaning and importance of these sayings would have been clearer to John's readers after Jesus' death than it was to Jesus' hearers, though Jewish leaders may have been infuriated by what they sensed was Jesus' subversive self-identification with God. See, for instance, their reaction to Jesus in Jn. 10.20. Jesus' words 'I am the gate' (vv. 7, 9) and 'I am the good shepherd' (vv. 11, 14) constitute an implicit attack on their stewardship of Israel, but also echo the name of Yahweh, an echo strengthened by the recollection of Yahweh's promise to care for his own flock in Ezek. 34.11–31.[22]

Our reading of the story of Moses' encounter with Yahweh suggests in a variety of ways that this event is not a mere dim and perhaps 'random' foreshadowing of Jesus, but an authentic expression of the God who was to be revealed most fully in Jesus, as well as an essential foundation for understanding that fuller revelation. What might 'preaching the incarnation' from this text entail?

Preaching the incarnation from the story of Moses

As Christian preachers we view all parts of Scripture, including the Old Testament, through the lens of the gospel of Christ, the one in whom God took human flesh for the salvation of the world. But even as we do that, we also seek to *listen* to all parts of Scripture, including the Old Testament, allowing it to fill out the meaning of that gospel and to enrich our comprehension of it in emotional as well as intellectual ways.

This double dynamic is at work as we preach from the story of Moses' call. We come to it with a particular Christian *interest*, but that does not predetermine what we will discover. Early Christian theologians regularly identified the 'angel' in the bush with God the Son,[23] but this is not the only way of reading the text 'Christianly'. Rather, we should seek a fruitful conversation between gospel and Scripture, theology and text, in which each informs and illumines the other while respecting its integrity. With that in mind, four areas of special interest arise from Christian faith in the incarnation, all of which we have touched on: the nature of God, God's relation to humanity, God's revelation in history and God's identification with a people's destiny.

The nature of 'God'

The Nicene Creed declares that Jesus is 'God from God, light from light, true God from true God'. Clearly Christians have a primary interest in the content of the word 'God' and the nature of the one so designated. We approach any testimony to, or discussion about 'God', in Scripture or elsewhere, in the light of our belief that the ultimate definition of God is found in Jesus.

When early Christians spoke of Jesus as 'Son of God' or—in due course—simply as 'God', the meaning of the word 'God' was drawn from the Israelite identification of 'God' with the Yahweh who, they believed, had pledged himself in covenant to them. When we read the stories of the Israelites' relationship to this Yahweh, we ask, In what ways do these stories give meaning to the assertion that Jesus was 'God' or 'God's Son'? This question is especially important in a multicultural society, where the word 'God' has such varied connotations. There is little point in exploring the idea that Jesus is the 'Son of God' without also unpacking the Christian content of the word 'God', which is inherited entirely from Judaism.

This Yahweh is surprisingly unlike many of the vague notions so often attached to the word 'God'. He is near and not far, he is down to earth and not ethereal, he speaks and hears and feels. He shows himself in and through his creation. In Exod. 3.1–15, he is mysterious and holy, yet committed, earthed, involved. Historians of Israelite religion are no doubt right to say that especially in very early times he was envisaged as one tribal god among many, even though he came to be recognized as their superior, eventually relegating the others to virtual 'nothingness'.[24] It is not surprising that he should be seen as deeply implicated in the liberation of a specific people and the destruction of their enemies—and, in due course, in intertribal warfare. Nor, however, is it surprising that the perception of his nature and character should be refined and deepened over time. The point is that if we as preachers want to teach believers and non-believers about Jesus' significance, and allow them to grow in appreciation of it, they need to be introduced to Yahweh.[25] Only then will they come to understand Jesus in his proper context, both as arbiter of all previous testimony to Yahweh and as its authentic culmination. They will find that it is not ultimately surprising, though it remains thrilling, that *this* God should make himself known in this embodied way in first-century Palestine.[26]

God's relationship to humanity

Christians believe that, in Jesus, God relates to humans in the fullest way possible: as another human. But the story of Yahweh's earliest dealings with his people shows that our belief is not a new one. Although Yahweh did not appear to Moses in human form, he engaged Moses in dialogue. He spoke out of deep empathy with the particular human family to whom he was related. This was a genuine relationship; Moses was able to answer and object to what Yahweh said.

Exod. 3.1–15 shows us two things about God's relationship with humanity. First, it shows us that his compassionate communication with humanity, which we know in Jesus, is thoroughly characteristic of him. Second, it shows us that Yahweh's agency and human agency in implementing Yahweh's purpose are by no means mutually exclusive. It is Yahweh who comes down to save his people, but it is Moses who must go to the Israelites and Pharaoh and begin the journey to liberation. Yahweh's activity in Jesus is the pinnacle of such divine-human partnership, but it is not the beginning of it.

The revelation of God in history

The incarnation conclusively demonstrates God's involvement in and affirmation of the historical process and predisposes us to look for signs of that involvement in times and places *other* than first-century Palestine. Belief in the incarnation requires that we see Jesus as the *definitive but not the only* statement of what this involvement means.

Thus in Exodus 3, God's entanglement in the *historical* affairs of Abraham's descendants leaps out at us. It would be selling this story (and the incarnation) short if we treated it merely as a fable illustrating certain timeless truths about God. This does not mean that we should treat Old Testament narrative in a 'fundamentalist' way, as if ancient historiography is like modern, as if only 'literal' truth (whatever that might be!) is 'real' truth, or indeed, as if there were *any* historiography unfiltered by the interpretative grid of the narrator. But it *does* mean that we recognize the remarkable, unique way in which, for Israelite and Christian faith, history is indispensable as a means of God's revelation.[27] The precise circumstances of the Israelites in Egypt, the date and nature of the Exodus, and even the exact sequence of the conversation between Moses and Yahweh—these are secondary matters theologically. The testimony to Yahweh's working in history is not.

God's identification with a people's destiny

God entered history in Jesus of Nazareth. But it was not world history in general that he entered; it was the history of a particular people. In scholarly circles this apparent favouritism is known as the 'scandal of particularity'. Once more, we can turn to the earlier episode of Yahweh's encounter with Moses to shed light on how this 'scandal' is related to the incarnation.

Yahweh's involvement with particular individuals and a particular family is clear throughout the Old Testament. That involvement by no means implies that they were always in agreement with Yahweh or that they are being held up as exemplary.[28] It does, however, set the scene very clearly for his coming as an Israelite among Israelites. The question then is What does this concern for Israel say about his care for, or involvement with, those outside that specific people, and with the world or creation as a whole?

Two interesting pointers to an answer emerge in Exod. 3.1–15. The first pointer is the burning bush itself, wherein a *particular* piece of God's creation becomes a vehicle for God's revelation. There are two ways to interpret this in the light of the incarnation.

One option is to say that the incarnation *affirms* such particularity. That is, through Jesus, a particular individual who lived in a particular time and place, we are strongly encouraged to listen and look for God in particular individuals, times and places; to be ready to be surprised by him as Moses was. But there will be other individuals, times and places that are *not* means of divine encounter of this kind—though the story of Moses may suggest that we should not assume in advance that we know who or what these will be.

The other option is to say that the incarnation *universalizes* the presence of God in his creation. That is, Jesus becomes the normative, reliable centre where God is to be found. He is accessible to anyone and everyone, and through him we discover that God himself is not tied to any locus. This is suggested by Jn. 4.24: no longer is any one 'mountain' to be seen as the place for worship; those who worship the Father will do so 'in spirit and in truth', i.e. according to the reality of his unique revelation in Jesus, the one through whom, John says, the Spirit is bestowed (Jn. 20.19–23). Viewed through this lens, the burning bush seen by Moses epitomizes an experience of God that may now, through Jesus, be mediated by any and every element of creation. Or in the poetic interpretation of Elizabeth Barrett Browning,

Earth's crammed with heaven,
And every common bush afire with God.[29]

Christian theology, I believe, can with authenticity hold both of these interpretations in tension. If we say that the incarnation points to the *particularity* of God's revelation, we affirm, in the tradition of Barth, the freedom of God to surprise and address us. If we say that the incarnation points to the *universality* of God's revelation, we affirm, in the tradition of Rahner, the creation as a sacrament of God's presence, such that we cannot exclude God from any part of the world, or fail to discern his hand, just because he does not address us there in a particularly striking way.

The second pointer to an answer concerning what Exod. 3.1–15 shows us about God's care for the world as a whole is God's promise to liberate the Israelites from Egypt. The particularity of this promise is echoed climactically in Jesus, which prompts us to ask, with Anthony Hanson, 'Have we the right to universalize the sympathy of God by means of the particularity of Jesus?'[30] In recent decades liberation theology has often placed the story of Exodus at centre stage, as an expression of God's abiding and active concern for the oppressed—of whatever race or era. The New Testament indeed testifies that Jesus' impact included a radical redefinition of the people of God. No longer were they limited to historical Israel; nor would members of historic Israel be included by mere right of birth. In the kingdom which Jesus inaugurated, not only was personal sin forgiven and overcome, but social disease and oppression were also removed. In this sense, the good news of Jesus as foreshadowed in Exodus is indeed good news for the poor and downtrodden, whoever and wherever they are (Lk. 4.18). And yet Christian proclamation will never be just a general announcement of God's care for the oppressed—as if the Exodus story could be extracted from the unfolding saga of a nation and made a mere symbol. It will, rather, always centre on the way in which Yahweh's purposes unfolded through history and reached their culmination in Jesus. The incarnation, too, is no mere symbol of a timeless truth. It is Yahweh's entry into human time and into the story of a specific people.

Thus it is vital to take seriously the Old Testament story *on its own terms* as a vehicle for Christian proclamation. It is insufficient to draw out some isolated 'points' such as 'the compassion of God' or 'the power of God to rescue his people', and use the story merely as a peg on which to hang them. Only by allowing ourselves and our hearers to enter the narrative on a deeper level will we gain and communicate a sense that the Yahweh who came in Jesus is indeed the Yahweh who showed himself to Moses and the Israelites. The story of Moses and the story of Jesus are part of the one story of Yahweh, the God revealed in and through the history of Israel. The story of Moses does not offer mere parallels to or foreshadowings of the story of Jesus: it has its own concrete significance as an earlier episode in the one larger story.[31]

The following sermon, by Thomas G. Long, demonstrates a helpful way in which the story of Moses' call can be preached.

Sermon: The God of good appearances

Thomas G. Long

Everybody wants to make a good appearance. There is, however, more than one way to do so. The first and most obvious way to make a good appearance is to come across as impressive in the eyes of others. When a highly-decorated U.S. Army general testified recently before a congressional investigative committee, talk-show host and *New York Times* columnist Dick Cavett tuned in on television to hear what the general had to say. Cavett reported, however, that he was distracted from what the military man *said* because of how he *looked*. Trying to impress the panel, the general wore a uniform heavy with awards and decorations, 'ornamented like a Christmas tree with honors, medals, and ribbons',[32] wrote Cavett. 'I guess what bothers me about it is the ostentation', Cavett remarked. 'This general is greatly accomplished. So is a brilliant actor, but the actor doesn't walk around with an Oscar, an Emmy, a Tony and a cluster of rave reviews affixed to his tunic'.[33]

The sight of the festooned general prompted Cavett to remember a time, during the Vietnam War, when the legendary comic Mort Sahl met General William Westmoreland. Sahl, who had encyclopedic knowledge of military decoration, looked at the cluster of ribbons and hardware on Westmoreland's chest and began reciting their names one by one—the Distinguished Service Medal, the Croix de Guerre with Chevron, the Bronze Star, the Pacific Campaign medal. When he finished the list, Sahl commented, 'Very impressive! If you're twelve'.

That's the thing with this first way of making a good appearance, our attempts to appear impressive to others. People can often see through them. We all want to come across with the best profile we can fashion, but our attempts to put forward a good appearance perhaps reveal more than we know, more than we desire. Like the general, we tend to adorn ourselves with clothing, jewellery, designer sunglasses, trophies, sporty cars, job titles, Botoxed faces and other trappings that make us look more important, slimmer, smarter, younger, hipper or richer than perhaps we really are. But in all honesty we know the truth, and often others can discern it about us as well, that these 'good appearances' are as much about concealing who we are than revealing ourselves. An amusing country song that climbed the charts recently contrasted the way the singer tried to appear on his MySpace web page with the hard facts. In reality, goes the song, he is five feet, three inches, overweight, asthmatic, works at the Pizza Pit and still lives with his parents. Online, though, he is six feet, five inches, has a black belt in karate, lives in

Hollywood and drives an Italian sports car. 'I'm so much cooler online, so much cooler online',[34] he croons.

According to the biblical story, this business of trying to put up a good appearance in the eyes of others while at the same time hiding our true selves has been in the human heart, causing sadness and trouble from the very beginning. Creation hardly gets going before a self-conscious Adam and Eve are sewing fig leaves together to appear innocent and are hiding from God in a grove of trees. The first recorded murder takes place not because of money, drugs, or sex, but jealousy over appearances: it seemed that Abel's offering made a better appearance to God than Cain's, and the result was hot rage and blood spilled on the ground. Jacob, wanting what was not rightly his, disguised his appearance, pretending to be his slightly-older brother Esau, thereby hijacking Esau's blessing from his deceived father Isaac. Then Jacob himself gets fooled by appearances. He became acquainted with two sisters, Leah and her beautiful younger sister Rachel. Desiring to marry Rachel, he made a deal for her with her father, Laban. But Laban was eager to marry off his older and less-attractive daughter, so he borrowed a leaf from Jacob's own trickster playbook and pulled a switch. On the wedding day, Jacob thought he was marrying Rachel, but when the morning sun rose over the marriage bed, it was Leah that Jacob discovered beneath the burka.

Impressing others while hiding our true selves is one way to make a good appearance, but it is important to recognize that there is another way. This second kind of good appearance is not a matter of coming across as attractive in the eyes of others but rather of showing up in the right place at the right time. The woman who reschedules two meetings and a hair appointment to be in the stands at her son's first soccer game is making a good appearance. The man who walks into the hospital room of a co-worker with a vase of flowers and a word of good cheer has made a good appearance. The teacher who notices that one of her students is practically in tears from trying to solve a math problem and kneels down beside his desk to say, 'Let's work on this together', has made a good appearance. The fire company which arrives before the flames consume the house has made a good appearance. When a lonely man sits in the darkness of his apartment, feeling friendless and isolated, and there is an unexpected knock on the door, and the next-door neighbour is standing there, saying, 'I accidentally ordered more Chinese food than I can possibly eat. Care to share it with me?' the neighbour has made a good appearance. To paraphrase Woody Allen, 80% of what matters in life is showing up, and this second way of making a good appearance is not a hiding of one's true self. To the contrary, it is a disclosure of the true self, a revelation of character.

Contrasting these two ways of making a good appearance takes us right into the heart of the story of Moses and the burning bush in Exodus 3. Among the many rich theological truths to be found in this story is the simple claim that here God has made a good appearance, in the second and richer sense of the term. The point of this narrative is not how God *looks*. The passage is actually quite coy about whether it was actually an angel or God who appeared in that burning bush, and as God will tell Moses later, any who try to capture God in an image have committed idolatry (Exod. 20.4–6). The point of the passage is not how God *looks*, but where God intends to *be*, what God intends to *do*, where God intends to *appear*. God has heard the misery of the Hebrew slaves in Egypt, and God has decided to show up and to do something about it. The Israelites are in distress, and God has decided to make a good appearance.

This good appearance of God described in Exodus 3, this divine good appearance at a critical moment in history, is quite consistent with what we have already discovered about God in Scripture. When the earth is a form-less void, God shows up with a plan for creation. When Adam and Eve get in trouble in the garden, God shows up to set things right. When Abram is seventy-five years old and wondering what he and his wife, Sarah, will do in their retirement, God shows up to call him to move to another land and to become a blessing to all the families of the earth. And now the God who has repeatedly shown up shows up again, to act to set people free. God is the God of good appearances.

In the story of the burning bush, when Moses famously asks God about his name, God replies with a phrase that consists entirely of variations on the Hebrew verb 'to be', a notoriously difficult phrase to translate. It could mean 'I AM WHO I AM', or 'I WILL BE WHO I WILL BE', or 'I WILL CAUSE TO BE WHAT I WILL CAUSE TO BE', or even 'I WILL BE WHO I AM / I AM WHO I WILL BE'. Biblical scholar Terence Fretheim likes this last translation best, saying that, in essence, God's name is an affirmation, 'I will be God for you'.[35] Or to put it another way, God's name is 'I AM THE ONE WHO WILL KEEP SHOWING UP FOR YOU'. The God of good appearances.

For Christians, of course, the God who keeps showing up showed up once again in a manger in Bethlehem and in the life of Jesus of Nazareth. There is much to say theologically about the meaning of the incarnation, but at its base the incarnation is the decision of God to show up in the midst of human life, to make a good appearance. 'God never seems to weary of trying to get himself across', writes Frederick Buechner. And so, Buechner says, God keeps showing up—showing up in Noah, in Abraham, in Moses, in David and in John the Baptist. And then, most fully, God shows up in Jesus, 'the *mot juste* of God'.[36] Buechner goes on:

2

Embodied Wisdom

PROVERBS 8 AND JOHN 1.1–14

Manifestations of Yahweh

The extraordinary thing about early Christianity is the speed with which the disciples of Jesus began to *worship* him. They were not content with regarding him as a rabbi whose teachings would guide them in Yahweh's ways. They accorded him the honour and prestige that in their Jewish tradition of faith were due solely to Yahweh.[1]

And yet they did not cease to be worshippers of Yahweh himself; nor did they set Jesus beside Yahweh as another 'god' in some pantheon of independent deities—relating to one another with more or less amity or rivalry, like the gods of Olympus. On the contrary: their claim was precisely that in Jesus, Yahweh, the covenant God of Israel, the creator God of the whole earth, had revealed *himself* with full and final clarity. Jesus was not somehow separate from Yahweh, but one with him. They expressed this conviction in many ways. One of the most characteristic was that Jesus was God's Son, about whom Yahweh had issued a royal proclamation of good news (Rom. 1.1–6).

It was this conviction that in due course led to the full development of the doctrines of the incarnation and the Trinity. But was this a bizarre and aberrant development from a monotheistic faith that (whether one shared it or not) at least had the attraction of simplicity and straightforwardness? Such has been the verdict, in various ways, of many non-Christians, not least many Jews and Muslims. An important part of the function of this chapter, like the previous one, is to seek to show that this is not the case. The Christian claim is indeed a startling one, just as Jesus made a startling impact on his disciples: all the evidence suggests that even those who most warmed to Jesus were far from expecting Yahweh to reveal himself like *this*. And yet the claim coheres with, and does not contradict, the

21

ways in which people had apprehended Yahweh in the past. As with the simplicity of Jewish monotheism, one cannot expect just to argue people into believing in the Christian doctrines of incarnation or Trinity. But one can, I think, demonstrate that those doctrines are coherent with the faith of Israel as attested in the Old Testament. Indeed, one can seek to paint that coherence with a beauty that appeals, not on account of some quasi-mathematical exactness or rigid structure of belief, but through its allusive, diverse, metaphorical disclosures of the characteristic glimpse, the recurring theme, the telltale pattern—all of which point to the single truth at the heart of all that is.

In Chapter 1 we explored how the very character of the Yahweh who showed himself in the paradigmatic encounter with Moses is thoroughly consistent, in key ways, with the character of the Yahweh who, we believe, showed himself ultimately in Jesus. In this chapter we explore the fact that Yahweh in the Old Testament adopts a variety of media or, perhaps better, personae to make himself known, and discuss one in particular, that of Wisdom. I am aware of the danger of applying too literal an understanding of the Latin *persona* (meaning an actor's 'mask') to the 'persons' of the Trinity; one can imply that God is simply playing a game of disguises. But in trying to describe the shifting, varied glimpses of Yahweh's nature and activity as the Old Testament actually bears witness to them, I do not believe the idea is inappropriate. Indeed, it may capture quite well the ambiguous nature of these mediating entities. For example, in passages such as Prov. 8.22–31, are we to understand Wisdom as an independent or quasi-independent 'hypostasis', as often suggested, or rather as a literary personification of the quality with which God rules, as suggested by James Dunn?[2] I take the latter view, but the idea of 'persona' covers both possibilities in a way that may helpfully replicate the actual ferment of first-century thought, which is usually much more confused and varied than later theologians seeking precise definitions would like to make it.

This and other personae turned out to be ready-made categories in which the early Christians were able to express the nature of Jesus, though there is much disagreement about the extent of this dependency.[3] That expresses the human side of the picture—and we need to do that: the disciples and New Testament writers were humans, like us, struggling to make sense of the world, its origins and purpose, and the events of its history—above all, the event of Jesus. But the narrative of faith gives also the other side of the picture: the media of Yahweh's manifestation were not merely human constructs, to be wrested from their original context by a small group of deviant first-century Jews to serve a new and alien end, the identification of a human being with Yahweh himself. Rather, they were authentic but partial disclosures of the one who would one day reveal himself in all his strange but consistent glory in Jesus of Nazareth.

What then were these 'personae' or manifestations of Yahweh? In Chapter 1 we encountered one of the earliest, 'the angel of the LORD'. This figure was not, however, to prove the dominant mode of his revelation, though he has connections with the others, just as they themselves are closely connected with one other. The 'personae' that were to become the vital media through which Yahweh was sought and experienced were his glory (*shekinah*), his law or teaching (*torah*), his Spirit (*ruakh*), his word (*dabar*) and, not least, his wisdom (*khokmah*).[4]

Aspects of glory, law and Spirit come together in the closely-linked 'personae' of Word and Wisdom. It is clear that Yahweh's 'word', which comes again and again to the prophets, is not something separate from him, any more than his 'glory', 'teaching' or 'Spirit' can be seen as separate from him. Yet it can be vividly personified, as if it were his messenger sent out from him to achieve his purpose in the world (Ps. 147.15; Isa. 55.11). For the Evangelist John, the Greek *logos*, which both echoed such Hebrew phraseology and had added connotations of 'principle of universal reason' from Greek culture, was a perfectly-fitted way in which to envisage how the invisible Yahweh could show himself in human form.[5] It was his *word* which was made flesh (Jn. 1.14). Moreover, there is wide agreement that John's use of 'word' owes much not only to the understanding of God's *dabar* (word) in the OT, but also to that of his *khokmah* (wisdom). We turn now to examine the key passage about that wisdom, Proverbs 8.

The craftswoman at Yahweh's side

The book of Proverbs falls into two parts. Chapters 1–9 concentrate on appeals to seek wisdom, whereas chs. 10–31 contain sayings that demonstrate what wisdom means in practice. At the climax of the first part comes ch. 8, in which wisdom is vividly personified as a woman, making a public appeal to all and sundry.[6] This comes immediately after an equally vivid warning by the main voice of Proverbs, the one who addresses 'my son', against the wiles of the seductive woman, who in the context of the book is not merely a prostitute or adulteress but a figure for anti-wisdom, the epitome of the way of folly. The call of Wisdom in ch. 8 then comes as a powerful rhetorical contrast, an invitation to the reader as well as the 'son' of the implied author to choose aright in the stark choice that always lies before us.[7] We may divide the chapter into the opening and closing appeal (vv. 1–11, 32–36), the declaration of Wisdom's present function

(vv. 12–21) and the story of Wisdom's origins (vv. 22–31). We will briefly highlight the tenor of each section and some theological implications for our present subject.

The appeal of Wisdom (Prov. 8.1–11, 32–36)

Wisdom calls out to humankind, exhorting them to learn prudence (vv. 4–5). She underlines the justice and truth of her words (vv. 6–9). Wisdom is more valuable than all other kinds of wealth (vv. 10–11). Those who pay daily heed to her are blessed; indeed, to choose wisdom is nothing less than to choose life over against death (vv. 32–36).

Proverbs devotes so much space to the fundamental exhortation to choose wisdom over against folly, yet wisdom itself is never defined in terms of a specific text or body of knowledge. Chapters 10–31 give many examples of wisdom in the everyday circumstances of life, but these are not presented as being exhaustive or, indeed, as a coherent or systematic code to which one could adhere. The single controlling clue to the finding of wisdom is presented in 1.7, where the parallelism of the verse structure means that 'knowledge', 'wisdom' and 'instruction' are almost synonymous. 'The fear of the LORD is the beginning of knowledge; fools despise wisdom and instruction'. Wisdom, like Torah, is a reality greater than can be tied down in any text. She is closely tied to Yahweh himself, and the only means of access to her is, precisely, the reverent orientation of one's life towards Yahweh himself.

What purpose, then, does this personification of Wisdom's appeal serve? Why does the author of Proverbs not simply say, 'Does not Yahweh call out . . . '? It gives concrete expression to the fact that the choice before human beings, to obey or not to obey Yahweh, constantly presents itself in specific circumstances and events. It is not a merely abstract or intellectual choice. The life-or-death decisions confront us, in truth, every day. The fact that such choices are presented as choices about *wisdom*, and the powerful enticement to possess what is of lasting worth—true wealth, true life—underline the fact that the decision to fear Yahweh is intensely practical, with consequences for the present and future of life in this world. Thus fearing Yahweh and attending to Wisdom are bound tightly together. Fearing Yahweh is not a merely religious option for those who happen to fancy it; it is the gateway to living life as it is meant to be lived, life in its fullness. Conversely, attending to Wisdom is not something that can be done just by following a handy list of rules or consulting a book of philosophy; the fear of Yahweh is the only route.

The function of Wisdom (Prov. 8.12–21)

In this section Wisdom outlines, as it were, her credentials and her serv-ices. The personification continues to be a picturesque device to entice the hearer/reader to seek the path of wisdom rather than the opposite.

Verse 12 might seem to be a mere statement of the obvious, a tautologi-cal build-up of nearly-synonymous terms. 'I, wisdom, live with prudence, and I attain knowledge and discretion'. Its function, however, is to show that wisdom is not a narrowly-defined concept. It is as if Wisdom is say-ing, 'I don't mind whether or not you get my name exactly right, or if you get to know me through my friends. Prudence, Knowledge, Discretion—we're all in it together'. It is reminiscent of Paul's exhortation to think about 'whatever is true, whatever is honorable, whatever is just, whatever is pure, whatever is pleasing, whatever is commendable, if there is any ex-cellence and if there is anything worthy of praise' (Phil. 4.8). He is clearly not concerned that his readers should learn fine distinctions between these various categories!

The next verse (13) reminds us that Wisdom does not stand alone apart from Yahweh. 'The fear of the LORD' returns here, not only as 'the begin-ning of wisdom' but, apparently, as almost synonymous with wisdom. To fear Yahweh is to hate evil, and that means that Wisdom in her per-sonified form can say she 'hates' 'pride and arrogance and the way of evil and perverted speech'—another build-up of terms, this time suggesting all that lies on the opposite side of the divide from Yahweh and his ways, again without concern for precise definition or narrow demarcation be-tween them. Verse 14 again sounds tautologous if we read pedantically. Isn't it obvious that someone called 'Wisdom' should have 'good advice and sound wisdom' and 'insight'? Once more, it is the rhetoric of entice-ment—almost as if the word 'wisdom' itself and its close associates, by sheer repetition, will draw the casual passer-by, like baskets of shiny fruit on a market stall.

The last attractive gift mentioned in this verse, however, is somewhat different: 'strength'. This hints at the fact that the way of wisdom is more than a way of moral guidance; it is an empowering way. This appropriately leads into vv. 15–16. It is by Wisdom's aid that those who rule justly are enabled to do so.

Verse 17 is tantalizing for those (and perhaps this is all who are at-tracted to her) who would really like Wisdom to draw a clear, unambigu-ous map of how to find her. Having called out to us to pay attention to her, she now appears to be playing a game of hide-and-seek. She assures us that she loves those who love her; yet the way to find her is simply to seek her diligently. She will not be tied down or identified with a particular system, pathway, philosophy or rule.

Wisdom goes on, in vv. 18–21, to display another rack of goods on her stall, described as 'riches and honor, wealth and prosperity'. Those who walk in Wisdom's way of righteousness and justice will find that she walks alongside them, filling them with good things (vv. 20–21). This surely is a controversial claim. Can Wisdom really 'deliver the goods'? The Old Testament Scriptures themselves contain profound questioning of the link apparently made here between wisdom (i.e. obedience to Yahweh) and material prosperity; see especially Psalm 73 and the entire book of Job. The New Testament questions this further still, with its strongly future-oriented vision in which those now poor and hungry are pronounced blessed (Lk. 6.20–21). To deal adequately with this subject and with the problems of 'prosperity theology' would take us far outside the purpose of this chapter. However, it is relevant at least to observe how Wisdom here may be defended against the charge of infringing some cosmic Trade Descriptions Act.

Prov. 8.19 explicitly places Wisdom's wares in a category far *above* material prosperity: 'My fruit is better than gold, even fine gold, and my yield than choice silver'. The question that follows from this is how to read vv. 18 and 21. Are we to understand the wealth and honour there promised in a metaphorical rather than a literal sense, in the light of v. 19—i.e. as a well-being not narrowly defined by physical circumstances? Such a reading could certainly be justified as a Christian one, in the wake of the debates in Job and in the light of Jesus' teaching. However, the very earthy nature of the faith to which the Old Testament bears witness, not least here in Proverbs, and the very fact that debates such as those in Job could occur—these suggest that sayings such as those in vv. 18 and 21 could well have been meant and heard in a quite literal way. The connection between obedience and tangible 'blessing' is rooted in the Pentateuch, Israel's foundational charter: see especially Deuteronomy. The story of the rise, decline and fall of Israel's monarchical existence in the books of Samuel and Kings is precisely a story, overall, of the disastrous *material* consequences of disobedience to Yahweh's Torah. And the cries of Job and of the Psalmists (e.g. Ps. 74) would lose their force if it did not seem fundamentally outrageous that *present* circumstances should be as they are. To these people, Yahweh seems to have gone too far: in his zeal to judge evil, he has allowed the mockers and the foolish to gain the upper hand, violence to stalk the land, and the oppressed to retreat in disgrace (Ps 74.18–21).

It may be better, then, to recognize a tension here. Wisdom's gifts are more than material, but not less. The absence of material signs of Yahweh's blessing, even when people are seeking the way of wisdom and obedience, was not the signal for Israel to 'spiritualize' her hope altogether. Rather, it was one of the triggers for the development of a more robustly future-oriented faith, which came to expression in later prophetic writings (e.g. Isa. 40–66; Ezek. 40–48) and in the 'apocalyptic' atmosphere which formed the more immediate context for the birth of Jesus. In other words, it was realized that Lady Wisdom might not (to continue her own language!) 'deliver the goods' straightaway; but that did not mean she was not to be trusted. The materiality of what Wisdom offers and bestows leads directly to the striking affirmation of the material in the incarnation itself.

The origins of Wisdom (Prov. 8.22–31)

We come to the climax of Wisdom's speech, and the most intensely-suggestive part for our thinking about the incarnation. Prov. 8.22–31 is a wonderfully evocative and poetic picture of the act of creation. Wisdom portrays herself as a witness, a party to the exhilarating moment when earth and sea and sky and human beings first sprang into being. She herself was 'there' before any of it (v. 23), but not only as a witness. She was also a 'master worker', which can be translated 'foreman', 'artisan', or even (we might say) 'architect' (v. 30).[8] (The use of male gender-specific terms like the first one here may seem inappropriate, yet may also serve to highlight the feminine character of Wisdom more strikingly and subversively.) Yahweh the creator delighted in her, and she in him (v. 30). She rejoiced too in the world he had made, and particularly in its human inhabitants (v. 31).

What is this picture painted by personified Wisdom saying to us? Before we start thinking about the implications of there being, apparently, another 'entity' alongside Yahweh at the creation, let us remember the context of this vivid glimpse into the origin of all that we know. Wisdom is making an appeal to all and sundry to pay attention to her. This is a rhetorical device by the writer to underline the urgency, attractiveness and practical import of seeking and following Yahweh's ways. Wisdom has just declared her key role in the right governing of peoples and the bestowal of honour and prosperity. By now putting into Wisdom's mouth the claim to have assisted at the creation of the world, the writer is asserting that her qualifications go further and deeper still. She is actually the brains behind the universe, the creative intellect conceiving and holding together the mind-blowing grandeur and complexity of all that is.

But—let us underline the point again—the import of this is severely practical before it is in any way metaphysical. The writer is saying: Seek wisdom, by fearing Yahweh, *because in the most fundamental sense, this is the way the world works*. This is the basic principle on which everything 'ticks'. This is the way it was set up, the way it continues, and therefore the way by which human life may be safely oriented. In other words, the persuasive force of this passage is quite similar to that of Isaiah 40–55. There Israel is taught, or reminded, that her God, Yahweh, is not a merely local deity operating on arbitrary or eccentric principles. He is the very one who created the world. The 'wisdom' to which fear of Yahweh leads is not some kind of arcane gnosis, but the disposition that learns to see the world as it is and live within it accordingly. Craig Bartholomew expresses the point well.

> The fear of the LORD is . . . the beginning of wisdom in the sense that it represents the start of a journey of exploration and discovery which is creation-wide. . . . Education and exploration of all of life follow on from this foundation and beginning. Human wisdom is a correlate of the wisdom by which the world has been made. . . . Thus fear of the LORD evokes an attitude which takes the fabric of creation utterly seriously, because the design of the fabric comes from Yahweh. Fear of the LORD has creation-wide implications, and this is why wisdom in Proverbs deals with all aspects of life, and not just 'the spiritual'.[9]

Thus Proverbs cannot be interpreted as saying that simply by observing the created world, we will find wisdom (as in classic natural theology). As we have seen, the fear of Yahweh is to be the unambiguous starting-point for the search. Yet these verses do, surely, imply that we can expect to find our faith in Yahweh confirmed, exemplified, filled out in countless ways through the observation and exploration of his world, such that there is a constant interplay between the wisdom discovered through the inward eye of faith and that discovered through the outward eye of sight. This is Lady Wisdom's trump card and her answer to the suspicion of coy evasion raised by v. 17. *She is everywhere to be found.* Yet still, it seems, it is possible for us to miss her; so she must be sought diligently.

What, then, of this picture of Wisdom as Yahweh's right-hand person at the creation, the artisan or architect implementing his grand designs? Verse 22 was controversial in the early Church, for the Greek translation of the verse (echoed in the NRSV) said that Yahweh 'created' wisdom (*ektisen*). Yet here the Hebrew word, *qanah*, means 'get' or 'acquire'; Proverbs uses it several times in encouragements to human beings to 'get wisdom' and associated qualities (see e.g. 4.5).[10] Arius, condemned as a heretic, emphasized 'created' in an attempt to show that Jesus, the Wisdom of God, did *not* actually share the divinity of Yahweh but was a creature alongside all other creatures, albeit an exalted one.[11]

A recent judgement on this debate is surely (and appropriately) wise: 'We should not make the mistake of treating an Old Testament poetic statement about wisdom as if it were a doctrinal proposition about Christ'.[12] While agreeing wholeheartedly that points of Christian doctrine cannot be settled on the basis of texts such as this, I also, however, propose that the passage remains very significant for grasping how early Christian affirmations about Jesus fitted into, and did not overturn, the developing Jewish understanding of Yahweh. For what it surely shows is that belief in Yahweh as the sole creator of all was by no means incompatible with identifying—and personifying in daring fashion—an active, shaping 'principle' alongside him. 'Wisdom' in Proverbs 8 *is* surely, in ordinary literary terms, a personification; what is really being spoken of is Yahweh's own character and power at work in the making and ordering of the universe, a character and power to be sought, imitated and entered into in human life. Yet the glimpse of mutual rejoicing in v. 30 suggests something more; perhaps not yet a 'plurality' in the nature of God, but certainly a *relationality*. There is something irrepressibly outgoing about him. God is One, but he is not static, isolated, monolithic. This is a part of what makes this portrayal of Wisdom alongside Yahweh so fruitful a starting-point for understanding Jesus.

Yet the other side of this picture is equally important. Wisdom may indeed have been with Yahweh before the creation of the world. But it is *now* and *here* and *to human beings* that she makes her appeal. We miss the thrust of the passage if we focus solely on the relationship of Wisdom to Yahweh. Wisdom now turns her face to the human race, at whose birth she rejoiced, and summons them to listen to her, to love her, to seek her, in all the daily circumstances of their lives. It is this turning towards the human race in the turmoil of its existence that, equally, makes Wisdom such a fitting analogue and image of Christ.

Preaching the incarnation from Proverbs

As we have already seen, there has been widespread agreement that the figure of Wisdom in Jewish thought lies in some way behind some of the central New Testament statements about the identity of Jesus.[13] In Chapter 9 we will return to Wisdom as we consider Col. 1.15–20. At this point we will comment briefly on the significance of this background for the most famous of all expositions of the 'mystery of the incarnation', the fitting climax to countless Christmas carol services, Jn. 1.1–14.[14] Naturally, the reader must turn to the commentaries for detailed unfolding of this extraordinarily pregnant and extensively discussed passage. Here we will try to avoid losing the wood for the trees and focus on the startling simplicity of the profound claim being made.

The first five verses of John 1 sound like a reprise, in terser, more majestic form, of wisdom's exuberant proclamation in Prov. 8.12–31. Like Wisdom, 'the Word' was with God in the beginning. He is the agent of creation. Yet also like Wisdom, the Word is not to be regarded as separate from God; rather, he is a manifestation of God's very being. Like Wisdom, 'the Word' has a fundamental orientation not only to God but also to the human race. 'In him was life, and the life was the light of all people' (Jn. 1.4) might be taken as a summary of Wisdom's claim in Prov. 8.12–21 to be the giver of concrete blessing to humanity, as well as the bright picture in Prov. 8.31 of Wisdom 'delighting in the human race'. Jn. 1.5 then comes as the Evangelist's assertion of faith that, despite all possible evidence to the contrary, the Word (and by implication, Wisdom) continues to fulfil his/her function. The light for humanity that is the gift of God's Wisdom and Word *was never* extinguished by the 'darkness' of folly and rebellion which threatened to engulf it. John is placing himself in continuity with the faith expressed in Proverbs—that there is indeed a divine light at the centre of all things that can be sought and found by human beings.[15]

It is against this backdrop of belief in an unchanging divine Wisdom that John goes on to lift the curtain on the good news he has to tell. The reference to John the Baptist (Jn. 1.6–8) heralds the fact that this will be good news of a recent, historical event. The event turns out to be nothing less than this: that the light '*was coming into the world*' (v. 9, stress added), that 'the Word *became flesh*' (v. 14, stress added). In the process, the light encountered the darkness; the Word experienced the resistance that, all along, humanity had offered to Wisdom (thus necessitating Wisdom's urgent appeal). Yet for those who welcomed the Word, an exhilarating future opened up as children of God: a relationship of clarity and intimacy whose newness matched the amazing newness of the Word becoming flesh. Let us then crystallize four points about John's claim in view of its background in Proverbs 8.

First, *Jesus* is presented as true Wisdom and therefore as the embodiment of Yahweh himself. What is true of Wisdom is true of him. That means that in him, in this human being who trod the tracks of Galilee and Judea in the early first century, we find the clue to the meaning of the universe.

Second and equally important, Jesus is surely presented here as the true 'wise man'. In his human flesh—that is, in his entire disposition and behaviour as a human being—he displays what it looks like to heed Wisdom's call. He demonstrates what it means to be *in touch with* the meaning of the universe, to be alive to the summons of the one who from the beginning delighted in the human race.

Third, the gospel that John tells is therefore a reiteration in a new and urgent register of the call of Wisdom. Where once Wisdom cried out through prophets, wise men and the everyday circumstances of life, she now cries out supremely in one place, the place where she has taken human flesh. The gospel is good news of 'life in his name' (Jn. 1.12–13; 20.31). If Wisdom is at the heart of creation, then clearly she can still, in principle, be found in all kinds of places and voices; but just as in Proverbs the one *key* to wisdom is fear of Yahweh, so here in John the one *key* to wisdom, and therefore to life and light, is Jesus of Nazareth. He is the one to whom a true fear of Yahweh now directs everyone (cf. Jn. 3.21).

Fourth and finally, we repeat the point made in Chapter 1: those who preach on the incarnation cannot do so apart from the Old Testament background, in whose light alone the doctrine makes sense; conversely, we cannot preach on Old Testament themes and texts, such as those concerning wisdom, apart from the fuller light we have received on them in Christ. Our sermon here suggests one way in which we can take seriously the Old Testament portrayal of wisdom in our Christian proclamation of Yahweh's incarnation in Jesus of Nazareth.

Sermon: Personification

William Willimon

Does not wisdom call, and does not understanding raise her voice? On the heights, beside the way, at the crossroads she takes her stand; beside the gates in front of the town, at the entrance of the portals she cries out. (Prov. 8:1–3)[16]

Last year we visited Jerusalem. On our first morning, we entered the Holy City through the beautiful Damascus Gate. What a thrill to be entering this place of such spiritual grandeur!

Yet the grandeur of the moment was spoiled because of the incessant hawking of the street vendors who surrounded the entrance to the city gate.

Seeing that we are Americans, they began shouting out, 'Hey, mister! I've got great cigarettes here! Want a nice scarf? Look at what I've got here. Nice price. Not much money!'

The book of Proverbs says that 'wisdom' is just like those street vendors. Lady Wisdom sits at the gates of the city, shouting, hawking her wares, screaming out to everyone to come and get some wisdom from her.

It's not a very uplifting image of wisdom.

I'll let you in on a preacher's secret: whenever, in a sermon, we preachers lack a cohesive argument, or even a point that is worth making, we preachers find it helpful to fill the sermon with as much hot air as possible, fill up the balloon with helium, and let that waft over the congregation.

And you love it. You tend to think that 'religion' is about something vague that is 'spiritual'. Spiritual is when we all get together and are as nebulous as possible, ethereal and indistinct. Thus we dump a mess of generalities upon the congregation—redemption, atonement, inspiration, love, liberation, sensitivity, spirituality, blah, blah, blah—and we all come away feeling that something has actually happened in the sermon, though just what has happened, we couldn't say for sure.

Which makes all the more remarkable today's lesson from Proverbs 8. It's Trinity Sunday, and if a preacher can't be obtuse, vague and fuzzy on Trinity Sunday, when can you be? What Christian doctrine is more incomprehensible than the Trinity?

And yet today's text from Proverbs is uncooperative. Proverbs refuses to be 'spiritual' or otherwise elusive and indistinct. Today's text gets positively personal. In today's text the concept 'wisdom' is personified, made into Woman Wisdom. The Hebrew word for 'wisdom', *khokmah*, is made into a human being, given a face. It reminds one of the way John's Gospel opens with 'In the beginning was the Word, . . . and the Word was God'—high-sounding phrases, noble and uplifting, floating somewhere between the beginning of the world and where we are now, which is almost nowhere. And then John's Gospel becomes alarmingly concrete: 'and the Word became flesh'. Flesh. Meat. The Word, the eternal Logos, is personified, embodied, takes on undeniably and unavoidably physical form. God's eternal Logos is a Jew from Nazareth.

Something like that is happening here in Proverbs—wisdom is made flesh. 'Wisdom' is a noble word. But who really knows what we mean when we say 'wisdom'? Here Wisdom is more than a concept, an idea or a generality. Wisdom is an attractive woman who calls people to follow her, to receive her gifts. Wisdom stands before us, personified, and gives a long speech, offering a list of all the gifts that she bestows. Wisdom not only stands there before us but also reaches out to us, beckons us, allures. Lady Wisdom claims that she was present at the very foundation of the whole cosmos. Wisdom says that she is at the bottom of all true reality.

Truth has a face, a name, 'Wisdom'. Truth is not simply a set of ideas, a concept. Truth reaches out to you, speaks, beckons, stands there undeniably before you, making a personal claim upon you.

In one of his aphorisms, Nietzsche asks, 'What if truth were a woman?'—a statement that sounds sexist, and Nietzsche was not above sexism. But I take this to imply, 'What if truth had a face, a name? What if truth were not merely an abstraction but also a personality that reaches out to you, beguiles you, embraces you?' What if truth were more like a person than an idea?

Sitting in prison, awaiting his certain execution, punishment for a crime he never mentions, Boethius (executed in 524 CE) writes *The Consolation of Philosophy*, a book dearly beloved by the first Christian philosophers. Though he was a noble, well-educated Roman, Boethius spent most of his time in Greece, and it was there, no doubt, that he met Greek philosophy.

How to handle misfortune in life? When bad things happen, such as jail, how do you cope? Boethius contemplates his situation; then, surprisingly, a woman enters his prison cell. It is Lady Philosophy who enters and engages imprisoned Boethius in conversation. *The Consolation of Philosophy* consists of a dialogue between Boethius and Dame Philosophy about the nature of God, Providence, fate and grace.

Dame Philosophy convinces Boethius that happiness is the true end of humanity. We are made to find 'eudaemonia'. Despite life's setbacks, we are meant for happiness, but not happiness based on material things. Rather, we are made for philosophical happiness—detached, serene contentment—the consolation that the world's wrong cannot thwart, that home to which one can return during times of tragedy—this is the goal of philosophy.

Although the *Consolation* is an appeal to earnest philosophizing, it is significant that Boethius personifies Philosophy, as if Philosophy is something external to him, Truth that comes to him rather than his coming to Truth. There can be no real help to us, in this prison cell called life in this world, that is not external to us. Boethius portrays Philosophy as a person who encounters him in his misery, cajoles and challenges him, argues with and seduces him. The Truth that dares to speak to us, that reaches to us, is the Truth worth knowing. Sometimes we say, when some truth really comes to us, 'I got it!' when what we ought to say is 'It got me!' The *Consolation* presages the death of all earnest, heroic, subjective philosophizing, namely, in the advent of Jesus Christ.

We Christians don't just believe in 'God' or 'Spirit'. We also believe in the *incarnation*. We believe that God refused to be God by himself. God became flesh and moved in with us. God refused to be relegated to the realm of the vague and the indistinct. God has a face, a name, Jesus Christ. Something about this God refused to be God without us.

Lady Wisdom presages the incarnation, Jesus Christ. Our God doesn't just love us; God comes to us, speaks, reveals, reaches out to us when all the while we thought we were reaching out to God.

I think you know this already. That's why you are here this morning. You are here in church, not for a philosophical lecture, not for an enumeration of all the benefits of the Christian faith. You are here hoping to be met by the Word Made Flesh. True worship, in the name of the God we call Father, Son and Holy Spirit is always incarnational, personal, embodied. The deity of the gods of the Greeks was godliness of distance, aloofness. God? God is high, lifted up, distant and unapproachable. The God who met us in Jesus Christ is godly precisely in God's nearness, approachableness, availability and self-disclosure. Thank God that our God did not wait for us to come to God, but came to us, God With Us, Emmanuel.

During a discussion (i.e. bitter debate) about the upcoming budget in the church council one evening, some member of the council said in exasperation, 'I wish we could get off all this talk about money, money, money and get on with more spiritual matters'.

We wish. Something in us wishes that we could render the Christian faith into something spiritual, an idea that we could all discuss, a concept. No! The Christian faith is what happens when we are encountered by a person who says not 'Think about me' but rather '*Follow me!*'

This, said Bonhoeffer, is the whole point of a sermon. A sermon, says the great Christian martyr, 'enables the Risen Christ to walk among his people'. Don't you agree? A sermon is best, not as a listing of spiritual insights, a warm but fuzzy feeling engendered in people. A sermon is a sermon when it is used by God With Us as a means of intruding, invading, walking among God's people.

In a former congregation I had a man who drove an hour each way to be with us on Sunday morning. One Sunday I inquired into the reason for his making such an effort to be at our church. I hoped that he would answer, 'Of course, the brilliant preaching'.

He didn't. To my dismay he said, 'You know, most of your sermons are over my head. I only understand about one out of four of your sermons'.

Really? Then why did he keep coming to our church?

'Because', he answered, 'almost every Sunday I meet Christ. Somehow, someway, Christ comes to me, speaks to me, and I go away refreshed and more committed to follow Christ'.

Lady Wisdom reaches out to us, beckons us. So does The Word Made Flesh. Thank God our God was not content to be spiritual. Our God got personal. Thanks be to God!

Sermon commentary

This sermon captures the way in which God comes to us, taking the initiative to reach out to speak to us and meet us. It does so by evoking and echoing the call of Wisdom in Proverbs 8, connecting it to the incarnation of Christ and earthing it in the reality of present-day encounter with Christ in worship.

Note the way the preacher begins by declaiming a part of Wisdom's call. How much more effective an opening than 'my text today is . . . '! Straightaway we are *hearing* the word which will be unfolded as a summons to us. The story which follows of the visit to Jerusalem succinctly and vividly provides the background which makes sense of Proverbs' imagery: again, how much more effective than a ponderous explanation of personification. The preacher is respecting and echoing the form of the text itself, which dramatizes the way in which 'Wisdom, who observed the ways of the world from her window in Prov. 7.6, steps down into the arena and assumes the role of a preacher and teacher in the public forum of the town'.[17]

The sermon opening 'upsets the equilibrium',[18] raising the interest of the hearers and posing a problem to be worked at. It does so in two ways. On the one hand, it presents us with the shock of what an earthy picture of Wisdom this is. On the other hand, it exposes the way in which preachers and congregations can so easily drift into, and be satisfied with, a vague discourse about the 'spiritual'. The preacher's directness at this point chimes with the in-your-face hawking of Wisdom herself. There is at least an implicit challenge here to the widespread fascination with 'spirituality', often divorced from real Christian commitment or indeed any kind of commitment.

Willimon goes on to expose the thoroughly sub-Christian character of a mere interest in the 'spiritual'. He shows that the New Testament witness to the incarnation of Christ is in a clear line of continuity with the personification of Wisdom. Two fundamental features of God's revelation in Wisdom and in Christ are highlighted. First, God does not remain vague and indistinct, but takes specific form and makes specific claims upon us. Second, God does not wait passively to be found, but takes the initiative to come to us; otherwise we would never know wisdom, or know him.

All the way through the sermon, Willimon is 'embodying the word'.[19] I believe preachers are always called to do this, but it is especially appropriate in a sermon about the specific claims made upon us by the God who became incarnate! Nietzsche's aphorism 'What if truth were a woman?'

is memorable, links with the feminine portrayal of Wisdom and jolts the hearers into a fresh perception of the idea of truth. (It is also usefully provocative for any Christians who might think that nothing good could come from the mouth of Nietzsche!) The story of Boethius in his prison cell is not merely an 'illustration' of Wisdom coming to us from outside ourselves, but an *instance* of it, an example of it actually happening.[20] Then towards the end of the sermon we come right down to the present and discussions at a church council meeting. If we cannot be encountered by Wisdom in what we think of as the messy daily decisions to be taken about money, what does Proverbs 8 or the story of the incarnation mean?

The climax of the sermon returns to the idea of preaching itself and to what we should expect to happen when we gather for worship and to hear the word of God. It does so in a way which again exalts the initiative of God and his desire to meet with us. The man who keeps on coming all that way to church may not understand all the sermons, but he is met by the risen Christ. Wisdom is seen to be present, addressing God's children today. The preacher is brutally honest: this is God's doing, not his. And yet in his sermon he has gestured towards God's act[21] through his own incarnation of the Word.

3

'God with us'

MATTHEW 1.1–25 AND LUKE 1.26–2.21

The narratives of Jesus' conception and birth

Christmas focuses attention on the incarnation, yet preaching the incarnation by means of the Christmas stories is not as straightforward as one might assume.[1] There are three problems. First, a communicational one: the radical significance of the stories gets lost in a fog of sentimental familiarity. Second, an intellectual one: the stories raise serious questions of a historical and scientific nature for a thoughtful reader or listener. Third, a theological one: is there not a danger that if the truth of the incarnation is tied to the stories of the virginal conception, we will preach a 'hybrid' Jesus who is neither truly God nor truly human?

First, and perhaps easiest to deal with, is the *communicational* problem. Preachers have become accustomed to this, and many have become skilled at penetrating it. Indeed, this kind of penetration can itself become a kind of preaching cliché, as when Christmas sermons start to follow a predictable pattern of debunking Christmas-card or nativity-play diversions from 'the real meaning of Christmas' (a cliché itself if ever there was one!). However, as always, fresh language can yield fresh insight. Here are two examples.

Mary Cotes draws the hearer into the human dimensions of the manger scene, dispelling the idealism which often surrounds it. Invited into the darkness of the stable, the listeners find themselves awkward witnesses to the pains of Mary's labour.

'I'm never going through this again! I can't! I can't!' There is another scream, this time louder, tearing into us, and forcing us to be part of the pain. How much longer must we wait in the darkness? How much longer must we share the agony of this woman? How much longer before the coming of this baby?

'How silently, how silently, the wondrous gift is given'. Or so the carol goes. . . . But do you still believe it, now that you are standing in the stable?

'The little Lord Jesus no crying he makes'. Or so the carol goes.[2]

Giles Fraser, in an Ascension Day sermon, relates the truth of the incarnation to the ministry of St Martin-in-the-Fields, London, to the poor and homeless in its newly-reordered crypt.[3] This reminds us, incidentally, that the message of the incarnation is as pressing at Ascensiontide as it is at Christmas. Notwithstanding Jesus' withdrawal from sight, 'after the Incarnation [God] is at work in space and time in a way that he never was before'.[4] Criticizing what he perceives as a current Christian tendency to 'an introverted piety that spends its time gazing up into heaven [cf. Acts 1.11] and a practical indifference to the material conditions of those who live next door', Fraser goes on:

> It must be remembered then that Christianity is arguably the most materialistic of the world's religious faiths. For with Christianity, God is imagined not as a cloud, nor as a book, but as a human being, born in a shed, and at one with the physical reality of human life. With Christianity, God is to be found in the dirt and not in the sky. That's why the Ascension can be so misleading.[5]

However, he continues, there is another way of looking at the Ascension. The angels' question 'invites the disciples to bring their gaze down to earth and confront the measure of the task now before them. A heartbeat after Jesus' departure comes the terrifying question: "What on earth are we to do now?"'

> This remarkable church of St Martin in the Fields gives us a clue. Under our feet, deep within the earth, wonderful new facilities for London's poorest people have been dug out in a feat of the most extraordinary engineering. If you want to find God round here, follow the advice of the angels and cease gazing up into the sky. For God lives downstairs, alongside the homeless, the outcast and the refugee. Any church worthy of the name must be built right on top of a concern for the vulnerable, just as this church is quite literally.

'God lives downstairs': that certainly brings home the scandal of the incarnation in an arresting image that chimes with the story of Jesus' birth.

The second problem associated with preaching the incarnation from the Christmas stories arises from the modern *historical* and *scientific* questions posed to them. They are frequently seen as retrojections of

Christian belief into the narrative of Jesus' life, based at most on dubious tales, perhaps even fabricated out of Old Testament patterns and texts. The absence of any such stories in Mark and John is a sign to the more sceptical reader that they are no part of the 'essence' of the gospel and thus of dubious historical value. Such *historical* scepticism is linked to *scientific* scepticism about the possibility of any extraordinary event such as a 'virginal conception'.

Ignoring such scepticism is certainly not a valid option for the preacher. Serious questions like this are raised by many thoughtful people within the Church and beyond it, and indeed arise naturally from careful study of Scripture. Nevertheless, adopting a sceptical tone ourselves does not sit well with the proclamation of good news. So how are we to proclaim the Christmas gospel without retreating into an ostrich-like flat-earth approach? Below we will outline how sensitivity to the literary character of the texts may offer the best way forward.

Surprisingly, the third and most substantial problem with preaching the incarnation from the Christmas stories is *theological*. Is not the Christ presented here a God-human hybrid, rather than the unified person of orthodox belief?[6] Does not the language of virginal conception open the door to misunderstandings of incarnation as deriving from the sexual union of God and a woman?[7] This problem strikes closer to home than the others. For it is not simply a matter of how to commend the incarnation to those anaesthetized by a progressively watered-down Christmas, or to historical or scientific sceptics. It is a matter of understanding how two key texts in our tradition (Matthew and Luke) relate to the accepted summaries of our faith in the catholic creeds and conciliar formulations—and indeed to another key New Testament text, John, whose doctrine of 'the word made flesh' seems to express the unity of the person of Christ much more satisfactorily.

The subject of this chapter thus turns out to be a case study in the tension between Scripture and tradition, biblical narrative and creedal affirmation. I believe this tension is fertile, not fatal, and the more we inhabit its dynamics, the richer will be the proclamation engendered.

Matthew's birth narrative (Mt. 1.1–25)

I doubt if any exponents of storytelling today would recommend trying to 'hook' your audience by means of a list of forty-odd names! This opening section of Matthew is almost never read in public—and certainly not at carol services. But such strangeness should alert us to ask questions about the purpose of such a passage. Modern readers tend to find they keep being tripped up in this chapter. We will consider it under the headings of the surprises that keep being sprung upon us.

A surprising start

Why the genealogy in Mt. 1.1–17? It tells us three things. First, this is to be a book about a human being. Matthew is clearly concerned in detail with Jesus' human origins. Second, this is to be a book about 'the Messiah' (1.1). Matthew wants to defend Jesus' status to those who are unconvinced, and to give his Christian readers the resources to do likewise. Third, Jesus is attested as a scripturally-suitable candidate for Messiahship by being a descendant of Abraham and, above all, of David. Such reasoning is unlikely to convince many sceptics today, but within the world of first-century Judaism and Christianity inhabited by Matthew, these three points add up to a specific apologetic purpose: to show that the claim of Jesus' Messiahship is in accordance with the promises of blessing that would come through the descendants of Abraham (Gen. 22.18) and of an eternal throne to the line of David (Ps. 89.36). To put the point sharply. Matthew here is not concerned at all with the 'divinity' of Jesus (the Messiah of Jewish expectation was not in himself a 'divine' figure). The question of 'incarnation' is thus not here on the horizon. To a predominantly Jewish readership, Matthew wanted to show that the notion of Jesus' Messiahship is not contradicted (though it certainly could not be *proved*) by his pedigree.[8]

A surprising twist

The reader who has gotten this far may well be thrown off course again when reaching vv. 16 and 18. For here Matthew appears to shoot himself in the foot. Why go to such lengths to establish the genealogy of Jesus through Joseph if it turns out that Joseph was not his natural father after all? If Mary was found to be with child 'from the Holy Spirit' (v. 18), how could any argument from *Joseph's* ancestry carry weight? This puzzle may be partly to blame for a tendency to overestimate the significance of the virginal conception for Matthew. If it appears to us that the genealogy is rather pointless (or that its point depends on some flimsy theory about Jesus' legal status), we are more likely to latch on to the virgin birth as if it were Matthew's main point.

Yet the genealogy establishes an important Jewish legal point. The naming of Jesus commanded in v. 21 and carried out in v. 25 was the means by which, according to Jewish custom, Joseph took Jesus as his true adopted son.[9] Once Matthew's fellow-Jews could be persuaded to believe in this claim about *Joseph's* ancestry, they would not have a problem with the fact that *Jesus* was an adopted rather than a natural son. He too could be regarded as a true son of Abraham and son of David.

A surprising inclusion

The question now arises: why mention the virginal conception at all, when the very suspicion of anything irregular or shameful about Jesus' origins could be sufficient to discredit him and his followers in the eyes of opponents and unbelievers? Does this not spoil Matthew's apologetic, introducing a complication into an otherwise convincing (albeit, to us, arcane) argument about Jesus' Messiahship?

There may have been rumours about Jesus' irregular birth, and perhaps Matthew felt the need to set the record straight. Like Luke, he acknowledges that Joseph was not the natural father of Jesus. But against the obvious suspicions that would follow from this, Matthew and Luke affirm that it was by the agency of the Holy Spirit that Mary conceived. The stigma of illegitimacy may well have hung about Jesus as he grew up; a hint of this may be preserved in Mk. 6.3 and Jn. 8.41, as well as in the anti-Christian writer Celsus, refuted by Origen.[10] Matthew and Luke, who record Jesus' consorting with outcasts and ignominious death, would have seen the appropriateness of his bearing shame from the beginning. But equally, they would have seen here the sign of a unique bestowal of God's Spirit upon one set apart like no other to the will and purposes of God. One outwardly shamed was actually God's holy child.[11] Thus Mary is said to be with child 'from the Holy Spirit' (or 'from a holy spirit')—rather than, say, 'the Spirit of the Lord'—in Mt. 1:18 and 20. Against a background of slurs, is it the *holiness* of the unborn infant of which Joseph—and Matthew's readers—need to be assured? For Matthew, is the identification of God with the stigmatized more central to the truth of the incarnation than the mechanics of Jesus' conception? The theme of disgrace, and the appropriate response to it, continues to be central to Matthew's account of the circumstances of Jesus' birth in 1.18–25. Joseph willingly takes Mary into his care, notwithstanding the inevitable social stigma. He is strengthened to brace himself for awkward questions because he trusts God's word that 'the child conceived in her is from the Holy Spirit' (v. 20).

A surprising text

The final surprise is also the final clue to Matthew's account of Jesus' origins, helping us fit the various pieces together. In v. 21 the angel tells Joseph that he is to name the child Jesus, 'for he will save his people from their sins'. This is a straightforward example of the etymological significance often accorded to names in the Old Testament and Judaism; 'Jesus' is the Greek form of 'Joshua', meaning 'Yahweh saves'. Jesus will be a Saviour—in a more comprehensive sense than either Joshua or the 'judges' (alternatively rendered 'saviours') who followed him. In and through him, moreover, *Yahweh* will be seen as Saviour. But why then do vv. 22–23 make no mention of 'Jesus' or saviours, but cite Isa. 7.14 as the text being fulfilled? 'Look, the virgin shall conceive and bear a son, and they shall name him Emmanuel, which means, "God is with us."'

This odd transition suggests two things: First, the name 'Emmanuel' is not saying anything essentially different from the name 'Jesus'. Through drawing attention to both, Matthew wants to emphasize that Yahweh, the one true God, who has been with his people as a powerful saviour in the past, has come to them in the same way again. 'In Jesus Christ God has named himself afresh and supremely'.[12] Second, the promise 'The virgin shall conceive' is introduced here because of the reference to Emmanuel, not the other way round. Undoubtedly the word *parthenos* ('virgin'), the LXX translation of the Hebrew *'almah* ('young woman'), would have provided a useful link for Matthew with the conception of Jesus 'through the Holy Spirit' (vv. 18, 20), if those words are taken with the usually-accepted inference of a virginal conception.[13] But Matthew's main stress is on the nature of the child (both that in Isa. 7 and of Jesus) as a tangible, physical reminder of God's presence. This in turn reflects further on our understanding of the phrase 'from the Holy Spirit' (vv. 18, 20). Rather than specifying details about the manner of conception, this phrase then echoes the work of God through the ages, from the brooding of his Spirit over the waters in creation (Gen. 1.2) through the inspiration and direction of his prophets (e.g. 2 Kgs. 2.16) to the promise of a whole people renewed by the Spirit (e.g. Ezek. 36.26).

Thus Matthew is not trying to 'prove' anything by the citation of Isa. 7.14. A single text like this was not going to provide knock-down evidence of either Jesus' identity or a 'miraculous' birth. With his various Old Testament citations, Matthew is surely weaving a picture of Israel's story in which Jesus as Messiah can emerge as a consistent part.[14] Indeed, conservative readers of Scripture have a problem if they try to take Isa. 7.14

simply as a 'prediction' of Jesus' virgin birth. One cannot hold this view without seriously wrenching Isaiah's text from its literary and historical context. For whereas many 'Messianic' foreshadowings of Jesus in the Old Testament may be seen to have both an immediate historical reference and a *sensus plenior*, a fuller christological meaning, if it is the virgin birth we are thinking about, we have to choose: we cannot have our cake and eat it. 'Conservative' readers, least of all, could countenance a 'virgin birth' in the time of Isaiah. If they say that the Old Testament text affirms the uniqueness of Jesus in his birth from a virgin mother, they wrest that text from its context. If they take that context seriously, they have to admit *either* an eighth-century BCE virgin birth (compromising the uniqueness of Jesus) *or* some looseness and creativity in Matthew's use of the text, undermining any sense that he is using it as an intentional 'prediction' by Isaiah. This last option seems much more plausible.[15]

All this surely provides a sufficient answer to the theological concerns of those who fear that this birth narrative suggests not a unified Jesus Christ, but a 'hybrid' who is thus neither truly divine nor truly human. Matthew 1 places Jesus firmly within the human family. His legal ancestry through Joseph makes the claim of his Messiahship plausible for Matthew's readers, despite the surprising and even shameful circumstances of Jesus' birth. It is in his arrival as Messiah that God himself comes among his people, showing himself to be indeed their Saviour.

Joseph's role should not be understated. He was to be a willing servant through whom God's purpose could come about. He is prompted by God to extend God's mercy, love and protection to a woman who would otherwise have been at best disgraced, at worst killed, and so becomes one of the earliest manifestations of God's presence and character in the new epoch which is dawning. By his obedient naming and adoption of Jesus, he brings into the Messianic line one who would otherwise have remained an outsider to it. Thus he is instrumental in the demonstration to Jewish people by Matthew and others that Jesus truly fulfils the Scriptural qualifications for Messiahship. At the same time, Joseph's story—presumably willingly shared, just as it had been willingly entered into—is a paradigmatic case of God's choice not being tied to human descent, but a matter of his free and merciful promise (Rom. 9.8). And the 'promise' with which Matthew is concerned is not merely an isolated text about the conception of a child, but the entire hope revealed to Israel, apparently against all the odds, cumulating over the centuries—the hope that somehow, sometime, their God would come to save them, and also show himself as Lord of the whole world.

Luke's birth narrative (Lk. 1.26–2.21)

Luke's account of events leading up to and following Jesus' birth is worthy of sustained study in its own right,[16] but here I simply want to show how Luke in his own way gives a similar emphasis to that which we have seen in Matthew,[17] and thus likewise escapes the theological suspicion of propounding a 'hybrid' Jesus.

Luke prefaces the story of Jesus' birth with a chapter interweaving the remarkable circumstances leading up to it with those leading up to the birth of his cousin John. Luke 1 culminates in the story of John's birth and a note about his growth (vv. 66, 80) sandwiching a song of John's father, Zechariah, praising the God who 'has looked favorably on his people and redeemed them' (vv. 67–79). The chapter serves two purposes.

First, in linking Jesus and John, Luke stresses that the coming of Jesus was not an isolated event. A new era has already begun with the annunciation of John's birth. At the same time Jesus is marked out as greater than John: Jesus is the 'Son of the Most High' (1.32) while John is 'prophet of the Most High' (1.76). This build-up of God's activity serves to reinforce readers' faith, just as there is a mutual reinforcement of faith between Mary and Elizabeth (1.36–45).

Second, John the Baptist links the story of Jesus back into the story of Israel. Zechariah, Elizabeth and Mary are faithful Israelites who trust in God's promises, praise him for what he has done in the past and recognize his work in the present and the future (1.5–7, 39–56, 68–79). Just as in Matthew, then, the birth of Jesus is seen as an event in continuity with what God has done before, but bringing it to a climax. He is the one who will inherit the throne of David and reign over his people forever (1.33).

The virginal conception is given more emphasis in Luke than in Matthew, for it is part of the contrast drawn between Elizabeth and Mary. Elizabeth conceives in her old age, which was not unprecedented in Israel's history: Sarah is the prime example (Gen. 21.1–2). But Mary conceives without, it seems, the agency of a man—something truly new.

However, does the virginal conception have quite the prominent place here to which it has often been elevated? Note the phrasing of Lk. 1.35. In response to Mary's objection that she is a virgin, Gabriel responds: 'The Holy Spirit will come upon you, and the power of the Most High will overshadow you; therefore the child to be born will be holy; he will be called Son of God'. For the second half of the verse, the NIV has 'So the holy one to be born will be called the Son of God'. A modern reader expects the latter half of Gabriel's sentence to be 'therefore it's no problem that you're a virgin'. Whichever way the Greek is parsed, however, the stress is not so much on the power of God to cause Mary to conceive, as on the fact that the Holy Spirit will guarantee the holiness of the child (cf. Mt. 1.18, 20), and therefore his fitness to sit on the throne of David for which he is destined (Lk. 1.32–33), with the royal title 'Son of God' (v. 35). Perhaps for Mary the main problem arising from the annunciation is not disbelief in God's ability but the prospect of shame—the very thing the angel who appears to Joseph also addresses in Mt. 1.20.[18] The accent in Mary's song on God's mercy to the 'lowly' (1.48, 52) underlines the sense that the truly amazing thing God is doing is to take a shameful situation and turn it, not merely to good, but to his goal of glorious justice.

Luke is reticent about what happens between Mary's visit to Elizabeth and the birth in Bethlehem. Like Matthew, he is clear that Jesus is not Joseph's natural son (3.23). Mary had been a virgin when Gabriel appeared to her (1.27, 34); in 2.5 we are just reminded that Mary was engaged to Joseph, and told that by this point she 'was expecting a child' (2.5). The praises and proclamations that ensue focus entirely on the identity and destiny of the child, not at all on how he came into the world. But again, the overturning of conventional notions of shame and honour is to the fore: the first to go to see the baby are unclean, despised shepherds.

Luke, like Matthew, suggests that for God's peculiar purposes to be achieved, unusual methods have to be employed. In Matthew, a direct angelic visitation is needed to convince Joseph to adopt an otherwise socially-illegitimate child. In Luke, a Roman imperial decree is the means by which the destined Messiah ends up being born in the city of David. It was as if for God's grace truly to be highlighted in the Messiah's coming, he has both to fulfil and confound expectation. He is adopted as a genuine 'son of David', yet the stigma of unknown parentage hangs over his head. He is born in Bethlehem, but it is not 'home' to Joseph and Mary, and his first bed is an animal's feeding trough. Thus both God's faithfulness to his promises and his continuing power to do a 'new thing' (cf. Isa. 43.19) are brought to light.

The angel's words to the shepherds and the praise of the heavenly host in Lk. 2.10–14 are parallel to the declaration of Jesus as 'Saviour' and 'Emmanuel' in Mt. 1.21–23. At the heart of both announcements is the sense that *God has come to do in a new, final and decisive way what he has always been doing in the past.* This human child in a feeding trough is indeed a 'Savior', 'the Messiah, the Lord' (Lk. 2.11). This is news of great joy 'for all the people' (Lk. 2.10)—the same 'people' whom this Jesus will save from their sins (Mt. 1.21). And the upshot of this is that *God* is glorified and a new era of God-directed peace is ushered in (Lk. 2.14). The divine catches up the human, as we see time and again in the stories of Yahweh and his people.

Luke puts a particular accent on the way in which God's action has resonance and application for the 'pagan' world beyond Judaism. An altar of 'peace' had been built in Rome to celebrate the peace that the emperor was seen to have brought. The terms of the angels' proclamation echo words used of the emperor Augustus, as he was called a 'saviour' and even a 'god'. His birthday was said to have 'marked for the world the beginning of good tidings through his coming'.[19] And whereas 'all the people' in Lk. 2.10 has immediate reference to Israel, 'those whom he favors' in v. 14 indicates a much wider group.[20] (In Matthew this wider perspective does not become fully apparent until Herod and the wise men appear on the scene in ch. 2.) Jesus is the true 'god' who brings true 'good news' of 'peace', and in doing so challenges the claims of empire.

In his own way, Luke thus affirms Matthew's portrayal of a Jesus in continuity with Israel, in whom God's work with and among his people has come to a head. This is no hybrid Jesus, but a true human being, uniquely bearing the stamp of a God who can create a 'new thing' in the midst of oppression, shame and sin, while remaining faithful to all his past promises. Exactly how he will do this is the burden of the rest of these Gospels.

Preaching the incarnation from the narratives of Jesus' birth

The opening chapters of Matthew and Luke offer a wealth of material through which the truth of the incarnation may be explored and proclaimed. Let us summarize some of the main homiletical implications of our discussion under the heading of three kinds of sensitivity needed as we approach these texts.

Literary sensitivity

These narratives encounter the reader as tales rich with meaning. Their immediacy and colour, 'fraught with background',[21] deserve to shape and inspire sermons, so that congregations may feel their power afresh. Borg and Crossan suggestively describe them as 'parabolic overtures' to the Gospels.[22] Literary sensitivity will inspire us to enter and seek to re-present the stories in a positive way, rather than dismissing them as legend or fable. It will not deny hearers' serious historical and scientific questions but put them in perspective by focusing on the actual stories, not the irresolvable disputes about what exactly lies behind them. This allows hearers space to weigh their force for themselves. It is not for us to shield others from mystery by saying too much.

Historical sensitivity

Notwithstanding what we have just said, historical sensitivity is bound up with literary sensitivity. It is only through some understanding of the narratives' background in both Jewish[23] and Roman[24] worlds that we may apprehend their depth and resonance as literature. The fact that the nature of whatever historical events lies behind the narratives remains shrouded in mystery by no means implies that the narratives are not historically *conditioned* at every point, having significance within a first-century world of meaning. Our appreciation of the stories and ability to communicate them will be much enhanced by a growing familiarity with that world. Imagination will suggest different ways of communicating historical insight, without losing the engaging elements of a narrative style.

Theological sensitivity

These narratives are laden with theology, and to ignore this does them, and our hearers, great injustice. Yet we have seen that their theology is more subtle than is sometimes assumed. Matthew and Luke do not announce the incarnation as explicitly as John or Hebrews. The accounts of the virginal conception do not necessarily imply a full doctrine of incarnation; moreover, if they are taken that way, they may lead towards unhelpful ideas of a divine-human hybrid.

Rather, they trace the hand of God in the conception and birth of Jesus just as they trace it in his life, death and resurrection. This was a baby born in dubious circumstances, nonetheless to be recognized as the fulfilment of God's promises to Israel. Gabriel's words about the child being called 'Son of the Most High', inheriting David's throne and bearing holiness (Lk. 1.32–35) foreshadow Paul's post-resurrection description of him as '[God's] Son, . . . descended from David according to the flesh, . . . declared to be Son of God with power according to the spirit of holiness by resurrection from the dead, Jesus Christ our Lord' (Rom. 1.3–4).[25] This was the climactic example of God's propensity to turn human fortunes and verdicts on their heads (Lk. 1.46–55; cf. 1 Sam. 2.1–10). Mary's words about lifting up the lowly (Lk. 1.52) are prophetic of what will happen to Jesus himself, who is to be humbled and rejected, but then exalted by God (Acts 2.23–24, 33; 3.13–16; 4.10–12; 5.30–31).

Thomas F. Torrance helpfully explains how the teaching of the 'virgin birth' as attested by Matthew and Luke actually safeguards the genuine humanity of Jesus:

> That Jesus was born of the virgin Mary means that he was a genuine man, that his humanity was not docetic. The witness of scripture is that Jesus was really born of Mary, born through all the embryonic processes of the womb just as other human beings.[26]

Such theological themes may be woven into a preacher's literary and historical re-presentation of the stories. But what happens when, in a particular setting, the stories are very well known? When, perhaps, worshippers have just heard one of them read out yet again? Christmas, surely, is a time when, in the right setting, theology can truly take wing from the pulpit, without always having to rehearse the narrative details. Against the rich sounding board of these very down-to-earth tales of a young couple and their child in first-century Palestine, the full majesty of God's work in the incarnation can be opened up. Here, then, is a quintessentially 'theological' sermon from one of Britain's leading theologians.

Sermon: The joy and sorrow of God*

Rowan Williams

Eleven days ago, the Church celebrated the memory of the sixteenth-century Spanish saint, John of the Cross, Juan de Yepes—probably the greatest Christian mystical writer of the last thousand years, a man who worked not only for the reform and simplification of the monastic life of his time but also for the purification of the inner life of Christians from fantasy, self-indulgence and easy answers. Those who've heard of him will most likely associate him with the phrase that he introduced into Christian thinking about the hard times in discipleship—'the dark night of the soul'. He is a ruthless analyst of the ways in which we prevent ourselves from opening up to the true joy that God wants to give us by settling for something less than the

---

*Preached by Archbishop Rowan Williams at Canterbury Cathedral, Canterbury, UK, on 25 December 2007.

real thing and confusing the truth and grace of God with whatever makes us feel good or comfortable. He is a disturbing and difficult writer; not, you'd imagine, a man to go to for Christmas good cheer.

But it was St John who left us, in some of his poems, one of the most breathtakingly imaginative visions ever of the nature of Christmas joy, and who, in doing this, put his own analyses of the struggles and doubts of the life of prayer and witness firmly into an eternal context. He is recognized as one of the greatest poets in the Spanish language; and part of his genius is to use the rhythms and conventions of popular romantic poetry and folksong to convey the biblical story of the love affair between God and creation.

One of his sequences of poetry is usually called simply the 'Romances'. It's a series of seventy-five short, mostly four-line, verses written in the simplest possible style and telling the story of the world from the beginning to the first Christmas—but very daringly telling this story from God's point of view. It begins like a romantic ballad. 'Once upon a time', God was living eternally in heaven, God the Father, the Son and the Holy Spirit, with perfect love flowing uninterrupted between them. And out of the sheer overflowing energy of his love, God the Father decides that he will create a 'Bride' for his Son. The imagery is powerful and direct: there will be someone created who will be able, says God the Father, to 'sit down and eat bread with us at one table, the same bread that I eat'.

And so the world is made as a home for the Bride. Who is this Bride? It is the whole world of beings who are capable of love and understanding, the angels and the human race. In the rich diversity of the world, the heavens and the earth together, God makes an environment in which love and intelligence may grow, until they are capable of receiving the full impact of God's presence. And so the world waits for the moment when God can at last descend and, in a beautiful turning upside down of the earlier image, can sit at the same table and share the same bread as created beings.

As the ages pass on earth, the longing grows and intensifies for this moment to arrive; and at last God the Father tells the Son that it is time for him to meet his Bride face to face on earth, so that, as he looks at her directly, she may reflect his own likeness. When God has become human, then humanity will recognize in his face, in Jesus' face, its own true nature and destiny. And the angels sing at the wedding in Bethlehem, the marriage of heaven and earth, where, in the haunting final stanza of the great poetic sequence, humanity senses the joy of God himself, and the only one in the scene who is weeping is the child, the child who is God in the flesh: 'The tears of man in God, the gladness in man, the sorrow and the joy that used to be such strangers to each other'.

Well, that is how John of the Cross sets out the story of creation and redemption, the story told from God's point of view. And there are two things
in this that are worth our thoughts and our prayers today. The first is one of
the strangest features of John's poems. The coming of Christ is not first and
foremost a response to human crisis; there is remarkably little about sin in
these verses. We know from elsewhere that John believed what all Christians
believe about sin and forgiveness; and even in these poems there is reference to God's will to save us from destruction. But the vision takes us further
back into God's purpose. The whole point of creation is that there should be
persons, made up of spirit and body, in God's image and likeness, to use the
language of Genesis and of the New Testament, who are capable of intimacy
with God—not so that God can gain something but so that these created
beings may live in joy. And God's way of making sure that this joy is fully
available is to join humanity on earth so that human beings may recognize
what they are and what they are for. The sinfulness, the appalling tragedy
of human history, has set us at what from our point of view seems an un-
imaginable distance from God; yet God, we might say, takes it in his stride.
It means that when he appears on earth, he takes to himself all the terrible
consequences of where we have gone wrong—'the tears of man in God'; yet
it is only a shadow on the great picture, which is unchanged.

We are right to think about the seriousness of sin, in other words; but we
see it properly and in perspective only when we have our eyes firmly on the
greatness and unchanging purpose of God's eternal plan for the marriage of
heaven and earth. It is a perspective that is necessary when our own sins or
those of a failing and suffering world fill the horizon for us, so that we can
hardly believe the situation can be transformed. For if God's purpose is what
it is, and if God has the power and freedom to enter our world and meet us
face to face, there is nothing that can destroy that initial divine vision of what
the world is for and what we human beings are for. Nothing changes, however far we fall; if we decide to settle down with our failures and give way
to cynicism and despair, that is indeed dreadful—but God remains the same
God who has decided that the world should exist so that it may enter into
his joy. At Christmas, when this mystery is celebrated, we should above all
renew our sheer confidence in God. In today's Bethlehem, still ravaged by
fear and violence, we can still meet the God who has made human tears his
own and still works ceaselessly for his purpose of peace and rejoicing, through
the witness of brave and loving people on both sides of the dividing wall.

But the second point growing out of this is of immense practical importance. The world around us is created as a framework within which we may
learn the first beginnings of growing up towards what God wants for us. It

is the way it is so that we can be directed towards God. And so this is how we must see the world. Yes, it exists in one sense for humanity's sake; but it exists in its own independence and beauty for humanity's sake—not as a warehouse of resources to serve humanity's selfishness. To grasp that God has made the material world, 'composed', says John of the Cross, 'of infinite differences', so that human beings can see his glory is to accept that the diversity and mysteriousness of the world around is something precious in itself. To reduce this diversity and to try and empty out the mysteriousness is to fail to allow God to speak through the things of creation as he means to.

> My overwhelming reaction is one of amazement. Amazement not only at the extravaganza of details that we have seen; amazement, too, at the very fact that there are any such details to be had at all, on any planet. The universe could so easily have remained lifeless and simple. . . . Not only is life on this planet amazing, and deeply satisfying, to all whose senses have not become dulled by familiarity: the very fact that we have evolved the brain power to understand our evolutionary genesis redoubles the amazement and compounds the satisfaction.

The temptation to quote Richard Dawkins from the pulpit is irresistible; in this amazement and awe, if not in much else, he echoes the sixteenth-century mystic. So to think of our world as a divine 'prompt' to our delight and reverence, so that its variety, the 'extravaganza of details', is a precious thing, is to begin to be committed to that reverent guardianship of this richness that is more and more clearly required of us as we grow in awareness of how fragile all this is, how fragile is the balance of species and environments in the world and how easily our greed distorts it. When we threaten the balance of things, we don't just put our material survival at risk; more profoundly, we put our spiritual sensitivity at risk, the possibility of being opened up to endless wonder by the world around us.

And it hardly needs adding that this becomes still more significant when we apply John of the Cross's vision to our human relations. Every person and every diverse sort of person exists for a unique joy, the joy of being who they are in relation to God, a joy which each person will experience differently. And when I encounter another, I encounter one who is called to such a unique joy; my relation with them is part of God's purpose in bringing that joy to perfection, in me and in the other. This doesn't rule out the tension and conflict that are unavoidable in human affairs—sometimes we challenge each other precisely so that we can break through what it is in each other that gets in the way of God's joy, so that we can set each other free for this joy.

This, surely, is where peace on earth, the peace the angels promise to the shepherds, begins, here and nowhere else; here is where we understand what human beings are for and what they can do for each other. The delighted reverence and amazement we should have towards the things of creation is intensified many times where human beings are concerned. And if peace is to be more than a pause in open conflict, it must be grounded in this passionate and amazed reverence for others.

The birth of Jesus, in which that power which holds the universe together in coherence takes shape in history as a single human body and soul, is an event of cosmic importance. It announces that creation as a whole has found its purpose and meaning, and that the flowing together of all things for the joyful transfiguration of our humanity is at last made visible on earth.

> So God henceforth will be human, and human beings caught up in God. He will walk around in their company, eat with them and drink with them. He will stay with them always, the same forever alongside them, until this world is wrapped up and done with.

Glory to God in the highest, and peace on earth to those who are God's friends.

Sermon commentary

Not every local church would be the place to start a Christmas sermon with reference to John of the Cross. But this was not a local church: this was Canterbury Cathedral. And the speaker was the Archbishop of Canterbury, whose words on such an occasion quickly travel around the globe. They are the words of a preacher who is known to eschew the trivial and always to have important, if sometimes difficult, things to say. They are authentically Christian words, clearly spoken by one immersed in the Christian tradition (no easy pandering to populism here!), yet addressing the very heart of what it means to be human beings in God's world. To borrow a political slogan, they are the words of 'a serious man for serious times'.[27]

Even if the opening reference to John of the Cross would be strange to some hearers, we very soon down to what has been called 'primary damage'[28]—the exposure of something at the root of the human condition, our propensity to settle for something less than the real thing. To this propensity the sermon addresses the glorious gospel answer: the truth that God, the creator of all reality, is in love with his creation, determined to bring it to its proper fulfilment and potential. His incarnation is the ultimate demonstration of this.

John of the Cross not only offers us the striking ballad in which this great narrative is told from God's point of view. He also gives the preacher memorable poetic language with which to capture it. God and humanity sharing bread at the same table; 'The tears of man in God, the gladness in man, the sorrow and the joy that used to be such strangers to each other'. He enables Williams to highlight the truth seen by early Christian teachers such as Irenaeus, that though human sin is indeed a blight on God's world, in urgent need of a remedy, God's purposes derive from before there was sin and reach far beyond it into a scarcely imaginable future of joy.[29] This is certainly a bracing message to lift the human heart at Christmas or any other time; it is interesting that it is heard with such comparative rarity, focused as we so often are—both preachers and congregations—on our needs, troubles and failings, thinking that God has no other purpose, perhaps, than to sort them out.

What follows is equally exciting. a vision of the world, created and entered by God, as the arena in which we can learn what it is to fulfil the destiny God has in mind. Williams (with John of the Cross) believes that the incarnation affirms the potential of this world, even as it enables its necessary healing and restoration. It is from the variety of creation, and above all through our fellow human beings, that we can learn what it is to become a race and a world that will share the joy of God. With mischievous glee Williams is able to draw in the words of atheist scientist Richard Dawkins in support.

This God-founded yet world-oriented spirituality inspired by John's vision of the incarnation leads seamlessly to the necessary and urgent practical implications of the doctrine. If *this* is the world created by God, in which he has come to eat bread with us, how can we not be deeply attentive to it, and above all to our fellow human beings, whose form Jesus took? *This* surely is how the words of the angelic celebration will come true: when people have grasped the vision and turned their eyes in love to one another and to the creation.

It is a message for everyone; for the world, not just the Church. And preachers can learn much from the way it concludes. The joyous mood of Lk. 2.1–14 has been echoing all the way through. Now the text of Lk. 2.14 is spoken as climax of the sermon, rather than opening gambit, and the familiar words are heard freshly as a result of the unusual way in which Williams has opened up the significance of Christmas. This certainly is creative biblical theology and theological exegesis at their finest.

4

From infant to adolescent
LUKE 2.21–52

The human growth of Jesus

How could one say that Christ was manifested only in semblance in the world, born as he was in Bethlehem, and made to submit to the circumcising of the flesh, and lifted up by Simeon, and brought up on to his twelfth year (at home), and made subject to his parents, and baptized in Jordan, and nailed to the cross, and raised again from the dead?[1]

The all-too-brief glimpses given to us by Luke into the boyhood of Jesus compel us uniquely to face the reality of the incarnation. A superficial reading of the Gospels might lead us to the docetic heresy of saying that Jesus was an essentially 'supernatural' figure, attended by miraculous events, whose humanity and suffering were but a 'front'. It is not, however, so easy to evade the real humanity of Jesus when we note that his foreskin was removed (Lk. 2.21), that he lay in an old man's arms (2.28), or that he upset his parents (2.48). It is not even the details of these stories that impress this upon us so much as the fact that they are told. In a few tiny snapshots that make the reels and reels of modern childhood photography look faintly ridiculous, we realize that Jesus was not propelled as if by a rocket from amazing birth to amazing adulthood. He went via the normal route of infancy, childhood and adolescence.

In considering the stories of Jesus' birth, we saw that there is a fertile tension between the biblical narratives and the doctrinal formulations. So it is here too. How can we possibly predicate of this human, growing child that he is 'God'?

This was how the Fathers expressed the matter at Chalcedon (451 CE):

One and the same Christ, Son, Lord, Only-begotten, recognized IN TWO NATURES, WITHOUT CONFUSION, WITHOUT CHANGE, WITHOUT DIVISION, WITHOUT SEPARATION;

the distinction of natures being in no way annulled by the union, but rather the characteristics of each nature being preserved and coming together to form one person and subsistence, not as parted or separated into two persons, but one and the same Son and Only-begotten, God the Word, Lord Jesus Christ . . .[2]

However, it is one thing to affirm, as a matter of faith, that Jesus Christ possesses 'two natures' that 'form one person and subsistence'. It is quite another to see what that means in practice for understanding Jesus' earthly life and interpreting the stories which tell of it.

One way of looking at it, popular among the Antiochene Fathers and down to modern times, is to divide up the various aspects of Jesus' life into manifestations of the human and the divine. This approach easily slides into the idea that Jesus alternated between humanity and divinity—even that his 'divinity' helped him out of tight spots caused by his 'humanity'. Criticising Pope Leo's saying in the fifth century about Christ's two natures, that 'the one is resplendent with miracles, the other submits to insults', Hanson writes:

Nor yet are some modern apologists any more successful, when they suggest that the Incarnate Word normally restricted himself to the limits of his human nature, but could on occasion draw on the reserves of the divine nature, like an aeroplane using its reserve fuel-tank in an emergency. It is not so much that these explanations are inconceivable as that they are incredible. If we are driven to such shifts to explain how Jesus was both God and man, we should begin asking ourselves whether we have not got the wrong approach altogether.[3]

If this approach tends to turn Jesus into a split personality, however, there is danger in the other extreme, too, the tendency of the Alexandrian theologians so to emphasize the unity of the person of Jesus as the divine Word that his very humanity is undermined. Hanson is forthright in his critique of this approach too. It is seen in those who emphasize that even when he chose not to use them, Jesus possessed 'divine' attributes of omnipotence and omniscience—perhaps even from birth. Perhaps still more significant is the question of Jesus' self-consciousness. Responding to scholars, such as Karl Barth, who have stressed the initiative of God and the shocking newness of his coming into the world, and therefore postulate a 'divine' self-consciousness in Christ, Hanson writes. 'A Jesus who knew he was God is not a Jesus who is one of us'.[4]

How then are we to hear the stories of Jesus the infant, Jesus the adolescent—and Jesus in the wilderness, Jesus in Gethsemane, Jesus on Golgotha? How are we to speak of them? In what sense are we to proclaim the historic, orthodox faith of the Church that this man was and is 'God'? What is the outcome of such a claim when heard together with these stories?

Hanson is representative of those who find the Chalcedonian definition no longer adequate but who wish to retain a fundamental belief in the incarnation. He writes: 'I do not think that the concept of hypostatic union, the word uniting himself metaphysically to human nature, is compatible with the belief that Jesus Christ exhibited a real human personality'.[5] His solution to the problem is based on the centrality of the revelation of the *character* of God in Jesus. 'In Jesus Christ we can apprehend the revelation of God's essential nature as mercy and faithfulness, grace and truth in the Johannine sense'.[6] This is an attractive approach, which can be enriched and nuanced by the perception that various concepts profoundly analogous to 'incarnation' were present in first-century Judaism, including temple, Torah and the return of Yahweh. These formed a matrix within which we can imagine what it might have meant for Jesus to have a growing awareness of 'divinity' without in any way compromising his full-blooded humanity.[7] Such a solution allows for a 'normal' process of growth, in the sense of not bypassing the regular physical, mental and emotional dimensions of human development. It also affirms the validity and importance of tracing the historical lines of New Testament christology, without prescribing what the outcome will be. Thus N. T. Wright finds in Paul a frequent identification of Jesus with Yahweh, 'the *kyrios* of the Septuagint',[8] whereas Dunn traces a much more gradual development in christology;[9] but both are involved in the same valid enterprise. This enterprise in no way compromises an orthodox confession of faith in Jesus as God and man, for that confession concerns his identity in itself, not the process by which either he or his followers became aware of it.

Rather than being wholly 'other' to all previous human experience, as Barth suggests, the incarnation opens itself to our *apprehension* through the story of the Old Testament. Once recognized, however, the mystery of the incarnation cannot be truly *comprehended*, tamed and hemmed in by definition. The only adequate response is wonder and praise. Poetry and liturgy are often better at capturing such paradox than logical analysis.[10]

Welcome, all wonders in one sight!
    Eternitie shut in a span,
Summer in winter, day in night,
    Heaven in Earth, and God in man;
    Great little one! Whose all embracing birth
    Lifts earth to heav'n, stoops heav'n to earth.[11]

Seest though, my Soule, with they faiths eyes, how he
Which fils all place, yet none holds him, doth lye?[12]

Such praise leads to obedience. The sign that one acknowledges another as 'God' is the hold exercised by this 'God' over one's life. In the presence of Christ we are not permitted to wallow in purely mystic 'unknowing', which makes no difference to behaviour.[13] God appeared in human form, surely, precisely so that we *should* know what we should be. 'There was no other way for us to learn than to see our Teacher and hear His voice with our own ears'.[14] The measure in which we allow the pattern of Jesus to direct us is the measure in which we have grasped what the story of the God made man in Jesus of Nazareth is all about.

Luke's narrative of Jesus' infancy and adolescence

Circumcision (Lk. 2.21)

Luke's note about Jesus' circumcision and naming serves two purposes, which act as a curtain-raiser for the two longer stories to follow. First, it continues to show (following the stories of Zechariah, Elizabeth and Mary in ch. 1) that Jesus was born in an atmosphere of traditional Jewish piety. He comes into the world not from 'outside', but from *inside*—inside the covenant family of Yahweh, within which he would learn his identity and vocation, and within whose language of faith his followers would learn to speak of him. Second, it continues the pattern of God's word finding willing human response. Mary had obeyed (1.38), the shepherds had obeyed (2.16), and now Mary and Joseph name the child as commanded (1.31). The 'wisdom' ascribed to Jesus by Luke (2.40, 52)—a quality associated with obedience (cf. Ps. 111.10)—is thus seen not as an unprecedented characteristic, but one learned in a godly environment.

Presentation (Lk. 2.22–40)

This picture is expanded in the story of Jesus' presentation in the temple. This would have taken place when he was about six weeks old. Luke actually refers to two Jewish customs here: the purification rites for new mothers (Lev. 12.1–8) and the consecration of firstborn males (Exod. 13.2, 12).[15] Perhaps the two were regularly combined into one ceremony, especially when the family lived some distance from the temple.

But the important point is surely that Mary and Joseph are continuing to do what the law requires (2.23, 27, 39). The social dimension of the scene is accented: the offering made by Joseph and Mary is that expected of a poor family ('a pair of turtledoves or two young pigeons', v. 24; cf. Lev. 12.8).

The atmosphere of expectant faithfulness to Yahweh is enhanced by the appearance of the devout Simeon and Anna. To the outward eye, the infant Jesus was a 'firstborn male' like any other. But prophetic insight gives these elderly people a glimpse of his true identity. For Mary and Joseph, this must have reinforced the message of Gabriel and the shepherds' report of the angelic appearance. After all, Mary had 'treasured all these words and pondered them in her heart' (2.19). Yet there is a very realistic note struck by Luke's comment that they were 'amazed' at Simeon's words (2.33; cf. 2.18). This is a reminder that their receptivity to God's remarkable work did not entail some unclouded, uncomplicated faith in the child's 'divinity'. This was Mary's baby, and it is natural to assume that their faith in his unique identity and destiny had to be rekindled again and again. This surely was the pattern of Abraham's faith in Yahweh, and it remained so for all his spiritual descendants. There is also a reinforcement here for Luke's readers and hearers, who have followed the remarkable words and events from the angel's appearance to Zechariah right up to the circumcision of Jesus, and who wait to see how what they have heard about this child will come to fruition.

Simeon and Anna are steeped in Israel's faith and hope. Obedient to the law, they are yet not rooted comfortably in the past, but look forward eagerly to a future still to be disclosed. In George Caird's words, their 'loyalty to the law, so far from making them satisfied with its provisions, had kindled in them a flame of expectancy. . . . The piety of the Old Testament, properly understood, produced men and women agog for the coming of the Gospel'.[16] Thus in Jesus they recognize glory for 'your people Israel' (2.32), the people for whose 'consolation' or 'redemption' they and others looked (vv. 25, 38). But Simeon sees something more: that God has prepared this 'salvation', seen in Jesus, 'in the presence of all peoples' (v. 31). As Yahweh comes in Jesus to rescue his people, this event will be 'a light for revelation to the Gentiles' (v. 32). Yahweh is showing and vindicating himself before all the nations. This adds a special edge to the meaning of 'for glory to your people Israel'. What he does in Jesus for *all* peoples will demonstrate that this tiny, weak, apparently insignificant people are the true home of divine glory. Joel Green notes the irony of this: 'precisely in the center of the world of Israel, the Jerusalem temple, God discloses that salvation for Israel includes salvation for the Gentiles'.[17]

Simeon also speaks of Jesus as 'destined for the falling and the rising of many in Israel, and to be a sign that will be opposed so that the inner thoughts of many will be revealed' (2.34–35). The child will turn out to be like a measuring rod, against whom people are tested: a spirit level, against which the skewed is differentiated from the straight. He will have the magnetism to draw people's secret attitudes to the surface. Those who are obedient to God will find Jesus is the cause of their 'rising'; those who oppose him will find Jesus to be a stumbling block: their sin will be exposed, and they will show themselves to be ripe for judgement. Yahweh himself was known as a refuge, yet also a stumbling stone (Isa. 8.14).[18] By their reaction to Jesus, people will show either what it means to be for Yahweh or what it means to be against him.[19]

But there is another side. Simeon tells Mary that 'a sword will pierce your own soul too' (Lk. 2.35). Closeness and loyalty to Jesus would not exempt people from suffering. The career of Jesus signalled a crisis that would catch up both him and those around him in intense trial. Green suggests that the image of the 'sword' is closely related to the dynamics of the 'sign'. It 'relates to Jesus' mission of segregating those within Israel who embrace God's salvific will from those who do not'.[20]

We note Luke's emphasis on the *historical* role that Jesus is to fulfil. He will act as a 'sign', effecting salvation for his people and the revelation of God's light to the Gentiles, but also the 'falling' of those who oppose him. This 'falling' would later be epitomized in the catastrophe that overtook Jerusalem at the hands of the Romans. Jesus is the last opportunity for the nation as a nation to be restored. God's good purpose goes on beyond that judgement, but it is now worked out through an Israel radically redefined around Jesus. The glory that his people were destined to share in is to be channelled through Jesus alone. Green points to the echoes in this passage of Isaiah 40–66, in which the theme of God's 'servant' (often a designation for Israel) as a 'light to the nations' is prominent (Isa. 42.6; 49.6). Jesus takes on Israel's mantle. Green further observes that 'light' is a metaphor not only of salvation but also of revelation and of ultimate crisis.[21] Luke portrays Jesus as the pivot of history, for Israel and for the world.

Learning in the temple (Lk. 2.41–52)

Luke must surely mean us to see this vignette of Jesus' boyhood as in some way representative or typical, though it records a unique occasion. His summary notes about Jesus' growth in 'wisdom and . . . in divine and human favor' (2.40, 52) reflect standard ways of expressing the quality of a human marked out by their upright character and good fortune (cf. 1 Kgs. 10.1–9; Ps. 5.12; Prov. 3.3–4, 8.35; Lk. 2.14). Here the portrayal of *human* faith and piety—seen already in Zechariah and Elizabeth, Mary and Joseph, Simeon and Anna—is extended to the growing Jesus himself.

Jesus is seen as an active learner who engages intelligently with Israel's teachers at the symbolic heart of Israel's life, the temple, both asking and answering questions (2.46–47). It is interesting (and sad) that Christians sometimes give the impression of having little to learn; learning is a fundamental part of the human adventure, and here is Jesus doing it. He is beginning to make his own that identification with Israel's history, traditions and destiny into which he has been helplessly inducted in infancy.

Jesus' genuine humanity is revealed here in his conflict with his parents. It is fascinating that Luke has not suppressed this conflict, contrary to any idealistic notion of the child Jesus giving his family a trouble-free time. Jesus apparently didn't tell Mary and Joseph that he was staying behind ('typical teenager', do I hear parents saying?); when they found and rebuked him, he answered in what most parents today might regard as an unbearably precocious manner, blandly ignoring their anxiety. It is certainly true that we can never be sure of the tone of voice behind a written report. It is also true that for Luke, the story would be in line with Jesus' redefinition of his 'mothers and brothers' (8.19–21) and his encouragements to a cheerful lack of worry and fear (10.38–42; 12.4–7, 22–34). There is a consistency between the behaviour and attitude of the twelve-year-old and that of the adult. Yet the sense of family tension remains transparent. It is surely entirely in keeping with Jesus' real humanity that there should have been such tensions as he grew up.

If we see Jesus' humanity as a model for ours, the passage suggests that we should not be afraid of such tensions. It is easy to see things from both sides. On the one hand, here is a boy with a strong sense of vocation and a desire to learn. Few parents would want to discourage that! On the other hand, here are parents with a strong sense of care and protection. Few children (at least in retrospect!) would think that an ignoble thing. But sometimes it is precisely the highest motivations that conflict with each other. Recognizing the reality of such conflict in Jesus' family life is not incompatible with our belief that Jesus was a model human being. Indeed, it brings the model closer to us, opening the most revealing of small windows on to the emotions of adolescence and family relationships.

This sense of Jesus' humanity is not overturned by his reply: 'Did you not know that I must be in my Father's house?' (2.49). In calling God his Father, Jesus simply continues the theme of the chapter since v. 21: he is taking Israel's vocation on himself. Just as he receives Israel's role of God's 'servant', to be a light to the nations (v. 32), so now he shows consciousness of being God's 'Son', one of Israel's earliest names (Exod. 4.22–23). Not surprisingly, the significance of this was lost on Mary and Joseph (Lk. 2.50).

Lk. 2.51 completes the story in two important ways. First, it shows Jesus being 'obedient' to his parents. His sense of being God's Son was not incompatible with the normal respect due from child to parent. Might we even say that this was a case where Jesus '*learned* obedience through what he suffered' (Heb. 5.8, stress added)? Although Luke's comment here does not imply that previously Jesus had been *disobedient*, it does perhaps imply that this painful incident was an important step on the path through which Jesus discovered his deep and paradoxical vocation to submit to both divine will and human will. And again, this brings him closer to us, who know only too well that proper obedience—whether to God, parents or others—is not something given or learned automatically, or through simple adherence to a code of rules, but through experience that is often painful.

Second, this verse shows that Mary is not one of those whose incomprehension of Jesus causes her to reject what he says and stands for. She 'treasured all these things in her heart'. This is consistent not only with her response to the shepherds' visit in 2.19, but also with 8.19–21, where Jesus' mother and brothers are not portrayed as 'outsiders', separate from the disciples, as in Mk. 3.31–35, but are implicitly included, insofar as they, like anyone, 'hear the word of God and do it'. Mary thus becomes, like many others in Luke's Gospel, a model of true discipleship. She does not understand Jesus at first (who does?), but she is willing to ponder and learn from his words.

The picture emerging is of a Jesus fully integrated into the human family. He is distinct from, yet one with, his physical kin. His unique sense of vocation and identity arises not outside the circle of family, tribe and nation, but within it. He is marked out as wise and favoured, but his character has not been formed apart from those whose piety forms the backdrop of his early years (Lk. 2.21–40). Particularly in two ways he is bound closely to them. First, there is shared suffering. The parental pain evident in vv. 41–50 may be the first instance of the sword piercing Mary's soul (v. 35): it is the pain not merely of temporarily losing a child, but also of sensing that a gulf is opening up between him and you, that you do not understand him as you thought you did. But one may readily imagine the pain on Jesus' side too. Second, there is shared learning. Before the incident when he was twelve, Jesus, we are led to assume, learned from his parents; here we see him learning from the teachers in the temple; and afterwards he returns to Nazareth and continues in a posture of obedience (having learned more deeply through the whole experience). But his parents, too, are learners—Mary at least, who does not forget, but treasures all these things in her heart. All this is very revealing of Luke's approach to teaching what we call 'the incarnation'. He shows a Jesus who, in one aspect, is every bit as lonely a figure as in the other Gospels, as he heads to Jerusalem to meet his destiny. Yet this is also a vulnerable Jesus, who is dependent on others—not least his human parents—learns from them, and is formed in relationship to them. Conversely, Luke shows us a cast of first-century Jews who, in one aspect, are every bit as puzzled as they are in the other Gospels, and some are downright hostile. Yet these are people who are genuinely learning about Jesus and actually being formed into his pattern. The narrative of Jesus' journey to Jerusalem (Lk. 9.51–19.40) may be seen as Jesus' teaching about the way *of* the cross, as he treads his own way *to* the cross. Those who want to come after him are told that they must 'take up their cross *daily*' (9.23, stress added). On the night before his death, Jesus affirms the faithfulness of the inner circle, at least: 'You are those who have stood by me in my trials' (22.28). And as they wait for the power that will launch them into their task of being Jesus' witnesses, Mary the mother of Jesus is seen among their number (Acts 1.14). For Luke, human beings are not just the foils against whose dull sheen the uniqueness of the Son of God may shine more brightly. They are in a genuine reciprocal relationship with him, in which he learns from them, and they from him.[22]

Preaching the incarnation from the stories of Jesus' boyhood

The preacher must always press on beyond the question 'What did this story mean?' (in the experience of Jesus' family, for the early Christians, for Luke, for his readers) to the further question 'What is its significance *for us?*'

Our discussion suggests that it is simplistic to say that Luke is trying to underline the 'divinity' of Jesus here, and that therefore our preaching on these texts should have the main aim of showing how they 'prove' it. It is more in keeping both with Luke's thrust and our contemporary situation (in which 'divinity' is such a contested idea) to open up the human dynamics of the story, for it is precisely through these that the meaning of Jesus' divine nature will be disclosed. Of the many approaches one might take, I will mention three.

First, one can underline the fact that Jesus is presented to us (by Luke especially) as the model human being, one who has been through the various stages of human life and done so 'successfully'—certainly not as we usually think of success, but as the champion, the leader, the *archēgos*, or pioneer.[23] Irenaeus was one of the first to make this point:

> He came to save all through himself; all, that is, who through him are born into God, infants, children, boys, young men and old. Therefore he passed through every stage of life: he was made an infant for infants, sanctifying infancy; a child among children, sanctifying those of this age, an example also to them of filial affection, righteousness and obedience; a young man amongst young men, an example to them, and sanctifying them to the Lord.[24]

The American nineteenth-century preacher Phillips Brooks represented an Anglican emphasis on the incarnation at its best.[25] He preached a remarkable sermon aligning the stages of human life with those of the life of Jesus, as traced in the sequence of the Christian year. Jesus is seen as our pattern in his arrival or unique vocation (Advent), in his nativity and the solemnity of discovering an individual personhood (Christmas), in his self-manifestation and influence (Epiphany), in his suffering as the path to true maturity and glory (Lent and Easter), and finally in the widening of his influence after his earthly existence (Pentecost).[26] Such a sermon offers food for rich theological reflection. Brooks was careful to avoid the 'liberal' danger inherent in such an approach, that of seeing Jesus merely as a symbol for all that is best in humanity, rather than as the unique restorer of human relationship to God and to others:[27]

> We do not dishonor the humanity of Jesus when we thus make it the type of what ours may be. . . . Only remember He is not only pattern, but [also] power. We must be like Him, but we cannot be, save as He make us.[28]

Second, one can highlight the role of the other characters in the narrative as they relate to Jesus. Although various writers rightly warn about other Bible characters usurping the centrality of God or Christ in preaching, if we are to be true to Luke, we should highlight the genuine mutuality of Jesus' relationships. This will not weaken the truth of the incarnation, but rather strengthen it. Thus for a sermon on Lk. 2.41–52, I contrasted the glamorous portrayal of families on certain kinds of calendars with the reality both of normal family life and that of Jesus; I sought to evoke the congregation's empathy with both the twelve-year-old Jesus and his parents. A twelve-year-old was reported to be listening intently, to his parents' alarm!

Third, one can stress the role of Jesus as the fulfilment of Israel's hopes, and the turning point of history. This was the approach I adopted in the following sermon on Lk. 2.22–40.

Sermon: Signs of life and death

Stephen Wright

His parents couldn't have known just how it would turn out. A young black man, brought up in a Christian household in the southern states of America, in the days when your seat on a bus depended on what colour your skin was, went to college, grew in faith, awoke to the true inhumanity of the society he lived in. He would become a preacher, but so much more than a preacher. He would become a gathering point, a focus, a rallying centre, an icon of the unstoppable energy that would turn that society around and set it on a path of transformation that continues to this day, half a century later. And he would also become a sign that was spoken against, a stumbling block, a representative of all that the old vested interests feared, an object of resistance and hatred, abuse and arrest. In later years he would find himself distanced too from those who shared his goals but not his non-violent methods. Eventually he would be shot and killed, before he had reached the age of forty: forty years ago this year.

And Martin Luther King was doing no more and no less than living out, and dying out, the consequences of that ancient prophecy, spoken by an old man to a young couple with an infant child: the mother certainly still a teenager, the father probably not much older. To all outward appearances, they were like any other young family: a little nervous and overawed to be in the magnificent temple of Herod, no doubt; but a glow of pride and joy on their faces.

These words of the old man, though, spoke of what their child would become. That's always difficult for any parent to imagine. When you're concentrating on cute smiles and insistent wails and dirty nappies, you never imagine the parents' evenings at school, the rebellious teenager, the radiant bride, the successful businessman. You never even think about it. When granny says the baby's going to be a pianist because she's got long fingers, you laugh indulgently. The future is another country. Now is the time for cuddles and wipes.

But when the old man took their precious little boy in his arms and said, 'Now at last I'm looking at the salvation of my people, and all peoples', this was more than fond speculation by granny or granddad. This was not something for mere laughter. This was something for amazement and wonder. And what he said next, turning especially to Mary, the child's mother, both deepened the mystery and sent a chill wind through the atmosphere:

> This child is destined for the falling and the rising of many in Israel, and to be a sign that will be opposed so that the inner thoughts of many will be revealed—and a sword will pierce your own soul too.

Actually, our modern translations miss something here. They smooth out the sentence to make it read better. But in the original, the sign and the sword come together:

> This child is destined for the falling and the rising of many in Israel, and to be a sign that will be opposed—and a sword will pierce your own soul too—so that the inner thoughts of many will be revealed.

What did he mean? Well, we know something of how the story unfolded.

Jesus became a rallying point, a focus, an icon for a change in attitude, direction and expectation among his people. They gathered round him in their crowds, at first barely understanding what he was saying and doing. But gradually it dawned on them—some of them, anyway—that he was proposing something different from all the options on offer for an oppressed people struggling to trust their God and protect their sacred identity. He wasn't advocating retreat into the desert, like the Essenes: he spoke of trusting God in the middle of life's messiness and anxieties. He wasn't advocating snuggling up to the Romans, like the priestly leaders: he had hard things to say about rulers and their style. He wasn't advocating armed rebellion, either: he seemed to say that you could live under pagan rule and still find the safe pathway of obedience to God, even though it would cost you something. Nor was he advocating a hardening and intensifying effort at maintaining all the traditions, like the Pharisees: he said that in their attempt to get all the details right, they'd lost the basic plot of God's will.

So you couldn't put him in a box. Because, as eventually some came to realize, he was calling for nothing less than a total reorientation of his people's lives, individually and corporately. And you couldn't remain neutral in the face of that. Your thoughts were drawn out of you: I think here of that graphic picture in one of the Harry Potter stories of Dumbledore literally pulling his thoughts out of his head and putting them in the Pensieve.[29] Though many were slow to understand what was going on, they were not slow to take sides. Jesus was deeply attractive to many, yet profoundly suspected and feared by many others. On both sides, they had realized, intuitively perhaps, that the tectonic plates were moving.

What Jesus was initiating was a falling and a rising. The nation must die to all its old patterns of thought and behaviour. And he would lead the way.

In the unremarkable face of that infant, with his young parents standing by, Simeon saw that the Lord sought by his people had indeed suddenly and surprisingly come to his temple. And, shaped as his thinking would have been by Scripture, he might well have mused, with Malachi: 'But who can endure the day of his coming, and who can stand when he appears?'[30]

Yes, Simeon celebrated the dawning of the light of God for Israel, and for the Gentiles. The glory of Yahweh returning to his temple, his people and his world is an event of incredible joy; it means the renewal of his whole creation. But the light of God is not only the light of guidance and safety in which we are bathed; it is also the light of discernment and judgement. The Lord comes as the refiner and purifier.[31]

And as the infant Jesus grows into manhood, he becomes the sign of Yahweh's return to his nation and his world. He is the lodestar pinpointing the location of the Creator. He is the portent displaying in his life and death the awfulness of judgement upon evil. There is no turning back. He triggers an unstoppable momentum of both restoration and justice. Response to him separates people out. It demonstrates their response to Yahweh's presence.

And for those closest to Jesus, the sign of God's return to his people, there is a sword to pierce their soul.

Where do we fit into this story? Well, first, we are—mostly, I guess—among the 'Gentiles' to whom God's revelation has come. The falling and rising which Jesus set in train was above all the falling of all racial or national limitations on people's thinking about God and his interests, and the rising to the dawn of a new universal and cosmic perspective on the Creator's concerns and actions. We celebrate that and revel in it.

But at the same time, we are warned by the story of Israel and the story of Jesus. The dangers that Israel fell into are equally dangers for us. And if Jesus refused to fit neatly into any of the boxes which they had ready-made for him, he will refuse to fit neatly into any of the boxes which we are inclined to make, too. If he went to his death as an Israelite, identifying with Israel in its falling, as a prelude to its rising as a new international community, then we can see now that more deeply still, he went to his death as a human being, identifying with all humanity in our falling, as a prelude to its rising as the first fruits of a new creation.

So for us too there is a falling before there is a rising. And for those closest to Jesus, the sign of that true humanity, there is a sword to pierce their soul. What will that mean for you and for me? I can't say, exactly, any more than we can ever know exactly what it meant for Mary. But I can say that it is uncomfortable to identify with a figure who wouldn't be boxed up. It is uncomfortable not simply to go along with one or more of the communities of which you're a part; not simply to agree with the way everything's done, not simply to find security in familiar patterns of behaviour—whether that be indulging in cheap mudslinging, or inducing cosy feelings through our particular style of worship music. It's uncomfortable to question accepted values and challenge what seem to be regarded as indisputable individual rights.

For example, it's difficult even to question accepted behaviour in our use of the natural world and our shopping habits. Many churches now have 'green groups' and actively advocate fair trade. But challenge the idea of driving your kids to school, despite easy access to public transport and free travel for children, and you'll probably hit a buffer. Challenge the kinds of washing powder or coffee that people buy, and people think it's just too much of an effort to think about it for their regular shopping—even if we've thought about it when buying for the church! It's not that we can always or easily answer the question 'What would Jesus do?' But it's a matter of putting ourselves in the uncomfortable, unboxed place, seeking to stand where Jesus stood. There we start to feel at least something of the pricking of the sword's point.

But for you and me, the words of Simeon have a particular resonance and penetration. For as preachers we are those called to put our heads above the parapet in a particular way. I don't mean that our calling is somehow more holy than anyone else's. As for all disciples, whatever our calling, the sword starts to prick as we gather round Jesus, the sign. But as public disciples *we ourselves become signs*: gathering points around which people's attitudes and behaviour start to crystallize.

If course, if we content ourselves with mouthing trivia and banalities, or with simply repeating old formulas, it won't make much difference to us—or to anyone else. If we allow ourselves to be simply placed in the standard boxes—'typical evangelical', 'typical *Guardian*-reading liberal'[32] etc.—we will get along quite comfortably, and our preaching won't make much difference in the long run. But I think we're called to something greater. I think we're called to struggle to express the unboxed Jesus, the sign of true humanity. If we do that, we'll often find ourselves in the scary position of being out on a limb. But we'll also find ourselves drawn more and more deeply into what it is to be truly human, and truly you and truly me. We will experience opposition and resistance—but we will also become a thousand tiny catalysts for the flooding of the world with his glory.

Sermon commentary

This sermon was preached during a training weekend for Anglican readers (lay preachers) in the Diocese of Rochester, on the Feast of the Presentation of Christ in the Temple, 2 February 2008. This was one of those occasions when I was privileged to continue discussion with the listeners later on, and I have tried to incorporate some of their reaction into this commentary.

I find the discipline recommended by Thomas Long of writing a 'focus' and 'function' statement for each sermon very helpful.[33] On this occasion the intended 'focus' of the sermon was 'the identity of Jesus as a sign to be spoken against'. The intended 'function' was 'to inspire the orientation of life around Jesus—especially as ministers of the word'. The use of the word 'inspire' was a reminder that I needed not only to explain a passage or state a truth, but also to communicate a vision, evoking the desire to do and be what the passage invites us to do and be. I sought to achieve this through the use of narrative elements and plenty of images (something noted, I'm glad to say, by the hearers!). In addition to the Gospel reading, Mal. 3.1–5 was read, and this gave an Old Testament aspect to the biblical roots of the sermon.

The truth of the incarnation will live today, I believe, insofar as we can see dimensions of Jesus' unique earthly life replicated in some way in our own. Seldom having heard a sermon on Jesus as 'a sign to be spoken against', I wanted to explore its ramifications for us. One hearer queried whether this focus had allowed me to do justice to the passage. Readers must judge! The question of whether one is faithful to the passage is not to be decided by whether one has dealt with every part in detail (which I obviously did not), but by whether one has focused on one part in such a way as not to *obscure* other important parts, or to unbalance the message of the whole.

The sermon was structured on three narratives—those of Martin Luther King, Jesus, and ourselves as contemporary disciples and preachers. I hoped that the way in which these narratives connected with one another would communicate a sense of our organic connection with Jesus, whose story was the pool into and out of which the others flowed. King and contemporary disciples and preachers are thus seen not merely as illustrations of Jesus, or believers in Jesus, or imitators of Jesus, but as deriving their very life, meaning and role from Jesus.

Sermon structure is not theologically neutral, and the structure I adopted here reveals something of my interpretation of Luke and his implications, outlined above. Since Luke–Acts presents disciples as those who genuinely imitate Jesus and continue his work, I believe it would not do the Evangelist justice simply to present Jesus as a lone and static 'sign', in whom either to believe or disbelieve. For Luke, the implications of the incarnation spread out from the life of Jesus himself to those around him so that they themselves become—in a derivative way, to be sure—embodiments of God in the world. Those who take Jesus' side become, in their turn, those who will act as signs of God's presence, to be spoken against or supported.

This highlights the appropriateness of a narrative presentation. Narrative allows a sense of roundedness and embodiment which bald statement does not. Thus I briefly told the story of Martin Luther King to introduce the way in which, throughout history, human lives have become 'rallying points' for particular causes. I filled out what Simeon's prophecy would actually mean in Jesus' adult life. I feared that this section about the various options available to first-century Jews would sound lecture-like, but the hearers apparently did not think so.

I used a range of images and phrases to convey the idea of a 'sign' as it is used by Simeon. One of them, the picture of thoughts being drawn out of one's head that occurs several times in the Harry Potter books, ran the risk of alienating any who either did not know or did not approve of these stories. This was probably a stumbling block to one or two—not, I think, reason enough to repent of using such a graphic image, or fiction steeped in vital (even Christian) themes, but perhaps reason enough to offer further explanation of such an allusion in the future.

Finally I moved on to the ways in which we are called, both as disciples and specifically as preachers, to embody the 'unboxed Jesus', who transcends our neat human pigeon holes. No doubt a closing story of a preacher closer to home than King might have strengthened this sense of how we, in the present, carry the joyful burden of being, in the very contours of our lives, the manifestation of God summoning our fellow human beings to decision.

5

'Who do you say that I am?'

LUKE 9.18–27

The most recent phase of my ministry has involved learning about being a teacher in a seminary. In the early days most of my energies were spent in preparing one new lecture after another, and my main worry was whether there would be enough material. Light began to dawn for me, and hopefully for my students, with the realization that although good input is important, a significant part of teaching involves asking the right questions. For asking the right questions is more likely to provoke deeper thought about the subject and help people to move from surface learning to deep learning. Lk. 9.18–27 is a passage which bristles with questions that challenge the reader to think deeply about the person of Christ and about the cost of following him.

Our first steps in biblical studies will have alerted us to the significance of this episode in the ministry of Jesus. For Matthew, Mark and Luke all make plain that when Peter blurts out the confession, on behalf of the disciples, that Jesus is 'The Messiah of God' (Lk. 9.20), this marks a decisive turning point in Jesus' journey to the cross. The preacher's task, however, is not simply to offer an arm's-length history lesson about what happened long ago, but to find ways of drawing our listeners into the story so that they can be personally addressed by the questions it raises. Anna Carter Florence seeks to do this in the sermon included later in this chapter.

In beginning to pay close attention to this text, it is worth observing how Luke removes any reference to Caesarea Philippi and underlines how this decisive episode took place 'when Jesus was praying alone' (9.18). Thus the revelation of his true identity which follows is no accident: it is the outworking of the divine purpose.

Rather than locate the confession of Jesus as the Christ at a place named for the Roman emperor and his tetrarch, the confession occurs where Jesus is at prayer to God with his disciples. Prayer is an important theme in Luke because it serves as another way of emphasizing that all Jesus does is part of God's redemptive plan.[1]

Who is this?

The earlier section of Luke 9 describes how the disciples have been out and about, proclaiming the kingdom of God and healing the sick (vv. 1–11). For Jesus, the death of John the Baptist underlines the fact that humanly speaking, his days are numbered; and so he sends his disciples out to challenge the nation to repent and believe the good news. On their return, Jesus draws upon their experience and conducts a bit of consumer research, with the question 'Who do the crowds say that I am?' (v. 18). The crowds have benefited from the feeding of the 5,000, but to what extent have they understood who Jesus is and what he has done?

The question Jesus asks is basically the same question which others have been asking throughout his ministry. For as the drama of Jesus' ministry unfolds in Luke's Gospel, we find that over and over again many people are asking the question 'Who is this Jesus?'

In ch. 5, when Jesus heals the paralysed man who had been lowered down through the roof by his friends, 'the Pharisees and the teachers of the law began thinking to themselves, "Who is this who is speaking blasphemies? Who can forgive sins but God alone?"' (Lk. 5.21 NIV).

In Luke 7, after Jesus has disturbed respectable guests at Simon the Pharisee's house by announcing that a sinful woman has been forgiven (v. 49), onlookers ask, 'Who is this who even forgives sins?'

Then one night on the Sea of Galilee when Jesus stills the storm (Lk. 8.25), the disciples are all shaken and stirred. Not surprisingly, 'they were afraid and amazed, and said to one another, "Who then is this, that he commands even the winds and the water, and they obey him?"'

That mood of questioning has reached high places, for when Herod hears reports about Jesus, he says, 'John I beheaded; but who is this about whom I hear such things?' (Lk. 9.9).

Whether those actors in the drama are aware of it or not, they are beginning to construct a basic christology; for at its heart all christology is an attempt to answer this core question: 'Who is Jesus?' As we allow this text in Luke 9 to get under our skin, what becomes apparent is that the process of finding answers to that question is far from being complete.

One of the ancient prophets?

It is not difficult to see why many of his contemporaries viewed Jesus as standing in the prophetic tradition represented by John the Baptist, Elijah and the prophets of old (Lk. 9.19). Prophets were uncomfortable people to have around, for they challenged injustice, risking life and limb to rebuke kings and princes. Driven by their experience of God rather than by public opinion, they called God's people to turn away from their sins.

For some Christians today the prophets are seen mainly as *foretellers*, predicting a cataclysmic future when those who are not true believers will be 'left behind'. Now, although biblical prophets did foretell the painful consequences which were sure to come if people ignored the voice of God, they were more than just *foretellers*. They were also *forth-tellers* who spoke forth God's living word into their own contexts; and in reading prophetic texts, it is wise to consider the prophets' immediate audience before jumping too quickly to interpret their words as predicting future doom, gloom and disaster. Alongside those foretelling and forth-telling roles, the Hebrew prophets were also *re-tellers*, whose calling was to re-tell the old, old story and call people back to covenant obedience.

Viewed from that perspective, it feels entirely appropriate to see Jesus as inheriting the mantle of the prophets. He was a *re-teller* who came to call Israel back to the paths of obedience; thus in his Sermon on the Plain (Lk. 6.17–49) he harks back to the divine intention lying behind the commandments which formed the historic heart of the faith of Israel. He was also a *forth-teller* who announced the dramatic arrival of the kingdom of God in the here and now of contemporary experience. In addition, as opposition grew, he read the signs of the times and became a *foreteller* of the judgement which was sure to fall if God's people continued to turn a deaf ear to his voice (Lk. 19.41–44).

It is popularly believed that the voice of prophecy had been absent from Israel for centuries before John the Baptist appeared in the desert, urging people to repent and be baptized. However, N. T. Wright points to the work of Robert Webb, who identifies three basic categories of prophets who were active in Israel during the inter-testamental period:

> First, there were 'clerical prophets', holders of priestly (and perhaps also royal) office, possessing prophetic powers apparently in virtue of their office. . . . Second, there were 'sapiential prophets', wise men belonging to various sectarian groups such as the Essenes, or the Pharisees. . . . Third, there were 'popular prophets', with a further subdivision: 'leadership popular prophets' and 'solitary popular prophets'.[2]

Building on the Gospel evidence, Wright has little difficulty in arguing that both John and Jesus can be seen as 'leadership popular prophets', speaking God's word and calling together a community of disciples. It is not surprising that the crowds viewed Jesus in this light, and at various points in his ministry it appears that Jesus acknowledges that he is functioning like one of the prophets.[3]

As the Gospel narrative unfolds, it is clear that Jesus is not your average, run-of-the-mill kind of prophet. He is 'more than a prophet', and that something more becomes visible when Jesus addresses the disciples who have observed him at close quarters and asks, 'But who do you say that I am?' As spokesperson for the rest, Peter answers: 'The Messiah of God' (Lk. 9.20).

The Messiah of God

Whilst some biblical words and metaphors may not immediately connect with our contemporaries, the term 'Messiah' is not one of the words which has fallen out of common use. Its use has strayed out of the religious realm: it is sometimes used, for example, to describe someone who arrives to turn around the fortunes of an ailing business. Thus early in 2008 the supporters of one professional football club in the North-East of England greeted the arrival of a popular manager for his second stint at the club as 'the return of the Messiah'—desperately hoping that he would be the one to transform the club's lacklustre reputation on and off the field.[4]

It is probably misleading to think about one clearly-defined messianic hope shared by all first-century Jews, for there were differing visions of Israel's coming king. For most Jews, he would probably have been a God-sent human figure, rather than divine in himself. However, it is clear that many longed for the coming of a Messiah who would transform their nation's ailing fortunes. Whilst there were different visions of what this Messiah would be like, Wright argues that what the disparate movements in first-century Judaism had in common

> was the expectation . . . that Israel's long history would at last reach its divinely ordained goal. The long night of exile, the 'present evil age', would give way to the dawn of renewal and restoration, the new exodus, the return from exile, 'the age to come'. Where royal hopes were cherished, it was within this setting: the king that would come would be the agent through whom YHWH would accomplish this great renewal.[5]

This hope for the arrival of an anointed leader who would deliver Israel from oppression is clearly visible in John's account of the feeding of the 5,000, which talks about Jesus knowing that the people 'were about to come and take him by force to make him king' (Jn. 6.15).

At this point in the proceedings, we might have expected Jesus to congratulate Peter and the others for at last putting two and two together and reaching the conclusion that he was the Messiah. Far from handing out bouquets, however, Jesus 'sternly ordered and commanded them not to tell anyone'. With such fervent nationalistic hopes for a Messiah, the potential for misunderstanding was too great. In this case any publicity would have been bad publicity, which would have inevitably brought down the wrath of Herod.

For the moment, keeping a lower profile was the wisest course of action. The so-called 'messianic secret' is not some attempt to hide away the truth. The harsh political realities of the situation mean that the 'messianic secret' needs 'to be maintained because unleashing the secret would just lead to a wrong appreciation of Jesus' aims. With Peter and the other disciples at Caesarea Philippi, Jesus ignores the messianic title in referring to himself. He goes on immediately to refer to himself as "Son of Man" (Mk. 8.29, 31)'.[6]

It may not be fully accurate to say that Jesus 'ignores the messianic title', but he certainly redefines it by speaking directly about the Son of Man who will suffer and die (Lk. 9.21–22).

Son of Man

One of my earliest forays into New Testament studies involved writing an essay trying to make sense of the debates about what Jesus meant when he spoke about the Son of Man. Thirty years afterwards, the discussions continue.

> The background of the use of 'Son of Man' in the Gospels is still vigorously debated. It occurs in Dan. 7.13, . . . where it seems to refer to the exaltation of the holy ones of Israel to God. Use of the term to designate an apocalyptic figure . . . is attested in later sources, as is the use of 'the son of man' as a circumlocution in Aramaic. Jesus may have used the term in its generic sense ('a human being') or as a self-reference. Alternatively, he may have used the term because it was sufficiently ambiguous to force the hearer to discern its intended meaning.[7]

In line with many others, we suggest that as an important first step to understanding what is meant by the term the Son of Man in Luke 9, it is necessary to recall Dan. 7.9–14, which speaks of 'one like a son of man, coming with the clouds of heaven' to be vindicated before the throne of God (7.13–14 NIV). This passage is best understood not as referring to a heavenly being descending to earth on clouds of glory. Rather, it seems to be pointing to an earthly figure, 'one like a son of man', or 'one like a human being', who represents and embodies the life of Israel as it faces the onslaught of the forces of evil. The dramatic, apocalyptic description of the one like a son of man 'coming with the clouds of heaven' to the Ancient of Days, points to the exaltation and vindication of God's people in the person of their representative. Hence, Wright states that 'as this text was read by suffering Jews in Jesus' day, the "son of man" became identified as the anointed Messiah; he, of course, would "represent" the true Israel in the *sociological* sense, standing in her place and fighting her great battle'.[8]

Read in this light, it is clear that Jesus' comments about the Son of Man do not represent an 'ignoring of the messianic confession' but should be seen as a confirmation and clarification of the distinctive kind of Messiah he is going to be. Peter's confession and Jesus' words about the Son of Man provide much more adequate answers to the question 'Who is this?'; but they also stir up other questions such as 'Why must the Son of Man suffer?'

Why must the Son of Man suffer?

In his response to Peter's confession, Jesus states that 'the Son of Man must undergo great suffering', and the word 'must' translates the Greek word *dei*. This word carries theological significance: as Howard Marshall explains, 'The verb *dei* expresses the divine purpose which 'must' be fulfilled in the career of Jesus'.[9]

At this point there is scope for preachers to create narrative tension, inviting their listeners to enter more deeply into this passage by pausing to ask, 'Why must the Son of Man suffer?'

At one level the answer to that question is simple: anyone doing what Jesus did and saying what Jesus said was bound to bring the wrath of the religious and political establishment down upon his head. Humanly speaking, he was on a collision course with too many vested interests, and from that perspective he 'must' suffer if he continued to pursue his God-given vocation.

The Church sees a 'deeper magic' underlying this story,[10] believing that the Son of Man 'must' suffer in order to bring about atonement and salvation for humankind. However, voices both within and without the Church express some unease about a God who appears to demand suffering before he is willing to forgive.

Not so long ago a very good Christian friend gave me an unusual Christmas present: a copy of Richard Dawkins' best-seller *The God Delusion*. He had not detected a defect in my faith, and it wasn't a mistake. He thought, quite rightly, that I already had plenty of Christian books and might find it interesting to read the book and consider my responses to Dawkins' criticisms of Christianity.

At one point Richard Dawkins expresses his reservations about Christian beliefs in the atoning work of Christ, in characteristically robust and dismissive language:

> I have described atonement, the central doctrine of Christianity, as vicious, sado-masochistic and repellent. We should also dismiss it as barking mad, but for its ubiquitous familiarity which has dulled our objectivity. If God wanted to forgive our sins, why not just forgive them without having himself tortured and executed in payment—thereby incidentally condemning remote future generations of Jews to pogroms and persecution as Christ-killers?[11]

In explaining that the Son of Man must suffer, it is true that the verb *dei* conveys a sense of divine necessity. There is a sense in which the Son of man *must* suffer in order to carry out God's plan to bring about atonement for the sins of the world. However, there is no need to take the step which Dawkins takes, and move on from this to conclude that this divine necessity means that there is a vicious, sadomasochistic Father in heaven, punishing his loving, innocent Son down on earth.

So why *must* the Son of Man suffer?

On the one hand, it was necessary for the Son of Man to suffer because sin was so deeply ingrained in the warp and weft of human nature that simply saying 'I forgive you' would barely touch the surface of the problem. As a result of sin being so deeply engrained in human nature, much more radical surgery was needed. The only way to break sin's power was somehow to put our sinful human nature to death upon the cross. For only through such a sacrificial death and resurrection could sin's power be broken.[12]

On the other hand, the reason for the cross was simply that a loving God was not willing to let human beings destroy themselves. Out of sheer love, God moved in to rescue us from ourselves. Motivated solely by love, God was willing to pay the price that was needed to save us and to save this fallen world from self-destruction.

Putting all of those things together, it becomes clear that far from the Christian doctrine of atonement being vicious, sadomasochistic and repellent, it is truly a love story where we see God the Father, God the Son and God the Holy Spirit united and working together to absorb sin's destructive consequences and break its power. There is a divine necessity about the suffering of the Son of Man because a loving God is at work, stopping at nothing in his rescue mission, coming to set people free from the power of sin and death.

Although the studies in this book focus upon preaching the incarnation, these reflections on Luke 9 remind us of the impossibility of keeping the person and work of Christ in separate compartments. For as Daniel Migliore explains,

> *The doctrines of the person and work of Christ are inseparable.* On the one hand, 'to know Christ means to know his *benefits*,' as Philip Melanchthon rightly insisted. On the other hand, to know *Christ's* benefits, we must know who he is. . . . It is by telling the story of Jesus, by narrating the whole gospel—his message, ministry, passion, and resurrection—that we are able to hold together the person and work of Jesus.[13]

The preacher's calling is to tell that whole story in ways which can help to dispel those false, frightening images of an angry Father punishing a loving Son, so that people can experience the love which transforms and sets them free to hear the call to discipleship.

From earliest times Christians have proclaimed this story of God himself coming to earth. We have claimed that Jesus was greater even than the Messiah of Jewish expectation. But today preachers live and work in a sceptical world, which questions God's existence, and in a religiously-plural world, where followers of other faiths may be willing to view Jesus as a prophet but feel unable to acknowledge his divinity. Such concerns may lead some to claim that in confessing that Jesus was the divine incarnate Word, Christians are imposing later doctrinal categories upon the biblical text, which does not itself make such startling claims. In listening to those concerns, the preacher reading this text will also need to ask questions about how Jesus understood himself.

Was Jesus mad, bad or God?

Richard Dawkins reacts against C. S. Lewis' assessment of the situation[14] and suggests that 'Jesus was honestly mistaken'. Along the way he states that 'the historical evidence that Jesus claimed any kind of divine status is minimal'.[15] From a very different faith perspective, Muslims are convinced that 'Jesus is not divine—he was no different from other prophets who brought God's message to their people. Jesus Christ is not the 'Son of God', for he was created by God'.[16]

It is clear from the Gospels that Jesus did not go around publicly declaring that he was the Messiah, still less God, for such a strategy would have brought his ministry to an immediate, premature end. However, we can gain a clearer idea of how Jesus understood himself and his mission by observing what he did. For the truth about character and identity is not revealed purely by a person's words, but more significantly by their actions and the whole course of their life.

This principle can be simply illustrated. For example, it would be possible for me to make public statements announcing that I am a very gifted concert pianist. However, actions speak louder than words, and when it comes to playing the piano, the sad truth is that my left hand literally does not know what my right hand is doing. Anyone observing my feeble attempts to make music would conclude that my claims were false, however good my publicity may have been.

If we observe the life of Jesus and pay attention not just to his words but equally importantly to his actions and to the whole course of his earthly career, then a clear picture begins to emerge. The whole narrative of Jesus' life narrates his identity in a clear and convincing manner. Thus we find N. T. Wright arguing that the evidence garnered from the life of Jesus as a whole is entirely consistent with the claim that Jesus was conscious of having a vocation as the messianic prophet called by God to bring in the kingdom of God.[17] However, Wright is very careful to explain what he does not mean:

> 'Awareness of vocation' is by no means the same thing as Jesus having the sort of 'supernatural' awareness of himself, of Israel's god, and of the relation between the two of them. . . . Jesus did not, in other words, 'know that he was God' in the same way that one knows one is male or female, hungry or thirsty, or that one ate an orange an hour ago. His 'knowledge' was of a more risky, but perhaps more significant, sort: like knowing one is loved.[18]

At first sight such comments may seem disturbing, but they are not in conflict with the Church's assured convictions that if we are to do justice to who Jesus was and is, we need to talk about one who is both fully human and fully divine. What Wright's comments highlight is that if we believe that the incarnation involved the Word taking flesh and becoming fully human, then this forces us to think carefully about how we understand the human experience of Jesus.

Perhaps it is helpful at this point to refer to Psalm 2, where the king who is being anointed is addressed by God, who says, 'You are my son; today I have begotten you' (v. 7). In the person of the king we see a human being who can legitimately be addressed as the 'son of God', who would in some way have been 'conscious' of standing in a privileged relationship with God on behalf of others. Perhaps in some analogous way, it is possible to view the fully-human Jesus as being aware of his privileged relationship as the Son of God as he reflected upon, and sought to interpret, his relationship with his Father and his prophetic and messianic vocation. In the light of the resurrection, the Church was able to look back in hindsight and conclude that the story of Jesus was simultaneously the story of the Word made flesh for us and for our salvation.

Who is this Jesus for today?

Earlier in this chapter it was suggested that all christology is an attempt to answer the fundamental question 'Who is Jesus?' and that the process of finding answers to that question is far from being complete. The process needs to continue because, as Migliore states, '*the living Jesus Christ is greater than all of our confessions and creeds, and he surpasses all of our theological reflection upon him.* The risen Lord continually upsets our neat categories and classifications of him and the salvation he brings. . . . No Christology can claim to exhaust the breadth and depth of the mystery of Christ'.[19]

In which case it should be important to listen to the answers that other believers are offering to the question 'Who is this Jesus?' because that will enlarge and enrich our understanding of the person of Christ. However, the sad fact is that many white, Western, male theologians have not been very good at this.

In a significant study of *Theology in the Context of World Christianity*, Timothy Tennent illustrates this by saying that

for many years, African Christians were not encouraged to reflect on this question for themselves. Instead they were taught to mimic what they had been taught. They were in effect, answering the question 'Who do the *missionaries* say the Son of Man is?' The Africans learned to faithfully repeat what they had been taught about Christ. But as the number of African Christians grew and theological reflection deepened, many Africans began to sense the Lord Jesus turning to Africans *as Africans* and asking 'Who do *you* say that I am?'[20]

In a similar vein, Douglas Waruta, a Baptist theologian from Kenya, contends that 'Africans have every right to formulate their own Christology, their own response to who Jesus is to them'.[21]

One of the ways in which people from different parts of the world have tried to answer the question 'Who do you say that I am?' is through art. Online access makes it easier to consider some of the ways in which Jesus is portrayed in different cultures.[22] Discovering how other people in other cultures 'see' Jesus should help us to realize that the way we understand the person of Christ is similarly shaped and moulded by our own cultural presuppositions.

A significant study of African christology has been carried out by Diane Stinton, whose research did not involve simply sitting down in libraries and reading about African ideas about Christ. She interviewed people in Kenya, Ghana and Uganda about their Christian beliefs, and she listened to their songs and praises to discover the christological insights embodied within them. Arising from this study, she was able to identify some of the dominant christologies present within African Christianity.

She identifies four main categories: (1) Jesus as Life-giver or Healer; (2) Jesus as the Mediator between people and God, the Supreme Ancestor; (3) Jesus as the Leader, as the Chief or King, as the Liberator; and (4) Jesus as the Loved One, as Family, as Friend.[23]

Tennent argues that Christians in the West should pay close attention to these developments, because as 'the gospel has been translated into Chinese, Indian, African and Korean, and other cultures, we gain more and more insights into the beauty and reality of Jesus Christ'. He refers to this as the 'ontic expansion of God in Jesus Christ' and explains that this expression 'does not refer to any ontological change in the nature of Jesus Christ himself; but rather, to how our own understanding and insights into the full nature and work of God in and through Jesus Christ is continually expanding as more and more people groups come to the feet of Jesus'.[24] He is conscious that developing christologies need to be evaluated, and he identifies criteria for evaluating them in the light of Scripture and tradition.[25]

All of this suggests that, in an increasingly-diverse world, the preacher's understanding of who Jesus is can be enriched by listening to believers in other cultures as they respond to the searching question 'Who do you say that I am?' Part of the preacher's vocation is to find fresh and appropriate ways of communicating Jesus' significance for their own cultural contexts.

Take up the cross daily

Mark Twain reportedly said, 'Most people are bothered by those passages of Scripture they don't understand, but for me, I have always noticed that the passages that bother me are the ones I do understand'.

Jesus' words in Lk. 9.23–26 are not all that difficult to understand, but they stop us in our tracks, for they run in the opposite direction to the self-centred, consumerist society which we inhabit. These verses challenge us not to preach the 'cheap grace' which Bonhoeffer warned about in those dark days as Hitler rose to power.[26] The gospel we are called to proclaim is not that Jesus will make us happy, but that he calls us to deny ourselves, take up the cross daily and follow him.

Alan Culpepper sums this up in a helpful way: 'There are only two impulses in life. One is the impulse to acquire, take, hoard, own, and protect. The other is the impulse to give and to serve'.[27] The clamouring voices in our society claim that the first approach is the only one that really matters; but the preacher's calling is to proclaim, without apology, that Jesus summons us to that second way, which leads to life in all its fullness.

Luke underlines the down-to-earth, matter-of-fact nature of discipleship by adding the word 'daily' to Mark's account of this episode (Lk. 9.23). Ian Stackhouse interprets this as an invitation to engage life in a slower gear:

> Cross-bearing for Luke is not so much the grand gesture, but daily fidelity to whatever God has put before us. . . . Christian living is not so much being eaten by the lions; in one sense that would be easy. Rather, it is more like being trodden to death by a flock of geese. It is a slow and daily process. But through the ascesis of living daily, something deep emerges.[28]

The $64,000 question?

This passage bristles with questions, and through it the living Christ confronts each one of us with the question 'But who you do say that I am?' Ultimately the answer which Christ desires, and the response which our preaching seeks, is to answer this question through a personal commitment to discipleship. For the truth which this passage entrusts us to preach is that 'we are becoming who we shall be. Who we say Jesus is now determines what he will say of us in the future. How we answer the question "Who do you say that I am?" through our day-to-day discipleship is the only answer that matters—but everything depends on that answer'.[29] In the sermon that follows, Anna Carter Florence presents the need to make such a personal response to Jesus' question in a direct and challenging way.

Sermon: Who do you say that I am?*

Anna Carter Florence**

[Jesus] asked his disciples, 'Who do people say that the Son of Man is?' And they said, 'Some say John the Baptist, but others Elijah, and still others Jeremiah or one of the prophets'. He said to them, 'But who do you say that I am?' (Mt. 16.13–15)

There is always a lot of scuttlebutt on the streets about who Jesus is. Everyone has an opinion: the bishop in the cathedral, the religion columnist in the local paper, the twenty-something blogger, the woman who cuts your hair.

Who do people say that the Son of Man is? Thumb through the Gospels, and you can't help noticing that *people say* a lot of things about Jesus. He is the King of the Jews. He is Mary's Son. He is the light of the world. He is a prophet without honor in his own country. Jesus is the one who can heal your child, cast out your demon, forgive your sins, lead your revolution. Jesus is the one you invite to dinner and then invite to leave the district. He is a Messiah, a prophet, a rabbi, a pain in the neck. He is alive, he is dead, he is risen, he will come again.

Ask around today, and you can't help noticing that *people say* a lot of things about Jesus now, too—theologically, historically, sociologically, pastorally, colloquially, politically, biblically—you name it. They say it out loud and on street corners. They say it across the kitchen table and on the Internet. They say it in classrooms and in pulpits. In just about any context you can imagine, *people say* all kinds of things about Jesus, because nearly everybody has an opinion. You don't have to be a follower of Jesus to understand that the man is big; he is as influential a figure as the planet is likely to see. So *people say* a lot of things about Jesus. They describe him, decry him, defend him, deconstruct him. They explain him, complain about him, and just plain old shoot-the-breeze about him. Jesus is easy to talk about in this world. Pick your context, pick your method, and go.

*A part of this sermon first appeared in *Lectionary Homiletics*, in the form of reflections on the text. Used with permission.

**Dr Anna Carter Florence is Peter Marshall Associate Professor of Preaching at Columbia Theological Seminary, Decatur, Georgia.

Who do people say that the Son of Man is? In the Church, this can get tricky. We have boundaries. We have orthodoxies. We have limits to interpretation. We even have exams, so we can monitor our educational and denominational processes. *People say* a lot of things about Jesus, but *you* can't, if you want to be a minister—not during an examination, anyway. Seminarians discover this in their first theology class; ordination candidates discover it when they meet with credentialing bodies. You have to learn the doctrine of a particular church, and honour it, as faithfully and with as much integrity as you can, so that what *your people say* about Jesus and what *you say* intersect. That's how we become part of a tradition, how we live in it, how we pass it on. What *people say* shapes us. And through the Spirit's power, what *people say* becomes so much more than their words ever could. We hear what *God* is saying, too—through us and in spite of us.

So how do you make the move from what *people say* . . . to what *you* say about Jesus?

Maybe it's a matter of growing up. That's what the confirmation rituals in some denominations are addressing: teenagers get a chance to stand up and confirm for themselves the baptismal vows that were made for them, on their behalf, when they were babies. They get a chance to say, 'I choose this for myself. I choose to say what my people say about Jesus'.

Maybe it's a matter of faith formation. That's what Christian practices are addressing: believers get a chance to grow into new places in their faith by participating in traditional practices of the church. Singing and praying. Serving and feeding. Testifying and protesting. Labyrinth walking and foot washing. The practices deepen our relationships with Christ and one another. They deepen what *we say* by plunging us into what *people say* about Jesus.

Maybe it's a matter of knowledge. That's what educational programs are addressing: you can take a Sunday school class or enter a degree program in order to learn more about history, doctrine, Bible, theology. You can finally learn what 'eschatology' means and how to pronounce it. You can take a Greek class and read Matthew in the original. You can memorize the names of saints and heretics, popes and emperors; you can become an expert on Jeremiah or a scholar of the Reformation. You can teach what *people say* about Jesus to others, simply because you have access to so much knowledge.

How do you make the move from what *people say* . . . to what *you* say about Jesus?

There must be many factors involved. I'm sure growing up has something to do with it; I'm sure faith formation is key, and knowledge helps.

Then again, there's always sheer nerve.

Jesus said, 'But who do you say that I am?'

And Peter answered, 'The Christ of God'.

Isn't it lovely to hear Peter get it right, for once? Although 'right' is not really the word for it; he isn't 'right' in the doctrinal sense. He isn't 'right' because he answers Jesus correctly, understands the terms (he doesn't! read on in the book!) or wins all the points for disciple maturity.

I think Peter is right because he sets aside what *people say* and listens to what God is unfolding in his soul. He allows God to tell him who Jesus is, and then he confesses it—which is an act of sheer nerve. You don't confess Jesus because you're *ready*. You confess Jesus because he's *right there*, and he asks, and you just do it: leave your nets and step out of the boat. You focus on him, take a deep breath, and go. Will you get it wrong and sink? Well, maybe. But he *is* right there, stretching out his hand—so what better time to try?

For each of us, I think the moment comes when what *people say* about Jesus is no longer enough. We can't hide behind it; we can't pretend it's ours. We can't substitute what *people say* for what *we* say. We have to listen closely to God . . . and speak up for ourselves.

For pastors, this is especially critical—and these days, poignantly difficult. The availability of resources on the Internet lets us access what *people say* about Jesus with more ease and speed than ever before. Wondering what your favorite preachers are saying about Jesus in this or that text? Click a few keys, and it's right in front of you. Some of those preachers have even given permission for you to use their words or preach their sermons, if you like! For most of us, that's like putting a crack dealer right in our laptops. On a good week, we aren't tempted, but throw a few wrenches into the schedule (a funeral or two, a pastoral crisis, a family meltdown), and we find ourselves alone and empty on a Saturday night, craving a sermon—any sermon. Wouldn't it be all right, just this once, to substitute what *people say* for *what I say*? After all, I don't plan to do it *every* week; just this once. . . .

. . . Until the *next* time I need a quick fix. . . .

I tell my students that the Internet is heroin: too easy to use and massively addictive. Don't even do it once, I tell them, because you *will* do it again; you're only human! And however good the intentions of those who tell us to go ahead and preach what *they say*, rather than what *we say*, the end result is the same: addiction to someone else's opinions and a shrivelling up of our own souls. Our parishioners hear it in us, too. They hear us citing what *they say* rather than confessing what *we say* about Jesus. It teaches them to do the same. And in a few years, the church loses its interpretive vitality and its confessional passion. Jesus himself could stroll into our worship services, casually ask us, 'But who do *you* say that I am?' and we wouldn't have a thing to say that wasn't a direct quotation of someone else.

Who do you say that I am? It might be the most radical question in Scripture, when you pause to think about it! Jesus is literally giving his disciples permission to do theology for themselves. He is not requiring them to pass an exam or finish the course before they open their mouths—and they *haven't* finished the course yet, not by a long stretch. There are days and days ahead of them, until Jesus leads them to Jerusalem. There are betrayals and denials on the horizon. There is a cross and an empty tomb. There is a fire on the beach, Jesus cooking fish for breakfast, and a chance to start over and feed his sheep. But how can we feed them if we don't leave our nets and blurt it out—who *we say* that *he is?*

Don't be afraid. Say it for yourself, out loud.

Trust that Jesus will take you where you need to go to learn the words you need to speak.

Amen.

Sermon commentary

At the start of preaching modules, I often ask students to think about what makes for a good sermon; and then to write down their current definition of preaching. Working through the exercise for myself leads me to a definition suggesting that preaching involves

> discovering the Word of the Lord from the Bible for this group of people at this particular time, and then delivering that Word in the power of the Spirit, in ways that people can understand so that they can respond in worship and service.

In the early stages of my preaching journey, I felt under pressure to cram the sermon as full as possible with information about the biblical text. Perhaps it was a defence mechanism against the fear, real or imagined, that someone would criticize me for omitting something vital. At times the net result of downloading so much material was probably spiritual indigestion for my hearers rather than inspiration.

With experience I have become more and more convinced of the need to listen carefully to the text as a whole, so that I can then select what needs to be said on this specific occasion. So rather than feeling obliged to tell the congregation everything that is in the text, on every occasion, my task is to discern a specific Word from the Lord, from this section of the Bible, for this group of people at this particular time. If preaching is to be effective, preachers need to make painful choices about what is just so important that it must be included in this week's sermon, and what can safely be left out for use on another occasion. Failure to make these critical decisions results in the main focus of the sermon being overwhelmed and lost amid a wealth of material. Maybe we preachers would do well to take heed of Cicero's quip that 'too much is more offensive than too little'?[30]

Anna Carter Florence demonstrates clearly how powerful preaching can be when it has a clear focus, and when the preacher resists the temptation to overload the sermon with lots of 'interesting' material which is not directly relevant to this particular message.

There is ample evidence here that she has been 'attending' to the biblical text with great care, and the sermon makes many connections with other parts of the Gospel narrative. At some point in preparing to preach from this passage, Florence was grasped by the question which Jesus asked his disciples.

David Schlafer suggests that most sermons are usually held together by an image, a narrative or an argument. He argues that 'in sermons that "work", in sermons that actually make the good news come alive, one of these three—*image, story* or *argument*—is the orchestrating, integrating principle that shapes the whole sermon'.[31] Maybe on this occasion the 'integrating principle' does not fall neatly into any of those three categories, for the sermon is built around the question 'Who do *you* say that I am?' The preacher does not work through three main 'points', but allows this searching question to determine the form which the sermon will take.

The skilful use of repetition helps to hold our attention, giving shape and energy to the sermon. In addition to repeating the question which Jesus asked his disciples, the regular refrain about what *people say* about Jesus today drives home the need for each hearer to give their own answer to that life-changing question. The preacher is insistent that relying on second-hand opinions leads to 'a shrivelling up of our own souls'.

This chapter has suggested that at heart all christology is an attempt to respond to the core question 'Who is Jesus?' The process of finding answers to that question is far from being complete. This sermon echoes that idea by affirming that 'Jesus is literally giving his disciples permission to do theology for themselves'. It implies that there is much to be gained from encouraging people to articulate their responses to Jesus' question 'Who do *you* say that I am?'

Preaching as Testimony is Anna Carter Florence's preferred description for her perspective on preaching.[32] She is giving testimony by describing clearly what she has seen in the biblical text, and by testifying to what she believes it means. This is no arm's-length, detached analysis of the grammatical structures of Luke 9; rather, it is the preacher's personal testimony to what she has seen and heard in the text. Having allowed herself to be addressed personally by God in and through the biblical narrative, her longing is that people listening will also find themselves being addressed directly by God through the sermon. This preacher is insistent that every hearer needs to bear testimony, to give voice to their personal response to the Jesus who persists in asking, 'Who do *you* say that I am?'

6

Struggling to obey God

MARK 14.32–42

So-called reality TV shows tend to follow a predictable format. Groups of ageing celebrities or wannabe celebrities are herded into a house or the jungle, and then subjected to make-believe pressures to provide entertainment for the masses. Being nosy and eavesdropping on people's private conversations are not generally applauded in respectable society; but millions ignore such moral scruples and tune in, hoping to see someone get into trouble.

Turning to Mark's account of Gethsemane, we find ourselves eavesdropping on a private and painful episode. As we tune in to this episode of *The Passion of Jesus*, we see the prime character enduring real stress—not to manufacture entertainment, but as part of a mission to secure salvation for all. Viewing Jesus struggling in the garden is not trespassing on private pain, but standing on holy ground.

The last few chapters of this book have followed the journey of Jesus from his surprising birth and precocious childhood to the pivotal moment when the mist cleared and Peter confessed: 'You are the Messiah'. At that turning point Jesus warned his disciples of the sufferings which lay in wait for the Son of Man; and now in Gethsemane the reality of that suffering begins to weigh him down.

At the beginning of Chapter 4 we noted the danger that a 'superficial reading of the Gospels might lead us to the docetic heresy of saying that Jesus was an essentially 'supernatural' figure, attended by miraculous events, whose humanity and suffering were but a 'front".[1] In Mark's account of Gethsemane, the events unfolding before our eyes dispel any idea of docetism by giving us a clear glimpse of the full humanity of Jesus.

Sonship

One of the challenges of preaching the incarnation is how best to affirm the core Christian message about 'our Lord Jesus Christ, at once complete in Godhead and complete in manhood, truly God and truly man'.[2] Turning to Mark's Gospel, we find the Evangelist proclaiming this profound message by telling the story of Jesus rather than trying to explain in minute detail 'how' incarnation 'works'.

This episode forms part of a Gospel which leaves the reader in no doubt that this Jesus was the divine Son. Right from the outset, readers of Mark's Gospel are alerted to the fact that the story it will tell focuses upon the Son of God. The opening verse simply announces 'the beginning of the gospel about Jesus Christ, the Son of God' (Mk. 1.1). At key points in the drama, the voice from heaven confirms that this Jesus is God's beloved Son (1.11; 9.7). Then, in ch. 15, as the story reaches its dramatic climax with Jesus dying on the cross, a foreign solider discovers the truth and declares, 'Truly this man was God's Son!' (15.39).

Readers whose ears are attuned to hear echoes of the Old Testament soon recognize that the way Mark tells this story serves to underline the divine identity of Jesus. In a brief introduction to Christian belief, Densil Morgan draws attention to the way in which the first eight chapters of Mark's Gospel portray Jesus as performing roles which the Old Testament attributed uniquely to Yahweh, the one true Lord and God.[3] So, for example, he refers to the way in which Mark 4

> depicts Jesus' revelation of himself as lord of the elements. Just as the sailor described by the psalmist turns to God in [Ps.] 107.28, so the storm-tossed disciples here turn to Jesus, at whose command the elements respond and become calm ([Mk.] 4.39; cf. Ps. 65.7; 89.9; 107.29). 'Who then is this', they ask, 'that even the wind and the sea obey him?' As it was God's prerogative in the Old Testament to rule the elements, so Jesus here displays an authority which is divine.[4]

After reviewing the evidence of the first eight chapters of Mark's Gospel, Morgan justifiably concludes that 'throughout these initial chapters in what is regarded as being the earliest of the New Testament Gospels, Jesus is identified as Yahweh, the Old Testament's single God'.[5]

Within the Gethsemane passage that note of sonship is evident when we hear Jesus calling out 'Abba, Father' (Mk. 14.36). Scholars have debated to what extent Jesus was unique in using this intimate Aramaic word *Abba* in his prayers to God. Even if absolute uniqueness cannot be proved,

James Dunn suggests that 'the likelihood remains that Jesus was marked out among his fellow Jews at least in the fact that *abba* was his characteristic and regular form of address to God in prayer'.[6]

If Jesus used this intimate word *abba* in his prayers, this suggests an intimate relationship with his Father in heaven. Dunn cautiously hints at the way in which this prepares the way for the Church's acknowledgement of Jesus as God's Son.

> The subsequent classic Christian understanding of Jesus as God's Son is firmly rooted in Jesus' own sense of intimate sonship to God. It is not that a unique category was thrust upon Jesus (the Son of God) to give him a status he had not claimed. It is rather that a less specific term of relationship (God's son), shared by angel, king, righteous individual or charismatic rabbi, and indicating God's approval and evident favor, became filled and absorbed by the distinctive character of Jesus' sonship, and thus came to be seen as uniquely applicable to him.[7]

In the previous chapter some questions were asked about Jesus' self-awareness. The prayer of Jesus in this passage draws attention to an intimate sonship to God, which is consonant with the Church's full confession of Christ's divinity. Some scholars suggest that the process of developing a 'high' christology was a much later development. If Morgan is correct that in Mark's Gospel we see Jesus being 'identified as Yahweh, the Old Testament's single God',[8] this suggests that a 'high' christology surfaced within the Church at a much earlier stage.

Struggle

At the same time as narrating a story which identifies Jesus as the Son of God, Mark's Gospel simultaneously tells the story of the Jesus who was truly man. As the passion narrative gains pace, the struggle of Jesus in Gethsemane brings the full humanity of Jesus clearly into view. At a very basic level, for example, his humanity is evident as Jesus brings his three closest friends to share this ordeal: 'the Son of God is human enough to need support at this testing time'.[9]

The sermon which follows later in this chapter depicts the garden of Gethsemane not as a peaceful garden full of fragrant flowers, but as a bloody battlefield. To understand the struggle going on in Gethsemane, it is important to see this as just one round of the fierce battle between God and the devil which raged throughout the ministry of Jesus. Recalling how

'Jesus was led up by the Spirit into the wilderness to be tempted by the devil' (Mt. 4.1), Pope Benedict emphasizes that this struggle with temptation was a reality 'during his whole life':

> Temptation comes from the devil, but part of Jesus' messianic task is to withstand the great temptations that have led man away from God and continue to do so. . . . Jesus must suffer through these temptations to the point of dying on the Cross, which is how he opens the way of redemption for us. Thus it is not only after his death, but already by his death and during his whole life, that Jesus 'descends into hell', as it were, into the domain of our temptations and defeats, in order to take us by the hand and carry us upward.[10]

From a Reformed perspective, Calvin similarly stresses that the struggle with evil was a constant part of the experience of the incarnate Christ. For 'far from being treated indulgently or softly, . . . while he dwelt on earth he was not only tried by a perpetual cross but his whole life was nothing but a sort of perpetual cross'.[11]

From the start of his ministry the tempter sought to distract Jesus from the path marked out for him by God. Now in Gethsemane, when Jesus, humanly speaking, is at his weakest, the temptation to turn from the way of the cross reaches full intensity, and Jesus struggles in prayer to find the strength to go on. The force of this testing time is briefly but powerfully described:

> [Jesus] began to be distressed and agitated. And he said to them, 'I am deeply grieved, even to death; remain here, and keep awake'. And going a little farther, he threw himself on the ground and prayed that, if it were possible, the hour might pass from him.[12]

The language is reminiscent of Psalms 42 and 43, where the righteous sufferer cries out again and again: 'Why are you cast down, O my soul, and why are you disquieted within me?' France wonders if 'Jesus' eventual acceptance of the will of his Father in Gethsemane owed something to his acquaintance with that psalm, where the mood of despair eventually gives way to a calm trust in God. "Hope in God; for I shall again praise him, my help and my God"'.[13]

In the sermon included in this chapter, one of the ways I tried to press home the reality of this struggle was with a quotation from R. E. Brown which portrays a Jesus 'for whom the future was as much a mystery, a dread and a hope as it is for us'.[14] There is an intense struggle going on as Jesus faces the fateful 'hour' when he must take the 'cup' of suffering and judgement. He is struggling to resist the temptation to give up on the mission God has entrusted to him. Perhaps up to the last minute he had harboured the hope that, against all the odds, Israel would respond to the good news of the kingdom of God? As that prospect recedes, he has to face up to the sobering reality of death, and he dreads experiencing abandonment by the God he called 'Abba'. Calvin comments:

> We have already seen the Lord wrestle with the fear of death, but now as He comes hand to hand with temptation, the ordeal is called a beginning of grief and sorrow. We gather that the true test of power only comes in the moment itself: then the weakness of the flesh betrays itself, which before was hidden and the inner emotions pour out. Though God had trained His Son in some preliminary bouts, now at the closer aspect of death He deals a heavier blow and strikes Him with unaccustomed terror.[15]

Calvin goes on to refer to Ambrose, who argued that Christ's experience of such terror casts no shadow on his divine glory, but served instead to equip him to save us. 'He did not assume the appearance of incarnation, but a reality. He had to bear grief in order to conquer sadness, and not shut it out: they do not have the praise of fortitude who are drugged by wounds and not hurt'.[16]

Surrender

Morna Hooker observes that 'it is difficult to believe that this scene would have been invented by Jesus' followers, for the tendency would have been to present him facing death calmly and serenely'.[17] Similarly, it is difficult to see why Christians would have invented a story which portrayed the premier group of disciples in such a poor light. Over and over and over again, they fail the test by falling asleep on the job; leaving Jesus to struggle on his own.

In contrast to their failure, we see Jesus reaching the point of surrendering afresh to God and to the course charted out for him. The answer to his prayer for the cup to be taken away from him was 'No'; and in response, Jesus surrenders himself to the path of obedience that will lead to the cross. This was no easy decision, as France explains: 'The Jesus who accepts his Father's will does not do so with a "docetic" indifference but with a mental as well as physical agony which will reach its horrifying climax in the cry from the cross in 15.34'.[18] For Jesus and for us, 'prayer . . . consists not in changing God's mind but in finding our own alignment with God's will'.[19]

Watch and pray

Each year a brochure arrives at our home with details of all the places where I could choose to go on a retreat. All sorts of personality types are catered for with preached retreats, silent retreats, plus retreats for those who want to develop their skills in painting or writing poetry. Normally the retreat centre is located in a tranquil part of the countryside, where you can escape from the stress of city life.

I am all in favour of retreats, but too often the implicit message of the advertisements is that prayer is much easier in idyllic, stress-free rural environments. The Jesus we see praying in Gethsemane is not retreating from stress, but facing it head-on. His prayerful surrender in that stressful context suggests that while prayer may be difficult, it is possible in the stressful contexts we face. The warning to 'watch and pray' (Mk. 14:38 NIV) is a constant reminder for Christians that without a prayerful dependence on God, our faith will crumple under the testing times which are sure to come our way.

Preaching incarnation

A generation ago some writers tended to see Mark's Gospel as a relatively-straightforward account of the life of Jesus which was rather lightweight in terms of theology. Theologically, the evangelist was not felt to be in the same league as someone like the apostle Paul. Certainly at first glance, the letter to the Romans may look more theological than Mark's Gospel; but it would be a big mistake to imagine that Mark was just a simple storyteller. The trend today is to acknowledge Mark as both evangelist and theologian.[20]

Mark is a significant theologian who proclaims the incarnation through the medium of narrative. Theology is woven into the fabric of all the stories about Jesus which Mark narrates; and as we indwell this story, the true identity of Jesus starts to emerge. We begin to see how this Gospel bears witness to the one who is truly God and truly human.

Mark's Gospel demonstrates how narrative can be an effective vehicle for conveying truth about the incarnate Son of God. This suggests that sermons on this kind of material are likely to benefit from homiletical strategies which are sensitive to the narrative shape of the text.

Sermon: Struggling to obey God*

Peter Stevenson

Last month a Christian community nurse from Weston-Super-Mare was suspended from duty for a period because she'd offered to pray for one of her patients. The lady she'd offered to pray for said, 'I have Christian beliefs myself and maybe she meant well. But it could perhaps be upsetting for some other people if they have different beliefs or thought that she meant they looked in such a bad way that they needed praying for'.

So what's the Christian thing to do?

Last July an Employment Tribunal found that Islington Council had unlawfully discriminated against one of their registrars, a Christian lady who felt unable to preside at same-sex civil partnerships. Then in December last year Islington Council won their appeal against the tribunal's findings. I don't know what's happened to that Christian registrar, but I can't help wondering . . .

In that context, what's the Christian thing to do?

A lady always stands outside the local branch of M & S offering to sell me a copy of *The Big Issue*. I don't really want to buy a copy, because money's a bit short and I'll never get around to reading it anyway.

In that situation, what's the Christian thing to do?

The way some church members behave drives me to distraction. It seems that some people have a special gift for rubbing others up the wrong way, taking offence at the slightest provocation and letting loose a barrage of wounding words. If I was their employer, I'd have sacked most of them years ago for aggressive and insulting behaviour; but it's not so easy to sack people in a voluntary organization like the church.

Faced with church people acting in the most un-Christlike way, *what's the Christian thing to do?*

You know, in this mixed-up world it's *not always easy to know* what God wants us to do; and in this mixed-up world, and as mixed-up people, it's *not always easy to do* what God wants us to do.

It's a struggle—but then it's not really surprising that it's a struggle to do what God wants.

It's not really surprising that it's a struggle because we live in a fallen world, a world that's turned its back on God. And in that kind of world, of course it's going to be difficult if we want to swim against the stream and live as God wants us to live.

---

*Sermon preached by Dr Peter K. Stevenson at the Rochester Diocese Reader Training weekend at Aylesford (UK) Priory on Saturday, 7 March 2009.

It's not really surprising that it's a struggle to do what God wants because we're all of us fallen human beings, and there's something inside each and every one of us which holds us back from doing what God wants us to do.

It's not surprising that obeying God is something of a struggle for us. *But what is surprising* is that obeying God is something which Jesus struggled with as well. And we get a glimpse of that struggle as we eavesdrop on the goings on in the garden of Gethsemane.

> They went to a place called Gethsemane; and Jesus said to his disciples, 'Sit here while I pray'. He took with him Peter and James and John, and began to be distressed and agitated. And he said to them, 'I am deeply grieved, even to death; remain here, and keep awake'. And going a little farther, he threw himself on the ground and prayed that, if it were possible, the hour might pass from him. He said, 'Abba, Father, for you all things are possible; remove this cup from me; yet, not what I want, but what you want'. (Mk. 14.32–36)

Last week Prime Minister Gordon Brown went to Washington to visit President Barack Obama, and he gave a speech to the joint houses of Congress. Every little detail of Gordon Brown's visit has been analysed, and various people have been looking closely at the two men's body language to see what it reveals about the nature of the special relationship between Britain and America.

The BBC's Matt Frei's assessment of Gordon Brown's meeting with Barack Obama was that 'Gordon Brown looked as nervous as someone on a first date in his meeting with the president'.

Janet Daley in *The Telegraph* yesterday said:

> It was painful to watch the contrast in body language when they sat together in the Oval Office for their (very brief) meeting with the press. Gordon grinned fixedly at Obama, positively cringing with eager sycophancy while the President sat facing stonily ahead of him, uttering mandatory words of friendship with which he seemed to feel uncomfortable.[21]

But on the other hand, a psychologist who's an expert on body language 'thought they got on pretty well'.[22]

Well, I don't know what we should read into Gordon Brown's body language; but if we pay attention to the body language of Jesus in the garden of Gethsemane, a very clear message emerges.

> [Jesus] said to them, 'I am deeply grieved, even to death; remain here, and keep awake'.

And going a little farther, he threw himself on the ground and prayed that, if it were possible, the hour might pass from him. He said, 'Abba, Father, for you all things are possible; remove this cup from me'. (Mk. 14.34–36)

- Can you see the anxiety etched on Jesus' face?
- Can you feel the terror throbbing in his veins as he throws himself on the ground and pleads for another way?
- Can you hear the fear in his voice as he cries out, *'Abba, Father, for you all things are possible; remove this cup from me.'*

There's a real life-and-death struggle going on here. As Jesus advances towards Jerusalem, the reality of his suffering and death comes home to him in an overwhelming way. And it's not just the pain of dying a brutal death that every fibre of his being reacts against. There's also the sense that he's the suffering servant of God who's taking upon his own shoulders the sins and burdens of a broken world.

One writer says:

Here for the first time Jesus experiences the silence of God, a divine estrangement that comes to expression finally in Jesus' cry of dereliction from the Cross. Gethsemane, then, does not so much demonstrate Jesus' anguish in the face of death as his fear of being abandoned by God.[23]

All of this leads me to conclude that part of the good news which emerges from this passage is *that being obedient to God is difficult for us, and that it was also difficult for Jesus.* And if Jesus has passed through that kind of experience, then he's well qualified to help us as we struggle day by day to obey God.

And certainly that's how this episode's interpreted in the letter to the Hebrews, which tells us:

In the days of his flesh, Jesus offered up prayers and supplications, with loud cries and tears, to the one who was able to save him from death, and he was heard because of his reverent submission. Although he was a Son, he learned obedience through what he suffered; and having been made perfect, he became the source of eternal salvation for all who obey him.[24]

- We're conscious that obeying God is a struggle.
- In Gethsemane we see Jesus struggling to obey God.
- And because he's shared our struggle, he's perfectly qualified to help us as we seek to know and do the will of God.

But there's a niggling little voice interrupting me as I say that . . . for there's a little voice within which says:

> Well that's all well and good, but . . . Jesus was the Son of God, so it wasn't really as big a struggle for him as it is for us.
>
> For didn't he know that there'd be a resurrection on the third day and that everything was going to work out fine?
>
> Yes, the cross would be painful, but he knew deep down that everything was going to work out OK.
>
> So how can Jesus really understand how hard it is for us to trust and obey God when we've got no guarantees that everything's going to work out OK? We don't have a divine overdrive like him that we can call on to get us out of trouble.

Now I don't know if you've ever heard that niggling little voice. But there's something very important at stake here, and if we take a wrong turning, we end up with a Christ who became *almost, but not quite human.* Throughout the history of the Church, Christians have affirmed that Jesus Christ was fully human and fully divine. Now most of the time we tend to put the stress on Christ being fully divine—truly this is the Son of God. But at the same time we also need to affirm that Christ was fully human.

When 'the Word became flesh and dwelt among us' (Jn. 1.14 NKJV), God came in the person of his Son to share our humanity and to identify with fallen human beings to the full. And Gethsemane's one of those episodes which shows us clearly that Jesus shared our humanity to the fullest extent imaginable.

His humanity's evident in the way in which he brought his three closest friends, Peter, James and John, into the garden. On the one hand, they were maybe there to stand guard and to warn Jesus about Judas and the religious authorities coming to arrest him. But on the other hand, they were probably there simply because this Jesus needed the support of his friends as he was facing testing times.

His humanity's evident in the way he struggles with his divinely-given vocation to be God's servant. This whole dramatic episode points to the truth that Jesus has shared our humanity to the full.

Let me read you the comments of one writer which sum this up in a clear and helpful way:

> A Jesus who walked through the world knowing exactly what the morrow would bring, knowing with certainty that three days after his death his Father would raise him up, is a Jesus who can arouse our admiration, but still a Jesus far from us. He is a Jesus far from a mankind that can only hope in the future and believe in God's goodness,

far from a mankind that must face the supreme uncertainty of death with faith but without knowledge of what is beyond.

On the other hand, a Jesus for whom the future was as much a mystery, a dread and a hope as it is for us and yet at the same time a Jesus who could say, 'Not my will but yours!'—this is a Jesus who could effectively teach us how to live, for this is a Jesus who would have gone through life's real trials.[25]

Now, reading the passage in this way doesn't in any way diminish our belief in the divinity of Christ: what it does do is to increase our sense of wonder that God so loved the world that the Word became flesh and dwelt among us; that Christ came to share our humanity in order to redeem us and open up the way to life in all its fullness.

And what we see here is that life in all its fullness involves surrendering ourselves to God. For the other thing to note here is that whilst there's a genuine struggle going on, that struggle isn't a revolt against God because having prayed three times for the cup to be taken away from him, Jesus accepts that the answer to his prayer is 'No', and he surrenders himself to God. He surrenders himself to doing God's will.

Abba, Father, for you all things are possible; remove this cup from me; yet, not what I want, but what you want.

Now if instead of being here this weekend, you'd decided that Spring is on its way and it's time to get your garden into order, you might've gone down to the Garden Centre to pick up all sorts of bits and pieces. And my guess is that amongst the 1,001 things that the Garden Centre wants you to put in your garden, you can buy a piece of garden furniture with these words carved into them:

One is nearer God's heart in a garden
    Than anywhere else on earth.[26]

And those words conjure up images of an English country garden: bright blue skies, the fragrance of roses, great bursts of colour, peace and tranquillity.

- It's a romantic picture!
- Its a romantic illusion!
- It's bad theology!

But perhaps the one place where it's true that you're nearer God's heart in a garden is in the garden of Gethsemane, where we hear the Son of God praying to his heavenly Father, in those intimate words *Abba, Father*.

But this garden is not a place of peace and tranquillity. The garden of Gethsemane is a battlefield—more *Flanders Fields*[27] than *Kew Gardens*.[28] For when we take off our rose-tinted glasses, we begin to see that there's a real battle going on here. It's a battle between good and evil, a battle between God and the devil. And it's the same battle that was running throughout the ministry of Jesus.

In this season of Lent we remember how Jesus was in the wilderness for forty days, being tempted, being tested by the devil. And those forty days were the opening rounds of this heavyweight battle for the championship of the world; and in this battle we hear the devil saying over and over again:

- If you are God's Son, turn these stones into bread.
- If you are God's Son, bow down and worship me, and all the kingdoms of the world will be yours.
- If you are God's son, jump off the top of the temple in a publicity stunt, and angels will surely come to your aid.

Over and over again, Jesus was being tested and tempted to turn away from God's way. And that battle, that testing, was going on throughout Jesus' ministry—and it erupts into view once again here in Gethsemane, where Jesus is put to the test. His faith and trust in God are put under pressure, and he's tempted to turn back, to turn away from God's way.

He's tempted to turn back from the way of the cross as that niggling little voice says, 'Surely there's some other way of saving the world which doesn't involve all that suffering and abandonment and death? Surely there's a better way of sorting out the world's problems than by dying a bloody death on a criminal's cross?'

- And Jesus struggles
- And Jesus prays
- And as he surrenders to God's will, he comes through this testing time on top.

It's Round 14 of this great heavyweight battle for the championship of the world, and once again Jesus comes out on top. And soon this battle will move on to the final Round, where through his cross and resurrection Jesus will be victorious over him who had the power of death, even the devil.

In the battlefield that was Gethsemane, Jesus' faith was put to the test, and he warns his disciples that their faith will be put to the test as well. Indeed, it was just before this episode in Gethsemane that Jesus had tried to warn the disciples that testing times were ahead:

> Jesus said to them, 'You will all become deserters; for it is written,
>
> 'I will strike the shepherd,
>   and the sheep will be scattered'.
>
> But after I am raised up, I will go before you to Galilee'.
> Peter said to him, 'Even though all become deserters, I will not'.
> Jesus said to him, 'Truly I tell you, this day, this very night, before the cock crows twice, you will deny me three times'.
> But he said vehemently, 'Even though I must die with you, I will not deny you'. And all of them said the same. (Mk. 14.27–31)

Peter and all the rest of the disciples said, 'Don't worry, Jesus, you can count on us ...'. In the *Friends* TV version of this story, we'd have the apostle Peter singing to Jesus, '*I'll Be There for You*'; but when the chips are down, Peter and the others aren't there to support Jesus because they're fast asleep.

> [Jesus] came and found them sleeping; and he said to Peter, 'Simon, are you asleep? Could you not keep awake one hour? Keep awake and pray that you may not come into the time of trial [into temptation]; the spirit indeed is willing, but the flesh is weak'. (Mk. 14.37–38)

- In their own strength there's no way that they can survive these testing times.
- In their own strength their faith will fail.
- In their own strength they'll turn back from following Jesus.

In their own strength there's no way they'll be able to stand, and that's why Jesus tells them

- to watch and pray.
- to pour out their anguish to God.
- to be honest to God about their questions and fears.

And when they cry out to God, they'll encounter the one who'll give them the power to say, '*Not my will, but your will be done*'.

A few years ago I visited one of my relations who'd gone to church regularly in earlier years, but who'd gradually found it harder and harder to believe. Listening to some middle-aged clergy left this person wondering whether their faith had withered as well? The temptation to give up on faith is still there. So where can we turn to for help when those testing times come?

Well, here in Gethsemane we don't see a helpless victim—but we see Jesus, who's master of his own destiny, the one who chooses to go to the cross; for at the end of this encounter, it's Jesus who's very much in charge.

> Jesus came a third time and said to them, 'Are you still sleeping and taking your rest? Enough! The hour has come; the Son of Man is betrayed into the hands of sinners. Get up, let us be going. See, my betrayer is at hand'. (Mk. 14.41–42)

As we focus on events in Gethsemane, we see a Jesus who faces and overcomes evil as he depends upon the power of God. This is the one who will overcome pain, suffering, evil and death by his cross and resurrection; and he's the one who can empower us to come through all those experiences which try and test our faith. He's the one who can give us the strength we need in Lent, and in life, to take up the cross and to go on following Jesus.

> Since, then, we have a great high priest who has passed through the heavens, Jesus, the Son of God, let us hold fast to our confession. For we do not have a high priest who is unable to sympathize with our weaknesses, but we have one who in every respect has been tested as we are, yet without sin. Let us therefore approach the throne of grace with boldness, so that we may receive mercy and find grace to help in time of need. (Heb. 4.14–16)

Sermon commentary

One of the things which helps keep both of us on our toes homiletically is the opportunity to preach to a group of people training to be preachers within the Anglican Diocese of Rochester. Each year one of us preaches during a training weekend and then responds to feedback and questions from the congregation. Chapter 4 reflects upon a sermon preached in 2008, and the sermon in view here was prepared for the 2009 group.

The questions which people asked in the feedback session helped me to reflect on the whole process of preparing the sermon. Sitting down to prepare this sermon on a familiar biblical passage, I was very conscious that my previous attempts had relied upon a simple three-point structure, using the headings 'Sonship', 'Struggle' and 'Surrender'. As the earlier part of this chapter suggests, those themes are embedded in this text; but for this occasion I wanted to use a narrative sermon structure more in keeping with the literary form of the text.

Moves and episodes

One way of reflecting on the sermon is to see it in terms of David Buttrick's ideas about sermons being made up of a number of 'moves':

> Sermons are a movement of language from one idea to another, each idea being shaped in a bundle of words. Thus, when we preach we speak in formed modules of language arranged in some patterned sequence. These modules of language we will call 'moves'.[29]

So, for example, the first 'move' in the sequence consisted of four brief scenarios which each raised the question 'What's the Christian thing to do?' In stitching these short stories together, the hope was that their accumulated impact would press home this fundamental idea that the Christian life is a struggle with no easy answers. This leads on into a second, shorter 'move', which might begin to disturb some hearers, suggesting that while we can see why for us obeying God is not easy in a fallen world, the Bible says that it was also difficult for Jesus.

Seeing the sermon as a sequence of 'moves', Buttrick points to the way that images combine to bring the sermon to life:

> A sermon, like a poem, is a structure of words and images. One 'perfect' flashing image will not make a poem. Instead it is an interaction of images within a structure that adds up to a fine poem. What makes a good sermon is not one single illustration, but a gridwork of interacting images, examples and illustrations.[30]

So within this sermon, alongside the big image of Jesus struggling in Gethsemane, other images are at work, such as the smaller images of an English country garden or the First World War battleground of Flanders Fields.

Another way of viewing this sermon is to see it as an example of 'episodic' preaching. Preparing for this sermon, I placed a sheet of paper landscape-style on the desk; and working from left to right, I started to jot down a series of boxes or speech bubbles. Each of these boxes represented an 'episode' in the story I wanted to tell about Jesus in Gethsemane. Some of the 'episodes' in the story were stories from the news, like Gordon Brown's visit to Washington. Other 'episodes' involved reading extracts from the biblical narrative. The challenge was to arrange these 'episodes' in sequences which would tell the story in a way that would engage and hold people's attention.

Appealing to the senses

Shortly before preaching this sermon, I came across Kenton Anderson's comment that 'one underappreciated aspect of Spurgeon's preaching is his use of the five senses to create an experience for his listeners'.[31] He gives some examples of the ways in which the 'Prince of Preachers' used affective language and argues:

> Spurgeon understood that preachers have it in their power to help the listener experience the presence of God through the way they use their words. 'God gives his ministers a brush, and shows them how to use it in painting life-like portraits, and thus the sinner hears the special call'.[32]

That suggested to me that it would be worth experimenting with sensory language in this sermon; to see if that might help people 'taste and see' what Jesus was experiencing in the garden of Gethsemane (Mk. 14.32–42). The point where I consciously tried to appeal to people's imaginations and senses followed on from talking about the body language of Jesus.

- Can you *see* the anxiety etched on Jesus' face?
- Can you *feel* the terror throbbing in his veins?
- Can you *hear* the fear in his voice?

On this occasion the congregation responded positively, and that encourages me to experiment further along these lines.

Raising questions

In general the feedback from my hearers was positive, although some would have preferred more answers to the questions raised by the sermon. In the workshop session there was scope to answer some specific questions about the way in which the biblical text had been handled. I was unapologetic, however, about raising questions without always answering them. My hope is that listeners will play their part in making the sermon work, and that they will go on wrestling with the questions long after the sermon is finished.

7

In the likeness of sinful flesh
ROMANS 8.1–8

It was the final year at theological college, and my turn had come to face the ordeal of 'sermon class'. Leading a service and preaching before faculty and students was enough to put the 'fear of God' into the most able preacher. In previous years we had been allowed to choose our own texts, but convention dictated that the principal selected the biblical passages for leaving students to expound.

One friend was asked to preach on Judges 21.25: 'There was no king in Israel; all the people did what was right in their own eyes'. So maybe I got off lightly when my allocated task was to preach from Rom. 8.1: 'There is therefore no condemnation . . .'.

Recently I stumbled across my sermon notes and some of the feedback sheets. They make sobering reading. One student thought that I probably 'preached too much judgement and not enough good news'; but then another person's advice for improving my preaching was rather puzzling: 'more aggression needed'. This novice preacher did not find Rom. 8.1–8 an easy passage to preach from. That is not really surprising: as I was to discover much later, 'the complex and powerful statement' of Rom. 8.3–4 is 'a sentence that has as good a claim as any to represent the very center of what Paul is saying in Romans 5–8, if not in his whole theology'.[1]

If such a great deal of theology is compressed into such a small space, what resources might Rom. 8.1–8 offer preachers interested in preaching the incarnation? At first glance it may appear that the focus here is less on incarnation than on the Spirit's role within the life of Christian believers. A closer look, however, unveils some important perspectives on incarnation.

The return of the king

As this chapter was being written, President Barack Obama was giving a landmark speech in Cairo. He was seeking to mend broken bridges in the Middle East and initiate a new era of relationships between the United States and the Muslim world.

In the centuries before the coming of Christ, in the period described by scholars as Second Temple Judaism, Jewish believers had many hopes for the coming of a new era; for the dawning of the Messianic age. The precise nature of those hopes provokes vigorous debates, which must be left for others to evaluate.[2] In terms of Romans 8, however, what can be said with some confidence is that the apostle Paul believed that Israel's hopes had been fulfilled in a surprising way by Jesus Christ. There is a clear sense in this passage that he believed that the coming of Christ signalled the dawn of a new era; the eschatological messianic age.

This eschatological dimension is signalled in Rom. 8.1 by the word 'now' (cf. 7.6). John Ziesler argues that the full force of the word 'now' needs to be acknowledged: 'It is not just a logical 'now', but a temporal one. Now in the New Age of Christ and the Spirit, new life is available'.[3]

The reason why there is no condemnation 'now' is because something of eschatological importance has taken place. In the light of the incarnation, crucifixion, resurrection and exaltation of Jesus Christ and the outpouring of the Spirit at Pentecost, the apostle is sure that this new age has dawned. For those who are 'in Christ', there is no condemnation to fear now or in the future because the eschatological verdict has already been announced in their favour. So the note of good news certainly does deserve to be sounded loud and clear.

This is not the sort of passage which is normally read at carol services, but in its own way it conveys the Christmas message that 'the hopes and fears of all the years'[4] find their fulfilment in the down-to-earth God who comes in the person of Jesus Christ, to share in our plight and usher in the long-awaited kingdom of God.

Cur Deus homo?

In thinking about the purpose of the incarnation, this passage offers several complementary answers to the question 'Why did God become human?'

To deal with sin

One answer is that the Word became flesh in order to set enslaved people free. Our shared human captivity is described here in terms of people being enslaved to 'the law of sin and death' (Rom. 8.2). We are powerless to set ourselves free, but God's act of liberation, in Christ through the Spirit, breaks the vicious circle of sin and death.

In that old student sermon, I tried to explore some of the things which enslave people; for one response to this passage could be for preachers to encourage people to reflect upon some of the things which enslave people today. In what ways do we need to be set free? It is worth underlining how Paul addresses every hearer of this letter individually, by using the singular 'you' when he declares in Rom. 8.2 that God 'has set you free'.

Paul is convinced that the law is 'good' (7.12), but that it is powerless to enable people to experience the abundant life towards which it points. The problem is that the divinely-given law has been abused by the power of sin to enslave people.

Many read Romans primarily as a challenge to those who think that they can justify themselves with God on the basis of the good works of obeying the law. The apostle Paul certainly makes it clear that justification is absolutely impossible on such a basis. However, the main target here is not the *torah*, or legalism, but the destructive power of Sin, which distorts the law and enslaves people.

Some may feel uneasy preaching about sin because the Church has an unenviable reputation for laying unnecessary burdens of guilt upon people. Talk of sin is often regarded as a pessimistic, intolerant, old-fashioned analysis of our human predicament. Those overly-optimistic voices are challenged by N. T. Wright, who argues that the troubled state of our world debunks the myth of ever-upward social progress and demands that sin is placed back on the agenda:

> It is time once again to hold out the analysis of human behavior offered in the New Testament. There is such a thing as Sin, which is more than the sum total of human wrongdoing. It is powerful, and this power infects even those with the best intentions. If it could make even the holy Torah its base of operations, how much more the muddled intentions of well-meaning do-gooders.[5]

As a sin-offering

Incarnation is a costly business, because breaking sin's power involves the sacrificial death of Christ. This comes into view in Rom. 8.3, where the phrase about God sending his Son 'to deal with sin' can also be translated in terms of the Son being sent 'as a sin-offering' (*peri harmartias*). Ben Witherington explains that 'this phrase is frequently used in the LXX to refer to a sin offering (cf. Lev. 5.6–7, 11; Num. 6.16; Ezek. 42.13). It certainly can mean that here as well, especially in the light of what follows and of what has been said in [Romans] ch. 5 about atonement'.[6]

Paul has already spoken about the atoning sacrifice which Christ has offered in Rom. 3.25; this further allusion to the sacrificial death of Christ is a reminder that the deep-rooted problem of sin cannot be dealt with by even the best of our human endeavours. If sin is to be wiped away and eradicated, then divine intervention is required.

Condemned sin in the flesh

These words make clear that the divine judgement upon sin which the law prescribed has been carried out, in the flesh on Jesus Christ. Paul does not say that Christ has been condemned, but that sin has been condemned in the flesh of Jesus Christ. So what might this unusual phrase mean?

It is clear that Paul believes that the Messiah Jesus is a representative figure whose death has consequences for others. One reading of this phrase would be to suggest that in his death, Jesus has taken the guilty verdict which others deserve, so that those he represents may hear the verdict of 'Not guilty'. This would fit with the judicial language of the opening verse of this chapter, which celebrates that there is now no condemnation for those who are in Christ Jesus.

In the light of Paul's earlier argument that 'the wages of sin is death' (Rom. 6.23), it can be argued that Christ's death involves him accepting the undeserved verdict of death on behalf of others. However, Paul is talking here not simply about being given a 'Not guilty' verdict; but about a divine act which somehow breaks and nullifies the power of sin. In order to break sin's power, something even more radical is called for.

Jesus the Messiah represents sinful, fallen humanity. As we shall shortly see, his identification with sinful human beings is complete and unreserved. By incarnation this representative figure takes upon himself mortal flesh, which is riddled with sin. This flesh is so contaminated and weakened by sin that the only way to put sin out of circulation is by putting it to death upon the cross. For only then can a new humanity, the humanity intended by God before the foundation of the world, come to be.

This process of condemning sin in the flesh certainly involves what takes place upon the cross. But what happens there is also the natural outworking of the redeeming process set in motion by the very act of incarnation. So we find C. E. B. Cranfield explaining: 'If we recognize that Paul believed it was fallen human nature which the Son of God assumed, we shall probably be inclined to see here also a reference to the unintermittent warfare of His whole earthly life by which He forced our rebellious nature to render a perfect obedience to God'.[7]

With the incarnation, death, resurrection and exaltation of Jesus Christ, a new humanity comes to be; and those who are 'in Christ' begin to share in the glorified humanity of their risen and exalted Lord.

Plumbing the depths of incarnation

Probably the most significant way in which this passage contributes to our understanding of incarnation is when it tells us that God sent his Son 'in the likeness of sinful flesh' (Rom. 8.3). Bundled up in these words is the amazing claim that when 'the Word became flesh and dwelt among us' (Jn. 1.14 NKJV), he assumed the selfsame, fallen humanity which all of us share. However, there is some biblical and theological work to be done to support this reading of the text.

Unfallen flesh?

Discussion centres upon how the word 'likeness' should be translated, because it might suggest that the divine Son assumed something 'like' but not quite the same as our sinful, fallen humanity. Thus some have argued that the choice of the word 'likeness' (*homoiōmati*) is a deliberate move to show that whilst the Son identified fully with people, his flesh was not exactly the same as ours. It resembled our fallen humanity, but it was not completely like it because it was unfallen flesh: the kind of flesh Adam had before the fall. This is probably what Witherington has in mind when he suggests that the 'likeness of sinful flesh' means that 'Christ had real flesh, but that it was not fallen and sinful flesh'.[8] This perspective was classically expressed by John Calvin:

> For we make Christ free of all stain not just because he was begotten of his mother without copulation with man, but because he was sanctified by the Spirit that the generation might be pure and undefiled as it would have been true before Adam's fall.[9]

Earlier in Romans the apostle Paul contrasted the actions of the first Adam with the redeeming actions of the last Adam, Jesus Christ (5.12–21). There is clearly value in telling the story of how the last Adam recapitulated the story of the first Adam, repairing the damage by obeying God at all those points where Adam failed. The idea of Christ assuming unfallen human nature, like that of Adam before the fall, would be compatible with this kind of re-telling of the Gospel narrative.

The assumption of fallen flesh

Nevertheless, bearing in mind Gregory of Nazianzus' assertion that 'what he has not assumed he has not healed'[10], the claim that Christ assumed unfallen human flesh suggests that our fallen human nature remains untouched and unredeemed. As Thomas Torrance bluntly states,

> If the Word of God did not really come into our fallen existence, if the Son of God did not actually come where we are, and join himself to us and range himself with us where we are in sin and under judgement, how could it be said that Christ really took our place, took our cause upon himself in order to redeem us?[11]

There are, however, good biblical grounds for claiming that the phrase in the 'likeness of sinful flesh' affirms Christ's wholehearted identification with us in our fallen state rather than suggesting that his human nature was of the pre-fall variety. So, for example, we find James Dunn arguing that '*Homoiōma* . . . does not distinguish Jesus from sinful flesh or distance him from fallen man, as is often suggested; rather it is Paul's way of expressing Jesus' *complete identity* with the flesh of sin, with man in his fallenness'.[12]

An interesting variation of this perspective is advanced by Cranfield, who suggests that Paul uses the word 'likeness' in Rom. 8.3 both to signify that 'the Son of God assumed the selfsame fallen human nature that is ours' and to indicate that 'fallen human nature was never the whole of Him—He never ceased to be the eternal Son of God'.[13]

A distinguished line of thinkers

Geoffrey Wainwright observes that

> in the history of theology there is a narrow but distinguished line of thinkers who per-
> ceive that the humanity which Christ assumed was not a humanity as it still was 'before
> the fall' nor yet a humanity as it will be in the definitive kingdom, but precisely a *fallen*
> humanity—though he himself remained without personal sin and was raised in glory
> at his resurrection.[14]

As samples of this 'distinguished line' of theologians, Wainwright mentions Gregory of Nazianzus,[15] Karl Barth[16] and Hans Urs von Balthasar,
who conveys this idea in dramatic language: 'The Son of God took human form in its fallen condition, and with it, therefore, the worm in its
entrails—mortality, fallenness, self-estrangement, death—which sin introduced into the world'.[17]

Thomas Weinandy's study of patristic, medieval and contemporary
writers leads him to conclude that 'the christological tradition definitely
confirms that the Eternal Son assumed a humanity which bore the birth-
mark of Adam. He became man in the likeness of sinful flesh'.[18] Weinandy is aware that there is a degree of ambiguity and tension in patristic
christology at this point. On the one hand, the principle, that what is not
assumed is not healed, leads to an emphasis upon the Son assuming flesh
like ours in order to be an effective Saviour. But on the other hand, stress
upon the obedience of the Son, who makes himself a perfect offering for
sin, tends to underline his dissimilarity to us. At this point it is not possible to resolve the ambiguities he highlights, but what his work makes clear
is that the idea of Christ's assuming fallen human nature is no theological
novelty, but a doctrine deeply rooted in the Christian tradition.

Incarnation and atonement

One of the consequences of seeing Christ's incarnation in this way is that
it acknowledges the essential connection between incarnation and crucifixion in the atoning work of Christ. Some models of atonement focus
on the death of Christ to such an extent that the life which preceded it
falls into the background. It is almost as if Christ simply had to avoid sin
for thirty-three years in order to qualify as the perfect sacrifice for sin.
Those who affirm that Christ assumed our fallen human nature affirm

that Christ remained sinless by the power of the Spirit, and that the whole of his life was part of the process of God's resisting evil and 'condemning sin in the flesh'. Thus we hear Thomas Torrance explaining, 'We must also say that in the very act of assuming our flesh the Word sanctified and hallowed it, for the assumption of our sinful flesh is itself atoning and sanctifying action'.[19]

Having advanced the case for affirming that Christ assumed our sinful flesh, it is appropriate to turn next to an historical case study illustrating one preacher's attempt to make this theme live for his parishioners. Later in the chapter we shall see a contemporary preacher tackling some of the same themes.

Preaching case study: John McLeod Campbell

In the course of affirming that 'the nature which God assumed in Christ is identical with our nature as we see it in the light of the Fall', Karl Barth[20] acknowledges the pioneering work of Edward Irving[21] in promoting this doctrine. One of the people directly influenced by Irving was the Scottish minister John McLeod Campbell (1800–72),[22] whose thoughts on this subject we now turn to.

Campbell was not a remote academic figure exploring abstract ideas in some distant ivory tower, but a working pastor whose theology was 'hammered out on the anvil of the parish ministry'.[23] His sermons were lengthy biblical and theological reflections which must have made severe demands on his listeners, even if they had longer attention spans than people today. For all his faults, here was a preacher who was trying to get his congregation to think seriously about some of the great themes of the Christian faith. This is not preaching as entertainment but as a vital strand of Christian formation.

In one of the sermons from his early ministry in Rhu in Dumbarton-shire (1825–31), John McLeod Campbell focuses directly upon Romans 8, but it appears in a very rare volume of sermons which is not generally accessible. However, in another sermon from the same period, based on Titus 2.11–14, Campbell summarizes his understanding of Rom. 8.3; and a copy of this sermon can be found in a recent study of Campbell's theology.[24]

God in our nature

In pointing to Christ's total identification with humanity, Campbell argues that Christ has identified fully with human beings by assuming their fallen flesh, and by his actions in our flesh he teaches us the truth about sin. Christ condemns sin, not by strident criticism but by revealing that it is not necessary for people's lives to be dominated by sin:

> Christ came in our nature—in our very nature—that he came into that very world in which we are, and enjoyed no privilege, no distinction to screen him from the power of the world, or from the oppression of the world—that he was exposed to all the attacks of Satan, and enjoyed no advantage to keep Satan from coming to deceive him, and attempting to destroy him.[25]

He argues that the human predicament, portrayed in Romans 7, is of people struggling unsuccessfully to overcome sin. This sorry state is brought to an end by Christ, by virtue of his coming 'in the likeness of sinful flesh'. For Campbell, the reference in Rom. 8.3 to the Son coming 'in the likeness of sinful flesh' does not mean that Christ came into something resembling sinful flesh, that was actually slightly different from it. He interprets this phrase to mean that Christ assumed a flesh which was the same as ours, thus providing proof for a genuine participation by Christ in our human nature and condition:

> You are not to suppose that this means in appearance merely. . . . Likeness of man means participation in manhood. It means taking that which is humanity—and the likeness of sinful flesh means that he took that flesh which we have for the purpose of condemning sin in it.[26]

This total act of identification not only has the negative effect of condemning sin by bringing it out into the open; for it also has the more positive purpose of revealing the truth about human life as God intended it:

> When I see before me the man Christ Jesus, denying ungodliness I see what I ought to be. I see what I am called to be. When I see him denying all worldly lusts I see, I say, what I ought to be, and what I am called to be.[27]

Christ has the Holy Spirit for us

In addition to revealing what people are intended to be, Christ shows that it is possible for people to live as God intended. He does not simply offer us an example of perfection and leave us with the impossible task of trying to follow that example. For the one who constantly received the Spirit from his Father has, since the resurrection, become 'the second Adam, the quickening Spirit', who pours out the Spirit upon his people (cf. 1 Cor. 15:45 KJV).

Campbell longs for his listeners to grasp that it is the power of this Spirit which makes it possible for people, in union with Christ, to live a new kind of life freed from the power of sin:

> Christ having condemned sin in the flesh—having presented himself without spot to God, through the Eternal Spirit, did this as a sacrifice for sin, and so put away our sin, and so we have our sin forgiven through the shedding of his blood, and he being exalted to the right hand of God, in reward of his holiness and righteousness, has received from the Father this high place, that now he is the second Adam, the quickening Spirit—that now he has the Holy Spirit for us to dwell in us by the Spirit that, through his Spirit in us, we might be what he was.[28]

In his glorified humanity, Christ stands in heaven as the second Adam, to whom God the Father has entrusted the Holy Spirit.[29] Describing the risen Christ as 'the quickening Spirit' does not imply a merging of Christ and the Spirit but highlights Christ as the one who pours out the Spirit on believers. He proclaims the incarnate Christ, who lived a godly life, and the ascended Christ, who supplies the Spirit who makes this new kind of life possible.

Jesus' purity can come in contact with our pollution and cleanse it

In a different sermon preached during his ministry in Glasgow, Campbell uses even more dramatic language to affirm that Christ assumed sinful flesh. Reflecting on Gal. 5.14–18,[30] Campbell wants the congregation to realize that 'man's soul is the theatre of a conflict between two powers, which try to draw him in two different directions'.[31] In this battle with the power of the flesh, human willpower is not sufficient to resist the reign of our fallen nature:

There is, deep in every heart, a fountain of pollution and darkness, deeper than we can fathom—deep as hell itself, and of the very essence of hell; for hell consists in a spirit that has no peace, being in rebellion against God, and having no resting-place either in God or man, because it has no trust.[32]

If human nature in general is in such a sorry state, does that also imply that Christ assumed a human nature like ours, afflicted by this 'fountain of pollution and darkness'? If there is an 'evil fire of enmity'[33] at work within the flesh, does this mean that there was an evil fire of enmity at work within the human nature assumed by Christ? The preacher does not hesitate to see Christ's plumbing the depths of our sinful existence in this way, because if 'every child of Adam has this flesh working in him',[34] then this is the only kind of flesh available for Christ to assume.

Campbell is not embarrassed to link Christ with such impurity because he is convinced that the power of Christ's purity is more contagious and powerful than the evil power at work in human existence. 'It is said, no one can touch pitch and not be defiled; but Jesus can touch the deep stream of pollution in our flesh, and yet not be defiled by it. His purity can come in contact with our pollution, and cleanse it'.[35]

The preacher portrays Jesus as the good physician who is able to supply the remedy to our fallen condition, as the one who 'is ever willing to impart His Spirit, as the power of holiness, the power of love to us'.[36] In Campbell's eyes the sinlessness of Christ is in no way compromised by this stream of pollution in human flesh, because Christ never submitted to its demands. The principle being followed here is the classic 'What is not assumed is not healed'. For only as the divine physician assumes such diseased flesh is he able to redeem it by the power of the Spirit.

An inner propensity to sin?

At this point it is appropriate to relate Campbell's approach to some recent discussions about Christ's assuming fallen human nature. Kelly Kapic observes that 'there is disagreement among those holding to the fallen position whether Jesus had an inner propensity to sin (i.e. concupiscence), some affirming and others denying'.[37]

So, for example, we find Thomas Weinandy's affirming on the one hand that 'our salvation is unconditionally dependent upon the Son's assuming a humanity disfigured by sin and freely acting as a son of Adam'. At the same time, however, he also takes great care in pointing out that he neither 'sinned personally' nor 'had an inner propensity to sin':[38]

While Jesus assumed our fallen condition and thus could be tempted, yet . . . he was filled with the Spirit from conception, thereby freeing him from the morally corrupting effects of original sin. Even though the New Testament does not make any distinction between temptations that arise from 'outside' and those that originate from 'within' a person (cf. Jas. 1.1–3), the received tradition seems to demand that Jesus' temptations could not have arisen from within him since he did not share our concupiscence, i.e., our propensity to sin.[39]

Questions can be asked about the precise nature of 'concupiscence' and whether this is synonymous with a propensity to sin, as Weinandy seems to imply. If 'concupiscence' is seen as immoderate or sinful desire, then the presence of concupiscence within the human constitution of Christ would be equivalent, in some traditions, to saying that Christ was a sinner.

However, it may also be possible to see our human propensity to sin in a different light. Perhaps this is one way of pointing to the common human experience that temptation to sin arises not simply from external factors, but also from deep-seated sources within human nature which need to be healed. Weinandy's obvious hesitations about ascribing to Christ an 'inner propensity to sin' introduce a degree of ambiguity into his account of the person of Christ. For if Christ did not experience and overcome this propensity to sin, which is the source of those temptations originating from 'within a person', then a lingering doubt must surely remain that a damaged part of human nature remains unassumed and thus unhealed.

The language employed by Campbell in his preaching points in a different direction. For it is hard to read his assertion that 'Jesus can touch the deep stream of pollution in our flesh, and yet not be defiled by it',[40] without concluding that Campbell believed that Christ had assumed a fallen human nature complete with its propensity to sin, but that he remained sinless by constant dependence upon the Holy Spirit. His preaching only makes sense on the assumption that Christ has faced and overcome this inner propensity to sin. For it is only if Christ has resisted the full force of external and internal temptation by the power of the Spirit that he can demonstrate that there is 'no necessity for our having sinned against God'.[41]

The perfect sacrifice of obedience

The incarnation functions as the just foundation of divine judgement against human sinfulness by demonstrating that sin is neither automatic nor inevitable. It is not just that the divine Son enters a world scarred by the fall and has to work within a creation groaning in travail, because the battle between good and evil rages within the very human nature he has assumed. This does not challenge core convictions about the sinlessness of Christ because at no point did he ever yield to this inner propensity to sin. It is this complete identification with fallen humanity which makes it possible for Christ to offer to God the perfect sacrifice of obedience through the power of the eternal Spirit.

Campbell's language may be difficult in places, but he often stresses that it was by the power of the Holy Spirit that Christ resisted temptation; and that the risen Christ is the one who pours out the Spirit, who enables people to live as God intends. In doing this he rightly picks up key themes from Romans 8 and demonstrates that thinking about incarnation forces us also to think about the Holy Spirit and the doctrine of the Trinity.

The origin of incarnation

Some representations of the atoning work of Christ have given the impression that we have a loving Son doing what is needed to placate an angry Father. Such misrepresentations are dismissed by Paul's comments explaining that we have been set free as a result of 'God . . . sending his own Son' (Rom. 8:3). As N. T. Wright explains, 'The condemnation of sin in the flesh of Jesus happened as a result of divine grace, of "God sending his own Son"'.[42]

The pre-existence of the Son

Talk of God 'sending his own Son' does not convince James Dunn that the pre-existence of the Son is in view here. He prefers to see this as another biblical text which needs to be interpreted in the light of an Adam christology.[43] A more traditional, incarnational perspective is advocated by Witherington, who asserts that 'in all likelihood "God sent" here and elsewhere in Paul implies a concept of pre-existence and so of incarnation. *Heautou*[44] is in the emphatic position—God's *own* Son was sent'.[45]

The topic of Christ's pre-existence will be re-visited in Chapter 8, where the focus falls upon Philippians 2. In thinking about this subject, there are two contrasting trajectories. On the one hand, Dunn follows a traditional historical-critical model, suggesting a long and slow development from New Testament times towards the high christology embodied in the creeds and confessions of the Church. The other contrasting perspective, championed by Bauckham and others, argues that the New Testament evidence suggests that from the earliest days of the Church there was a very 'high' christology.

As we shall see in Chapters 8 and 10, Bauckham detects across the New Testament a high christology of divine identity. He convincingly shows how Christ is consistently described as one who shares in the unique divine identity, who is given the unique divine name YHWH, and who shares in the unique divine sovereignty over all things.

Such a christology of divine identity, he claims, implies the pre-existence of the divine Son. If the claims that the New Testament makes about the Son are true, then this must have been true for all eternity:

> It is . . . all the more remarkable that early Christians included Jesus in the unique divine sovereignty not only eschatologically but also *protologically*, not only in the present and future but also from the beginning. . . . If Jesus is no mere servant of God but partici-pates in the unique sovereignty and is, therefore, intrinsic to the unique divine identity, he must be so eternally.[46]

The desire of divine love

Some models of atonement appear to concentrate so much on what Christ has *saved us from* that they lose sight of what Christ has *saved us for*. This can make it more difficult to see how the past event of salvation connects to the present experience of salvation. In a classic study of the atoning work of Christ, John McLeod Campbell explores how to hold together these two perspectives, which he calls the retrospective and prospective aspects of atonement: 'I have said above, that the atonement is regarded as that by which God has bridged over the gulf which separated between what sin had made us, and what it was the desire of the divine love that we should become'.[47]

Something of what that divine love desires to happen can be detected in Romans 8. As this chapter unfolds, it becomes clear that 'the desire of the divine love'[48] involves breaking the power of sin through Christ's in-carnation, death and resurrection, so that people can be set free from the law of sin and death and live as God's children in the power of the Holy Spirit. By virtue of the incarnation, sin's power is broken and the Spirit's power has been released. Thus by the power of the Spirit, believers can share in the Son's intimate communion with the Father, prompting them to cry out to God: 'Abba! Father!' (Rom. 8.14–17).[49]

The language and style may be that of an earlier age, but Campbell points us to something very important, because he was giving voice to a trinitarian theology of Christian experience where grace drives out legalism. James Torrance helpfully expresses the heart of this Trinitarian theology of persons in communion:

> Christ is presented to us as the Son living a life of union and communion with the Father in the Spirit, presenting himself in our humanity through the eternal Spirit to the Father on behalf of humankind. By his Spirit he draws men and women to participate both in his life of worship and communion with the Father and in his mission from the Father to the world.[50]

The Trinity and incarnation

At various points in this book, attention is drawn to the essential link between the person and work of Christ. This passage also prompts us to take notice of the way that thinking about incarnation and atonement requires us to think in trinitarian ways.

Although the word 'Trinity' cannot be found in the Bible, the biblical roots of the doctrine are not difficult to find within its pages. Daniel Migliore argues that

> the biblical basis of the doctrine of the Trinity is not to be found in a few 'proof texts' (e.g. Mt. 28.19). Its basis is the pervasive trinitarian pattern of the scriptural witness to God, foreshadowed in the Old Testament according to the Christian reading of it, and found more explicitly in the witness of the New Testament to the presence of the one and only God in the saving work of Jesus Christ and the renewing activity of the Holy Spirit.[51]

Something of that pervasive trinitarian pattern is clearly visible in Romans 8, which speaks of the God who sends his Son; of the incarnate Son, whose death breaks sin's power; and of the life-giving power of the Holy Spirit, who indwells Christians. The doctrine of the Trinity is not some mind-numbing problem to be solved, but an invitation to participate in the trinitarian life of God, relating to the Father through the Son in the power of the Spirit. This means that prayer, worship and mission are not ultimately about what we can do; but about sharing in what the triune God of grace is already doing as he works out his loving purposes in the world. N. T. Wright sums up the missiological challenge which this passage sets, in a most helpful way:

It is time for a genuinely incarnational theology to be let loose again upon the world, so that the rumour may become a report, and the report a life-changing reality. And for that to happen it is vital to grasp as well that the God who sent the Son now sends the Spirit of the Son. A fully Trinitarian theology, calling forth worship, love and service, is the only possible basis for genuine gospel work that will bring life and hope to the world.[52]

The very centre of what Paul is saying in his whole theology

Rom. 8.1–8 contains a wealth of material offering resources for many different kinds of sermons. It highlights the sending of the incarnate Son, who plumbed the depths of our plight by assuming our fallen flesh in order to redeem it. This emphasis upon Christ coming 'in the likeness of sinful flesh' rules out of court any idea of Docetism, that Christ only appeared to become human. The God we proclaim is not one who plays safe, dealing with humanity at arm's length, but one who embarks on a journey of costly and total identification with fallen humanity in order to set them free and give them life and hope. God's glory is not compromised or contaminated by virtue of Christ's assuming our fallen nature because 'His purity can come in contact with our pollution, and cleanse it'.[53] This act of divine condescension and generosity is the basis for Christian faith and worship.

I fear that my student sermon barely scratched the surface of this passage, which contains in concentrated form the centre of the apostle Paul's theology. In the sermon that follows, one of our colleagues, Dr Calvin Samuel, puts his finger on the theological heart of this passage.

Sermon: In the likeness of human flesh

Calvin T. Samuel*

Introduction

Romans 8 begins with that wonderful and well-known declaration in vv. 1–2. 'There is therefore now no condemnation for those who are in Christ Je-

*Revd Dr Calvin T. Samuel is part-time Tutor in New Testament at Spurgeon's College, London, and a Methodist minister serving in the Orpington and Chislehurst Circuit as Chaplain to Farringtons School.

sus, for the Law of the Spirit of Life has set you free from the Law of sin and death'. This declaration forms, if you will, the headline statement of the chapter, affirming profound truths of our liberation in Christ from judgement, condemnation, sin and death, as well as its glowing promise of the Spirit of life. The 'now' of v. 1 carries an eschatological nuance: it declares that in light of the definitive act of Christ, through which the end has broken into the present, we have, now, the benefits of the end, which include the glorious freedom here described. It is a most wonderful truth.

However, perhaps a greater truth is to be found in the next verse: 'For God has done what the Law weakened by the flesh could not do: by sending his own Son in the likeness of sinful flesh and to deal with sin, he condemned sin in the flesh, so that the just requirements of the Law might be fulfilled in us. . . .'

What does verse 3 mean in declaring that God has sent his Son in the likeness of sinful flesh? And in what way is this related to our being set free from the Law of sin and death? Put another way, in more overt theological terms, how does Rom. 8.3 understand incarnation? And in what ways are incarnation and soteriology linked?

In the likeness of human flesh

The phrase 'in the likeness of sinful flesh' is both interesting and open to a range of interpretations. On this verse, Fitzmyer observes: 'This is the closest expression in Pauline writings to the idea of incarnation'.[54]

But how exactly is incarnation understood here? Does Paul mean that Christ had only the appearance of sinful flesh? The Greek word used here, *homoiōma*, usually denotes likeness, copy, or form, indicating less than a full identity. Might this suggest that Jesus is only *like* sinful flesh but not quite the same? I think not. Paul does not imply a docetic Christ, who only appears to share our sinful humanity but actually does not; rather, Paul understands incarnation in terms of one who actually shares our sinful flesh. The Son was born as we are born, died as we die, is subject to temptation and weakness as we are, and experienced the effects of sin as do we.

As already observed, that Paul chooses this form of words is interesting; perhaps he does so in order to make the point that though the Son shares our sinful flesh, he nonetheless does not share our sinful acts. Put another way, though he becomes part of a sin-oriented human race, he himself does not sin. Thus sinful flesh, *sarx hamartias*, in this context denotes not a guilty human condition but rather the proneness or orientation of humanity towards sin.

To deal with sin

However, God has not sent the Son in the likeness of sinful flesh merely on a fact-finding mission; rather, he has been sent to deal with sin and to condemn sin in the flesh. What a curious expression! It needs further unpacking.

What does it mean for sin to be condemned? Here, as in many other places in Romans and indeed the wider Pauline corpus, sin is personified. Sin, represented as a power which holds us in its thrall, is perhaps most poignantly described in Romans 7. It is this malevolent power which Christ has come to deal with and to condemn. As previously noted, Romans 8 begins with the affirmation that there is now *no condemnation* for those who are in Christ Jesus. Instead, condemnation, meaning judgement, has been declared upon that enslaving power: sin.

Recognize, however, that Christ condemns sin *in the flesh*, a phrase which denotes not the locus of sin but the locus of its judgement. Put more simply, in his assumption of sinful flesh, in living sinlessly, in facing the cross, and in his sacrificial death and resurrection, God in Christ passed definitive judgement on both sin and its by-product, death, and declared them in the wrong. In and through his actions in this sinful flesh, then, Christ condemns sin.

That Christ condemns sin *in the flesh* makes a profound statement about incarnation, for it is through taking on our sinful flesh and redeeming it in himself that the dominion of sin is broken. Moreover, if it is not our sinful flesh which Jesus has taken upon himself, then the benefits of his redemption do not redound to us. One of the Church Fathers, Gregory of Nazianzus, put it far more cogently: '*What is not assumed is not redeemed*'. If it were not one of us who faced the cross and triumphed over it, of what relevance to us is that victory over sin and death? It is, thus, critical that it is *in the flesh* that Christ condemned sin, so that the just requirement of the Law might be fulfilled in us who walk not according to the flesh, but according to the Spirit.

The miracle of incarnation

Thus, in his incarnation Christ condemned sin in the flesh, which is for us a marvellous outcome. However, the greatest achievement of Christ's incarnation is not that God has become what we are, incomprehensible though that may be, 'the Godhead contracted to a span, incomprehensibly made man', as Charles Wesley wrote, the creator becoming a creature, the infinite finite, the invisible visible, the immortal mortal; yet this is not the greatest miracle of incarnation. Rather, the greatest miracle of incarnation is that he who became what we are enables us to become what he is. This is why it is so important to recognize that Christ has taken *our* sinful flesh, for it is that sinful flesh that he enables to become like him. Those who are *in Christ Jesus* can fulfil the just requirements of the Law if we walk not in the flesh but in the Spirit.

We must not overlook the trinitarian structure of these verses depicting the God who sends his own Son for the benefit of those who walk in the Spirit. Incarnation is a trinitarian undertaking and thus requires trinitarian understanding in terms of the sending of the Son, by the Father, in the power of the Spirit.

Conclusion

In the incarnation, God has sent his Son in the likeness of sinful flesh, to deal with sin and to condemn sin in the flesh. The Son has become what we are in order that we might become what he is. Those who are in Christ, and thus have a share in the benefits of his redemption, are to mirror both that submission to the Father and that empowering by the Spirit which underpin his incarnation. Only then can we hope to experience what incarnation alone can reveal to us, what it means to be genuinely human as divinely intended, humanity in perfect fellowship with God.

No wonder, then, that there is now no condemnation for those who are in Christ Jesus, for the Law of the Spirit of Life has set us free from the Law of sin and death.

Thanks be to God! Amen.

Sermon commentary

Searching for homiletical wisdom, James Thompson suggests that preachers today would be well advised to learn from the apostle Paul.[55] As the apostle's letters were probably dictated to a secretary and were intended to be read aloud in the churches, they contain clear echoes of his preaching. Listening to these echoes helps us catch glimpses of Paul's approach to preaching, which integrates proclamation and teaching. Such an approach, Thompson argues, which combines evangelistic and pastoral preaching, has continuing relevance in our current missionary context.

In part, his recommendations are a response to the weaknesses he perceives in the New Homiletic. In a culture where listeners are familiar with the Christian story, the parabolic indirectness of some forms of narrative preaching assumes listeners with sufficient biblical knowledge to fill in the gaps for themselves. In a post-Christian context where many know little about the basics of Christian faith, something more than indirect, parabolic preaching is needed to establish and sustain Christian communities.

Part of the remedy he suggests involves 'preaching like Paul', in the sense of preaching that is more overtly theological. The evidence of the Pauline epistles is that the apostle's way of doing theology was a practical response to issues and questions facing the churches. Faced with the current situation, where so many people know so little about Christian faith, Thompson argues that theological preaching is essential. For 'in the absence of theological preaching, the church's message is reduced to trivia. Its mission and goals rest on the will of the majority rather than the church's memory'. In contrast, he claims, 'theological preaching . . . is necessary to bring the church to consider the great themes of the Christian faith as it charts its future course'.[56]

Calvin Samuel's sermon on Rom. 8.3 offers a helpful example of clear, direct theological preaching. The sermon structure, which carefully develops an argument step by step, is an appropriate way of handling a passage in which Paul likewise develops his argument in a detailed and careful way.

At the outset the sermon *orients* its hearers by repeating and affirming 'that wonderful and well-known declaration' that 'there is therefore now no condemnation'. To some extent the preacher then *dis-orients* his listeners by claiming that 'perhaps a greater truth' can be found in Rom. 8.3. Finally, having explored the meaning of the Son assuming sinful flesh, the sermon *re-orients* its hearers by returning to the theme of 'no condemnation'. Having probed the gospel in microcosm in Rom. 8.3, there is even greater reason for believers to celebrate and affirm that 'there is therefore now no condemnation'.

Starting off in preaching, there were times when I skipped over difficulties in the text and hoped that the congregation would not notice. As time has passed, I have come to realize that paying attention to those difficulties and questions is often the very thing which helps to catch and hold people's attention.

In this sermon, instead of avoiding the problems, Calvin Samuel draws attention to them. For example, he highlights the reference to Christ's coming 'to condemn sin in the flesh' by saying, 'What a curious expression!' This provides a springboard for the next phase of the sermon, which seeks to explain how the malevolent power of sin has been condemned and judged by Christ.

Thompson warns that 'preaching of the Bible is no guarantee of the preaching of the gospel'.[57] The danger he fears is of focusing on a few biblical verses whilst losing sight of the bigger picture of Christian faith. In this sermon, Calvin Samuel demonstrates his firm grasp not only of Pauline theology but also of the larger story of the faith of the Church. As he reflects on 'the miracle of incarnation', he echoes the language of the Great Tradition of the Church as he points to the even greater miracle of incarnation, 'that he who became what we are enables us to become what he is'.

With enviable clarity, this sermon proclaims the miracle of incarnation and provides further confirmation that 'the complex and powerful statement' of Rom. 8.3–4 is 'a sentence that has as good a claim as any to represent the very center of what Paul is saying in Romans 5–8, if not in his whole theology'.[58]

8

The self-emptying Christ
PHILIPPIANS 2.1–11

No crying he makes?

Chapter 3 explored some of the resources which the Christmas stories offer for preaching the incarnation. Listening to familiar Bible readings and singing traditional carols brings home the message that the birth of this particular baby signifies the coming of 'the one who takes our humanity'.[1] Each year for me, the first carol service of the festive season evokes memories of an increasingly distant childhood, and of nativity plays with our children playing out the story that there was 'no room at the inn'.

One feature of most of the nativity plays I have attended is the singing of 'Away in a Manger'. I have to confess that my theological antennae twitch a little during the verse which says:

The cattle are lowing,
the baby awakes,
but little Lord Jesus,
no crying he makes. (anon.)

No doubt the lyrics, such as 'little Lord Jesus, / no crying he makes', seek to underline the fact that Jesus was a very special kind of baby. Now, every baby I have ever come across has cried; and if there was 'no crying' with the little Lord Jesus, then either he was very, very ill or he was not really fully human. Perhaps it is reading too much into poetic language; but maybe in seeking to celebrate the special nature of Jesus in this way, the lyricist runs the risk of painting a rather docetic picture of a Christ who *almost* shared our human situation to the full.

With some reason, the comment is often made that many Christians learn their theology from hymns and songs. If that is indeed the case, then some questions need to be asked about the kinds of theology people are

127

imbibing as they sing certain songs and hymns. Instead of conducting a purge of theologically-questionable hymns, however, this chapter focuses on Phil. 2.1–11, which includes a hymn full of rich and deep theology.

Trouble in the text?

Judging from how frequently Phil. 2.6–11 occurs in the liturgical lectionary (every year on New Year's Day and on Passion Sunday, and once every three years on Proper 21), this pericope should be one of the best known and most appreciated passages in the Bible. However, judging by the amount of scholarly debate it has occasioned, Paul's so-called 'Christ Hymn' must be one of the most difficult and provocative sections in the Christian Scriptures.[2]

At this point I have to confess that Paul's letter to the Philippians is one of my favourite books in the Bible. A series of sermons I heard as a teenager helped to kick-start my love for this prison epistle. Since then I have returned to it often and have preached several series of sermons on it. There is plenty of material here to nourish God's people in sermons and Bible studies; and at the heart of this joyful letter stands the inspiring Christ-hymn.

A comfortable familiarity with the text is challenged by the claim that the Christ-hymn is 'one of the most difficult and provocative sections in the Christian Scriptures'. There are quite a few other passages in the Bible which could claim to be more difficult; but there certainly are some big questions to consider as we look closely at this text. Rightly handled, such difficulties can provide the preacher with valuable resources. For as Eugene Lowry suggests, it is often a good idea for preachers to look for trouble in the text, because 'trouble, in, around, with, and about the text is often the occasion for a fresh hearing'.[3]

A pre-Pauline hymn?

Although there is wide agreement that Phil. 2.6–11 represents some kind of hymn (or poem),[4] there is a bit of 'trouble' in the text in the sense that scholars have engaged in lengthy debates about its origins. Perhaps, as Richard Bauckham suggests, 'Paul himself composed it';[5] and the apostle's other contributions to the New Testament certainly contain ample evidence of his skill as a writer and as a theologian. Maybe it was a hymn composed by someone in the early Church which was known by the believers in Philippi. Less likely is the older view suggesting that it might have been a 'Gnostic' hymn about some heavenly figure, which Paul adopted and adapted.

For the preacher, such speculation is not really troubling because it does not materially affect our interpretation of the passage. For as George Caird once put it:

> Whether Paul wrote the passage in the course of writing his letter or quoted his own or someone else's hymn, it was he who put it in its present context; and he did so because he believed that it said what he wanted it to say. Here as always we must pay proper respect to the law of contextual determination, that words, singly or in combination, mean what the writer or speaker on any given occasion intends them to mean. The meaning of this passage *in Philippians* is the meaning Paul intends it to have, the meaning he imposed on the ambiguities of its language.[6]

The pre-existence of Christ

One person well aware of the power of hymns to teach theology was Charles Wesley; and one of his best-loved hymns seems to provide a happy commentary on these verses from Phil. 2.5–11.

> He left His Father's throne above—
>   So free, so infinite His grace—
> Emptied Himself of all but love,
>   And bled for Adam's helpless race.
> 'Tis mercy all, immense and free;
> For, O my God, it found out me.[7]

Now whilst the technical language of incarnation may not be uppermost in their minds, many Christians singing, 'He left His Father's throne above', instinctively feel that the incarnation of a pre-existent divine being is in view when Phil. 2.5–7 talks about the one who 'was in the form of God' and 'emptied himself'.

For anyone interested in preaching the incarnation, there is a greater potential for 'trouble' in the text at this point, because some scholars argue that this ancient hymn is not necessarily describing the incarnation of a pre-existent divine being. The basis for such a claim lies in the suggestion that a contrast is being drawn here between Adam, who grasped at equality with God with disastrous consequences, and the last Adam, who did not count equality with God as a thing to be grasped.

One of the clearest expositions of this point of view is found in James D. G. Dunn's *Christology in the Making*, first published in 1980.[8] Parallels and echoes of Adam's story lead Dunn to conclude that

> The Christ of Phil. 2.6–11 . . . is the man who undid Adam's wrong: confronted with the same choice, he rejected Adam's sin, but nevertheless freely followed Adam's course as fallen man to the bitter end of death; wherefore God bestowed on him the status not simply that Adam lost, but [also] the status which Adam was intended to come to, God's final prototype, the last Adam.[9]

There are some grounds for suggesting that the notion of an Adam christology may shed some light on Philippians 2, but the waters become rather muddied when Dunn appears to question whether the idea of a pre-existent divine being is in view:

> The Philippian hymn does not intend to affirm that Jesus was as historical or as prehistorical as Adam, but that the *choice* confronting Christ was as *archetypal* and determinative for mankind as was Adam's; whether the choice was made by the pre-existent Christ or the historical Jesus is immaterial to the Philippian hymn.[10]

In a more recent study of Paul's theology, Dunn takes note of his critics but re-affirms his conviction that the Philippian hymn is one of the fullest expressions of an Adam christology in the New Testament. So, he asks, 'where does that leave the issue of the preexistent Christ? Here it needs to be stated again that the issue is independent of finding an Adam christology in the Philippians passage'.[11] In a footnote he concedes that his earlier discussion of an Adam christology had not closed off the possibility of detecting some kind of pre-existence in this passage. Noting the poetic language of Philippians 2, he observes that this allusive poetry has 'set in motion the thought of Christ's pre-existence',[12] but this is viewed not so much in terms of personal pre-existence, but rather as the pre-existence of the divine Wisdom.

Dunn's views are firmly rejected by Morna Hooker:

> Although some have tried to exclude the idea of pre-existence from Philippians 2 and have argued that it is the actions of the human Jesus that are contrasted with those of Adam, it is difficult to make sense of v. 7 without acknowledging that it was the *pre-existent* Christ who became man.[13]

Bauckham is similarly sure, along with the majority of exegetes, 'that the passage begins by speaking of the pre-existent Christ in eternity and proceeds to speak of his incarnation'. He makes it crystal clear that he does not 'think the passage embodies an Adam christology. If Adam is in view at all, he is in view only very indirectly'. In Bauckham's view, 'Adam has proved a red herring in study of this passage'.[14]

Believing that the personal pre-existence of the divine Son is being referred to in verse 6, Gerald Hawthorne suggests that talk about Christ being 'in the form of God' (*en morphē theou*) implies that the pre-existent Christ possessed all the characteristics belonging to God. For him, the 'somewhat enigmatic expression' about the form of God is

> a cautious, hidden way for the author to say that Christ was God, possessed of the very nature of God, . . . without employing these exact words. It appears to be a statement made by one who perhaps, although reared as a strict monotheist and thus unable to bring himself to say, 'Christ is God', was compelled nevertheless by the sheer force of personal encounter with the resurrected and living Christ to bear witness as best he could to the reality of Christ's divinity'.[15]

Reaching such positive conclusions about the personal pre-existence of Christ may help us sing the hymn 'And can it be' with conviction and gusto; but it is only the first of the many challenges facing the preacher wrestling with this text.

Searching for the meaning of *harpagmos*

The next difficulty to contend with has to do with how best to interpret the choice, described in verse 6, which the pre-existent Christ made. The crux of the argument revolves around how best to translate the unusual word *harpagmos*.

Does the word *harpagmos* refer to snatching or grasping after something, or might it suggest clinging on to something valuable? Ralph Martin's classic study warns us that in terms of *harpagmos*, part of the trouble is that 'there is no help available from contemporary usage of the word. It is *hapax legomenon* in the New Testament; and it is not found at all in the LXX. It is very rarely used in Greek literature generally, and such occurrences as there are shed very little light on the Biblical usage'.[16]

In the context of Phil. 2.6, much of the discussion revolves around whether *harpagmos* refers to something precious which Christ possessed but refused to cling on to, or if it implies that equality with God was something valuable which Christ did not yet possess but might be tempted to grasp. Most translations (e.g. NIV, NKJV, TEV) opt for the sense that Christ refused to cling selfishly on to equality with God.

More recently, discussion has moved in a different direction. Thus Morna Hooker states that 'the most likely interpretation of *harpagmos* is that it refers to "something to be exploited"'. In this view, equality with God was something that Christ already possessed, but which he chose not to use for his own advantage'.[17] This perspective is reflected in both the NRSV and TNIV translations, which affirm that the one who was in the form of God

- did not regard equality with God as something to be exploited (NRSV).
- did not consider equality with God something to be used to his own advantage (TNIV).

The repercussions of the 2008 collapse of major financial institutions and the worldwide banking crisis that followed in its wake will reverberate for some time to come. In this post-credit-crunch era, there is a widespread feeling that many powerful people in the financial world yielded too readily to temptation, using their positions for personal enrichment, rather than seeking to work for the common good.

Phil. 2.6 focuses upon Christ, who had the most prominent and privileged position imaginable: 'equality with God'. However, he did not see this position as an opportunity to take more and more for himself; he viewed it rather as an opportunity to give himself away in order that others might be blessed.

Conscious that 'all power corrupts; absolute power corrupts absolutely', it is not too difficult to think of powerful people who have used their position to protect and enrich themselves. Set against such a demoralising backdrop, talk about someone who 'did not consider equality with God as something to be used to his own advantage' begins to deconstruct standard understandings of power and position. That is how it should be, because this passage moves on, step by step, to turn our everyday assumptions about power and about God upside down. All of this raises questions about how our preaching can help to wean people away from the love of power so that they might become converts to the power of love.

Emptied himself of all but love

The next direct assault on our assumptions about the nature of power, and about the nature and power of God, comes when Paul tells us that Christ 'emptied himself' (*heauton ekenōsen*). What has troubled many scholars has been trying to work out what this *kenōsis*, emptying, actually means; for what does an infinite God have to empty himself of in order to assume finite human nature?

During the nineteenth century a number of theories were advanced to explore what Christ might have given up when he emptied himself during the incarnation. Within these kenotic understandings of christology, some writers suggested that the incarnate Christ emptied himself of 'relative' attributes such as omnipotence and omnipresence, whilst retaining the 'essential' divine attributes of holiness and love. Wesley's hymn 'And can it be?' was written before these kenotic theories became popular; but if the hermeneutics of suspicion is applied to the phrase about the Christ who 'emptied himself of all but love', it might imply that Christ divested himself of relative attributes whilst retaining the essential divine attribute of love.

Other writers suggested that *kenōsis* involved not the relinquishing of divine attributes, but rather their 'retraction', withholding them from use during the period of the incarnation. Within Phil. 2.5–11, however, there is little evidence that the apostle Paul was speculating about Christ divesting himself of any divine attributes. Hawthorne says,

> One need not imagine that the phrase means that Christ discarded divine substances or essences. . . . Rather, it is a poetic, hymnlike way of saying that Christ poured out himself, putting himself totally at the disposal of people (cf. 1 John 3:16), that Christ became poor that he might make many rich (2 Cor 8:9; cf. also Eph 1:23; 4:10).[18]

The root problem here is of adopting an *a priori* approach to doing theology whereby theologians assume in advance (usually on the basis of certain philosophical assumptions) that they already know what God is like. Such assumptions about God's nature and power then make it difficult to work out how such an omnipotent, omniscient, omnipresent God could possibly squeeze into human flesh.

On the other hand, if an *a posteriori* approach to the theological task is adopted, things begin to look quite different. This approach allows the way in which God has chosen to reveal himself to form the basis for the way in which we think and talk about God. If we do theology in this way, permitting the Gospel story to shape how we think of God, then we are forced to think about the nature of God in surprisingly different ways.

This point is affirmed by Karl Barth in dramatic and vivid language. In his treatment of 'The Way of the Son of God into the Far Country', Barth affirms that

God is always God in even in his humiliation. The divine being does not suffer any change, any diminution, any transformation into something else, any admixture with something else, let alone any cessation. . . . He humbled Himself, but He did not do it by ceasing to be who He is.[19]

If we think that this is impossible it is because our concept of God is too narrow, too arbitrary, too human—far too human. Who God is and what it is to be divine is something that we have to learn where God has revealed Himself and His nature, the essence of the divine. And if He has revealed Himself in Jesus Christ as the God who does this, it is not for us to be wiser than He and to say that it is in contradiction with the divine nature.[20]

In other words it is a waste of time wondering about which attributes of God have somehow been hidden out of sight during the incarnation. The amazing mystery is that the Christ who emptied himself, taking the form of a slave, did not conceal God but rather revealed him. Morna Hooker puts it well:

Christ did not cease to be 'in the form of God' when he took the form of a slave, any more than he ceased to be the 'Son of God' when he was sent into the world. On the contrary, it is *in his self-emptying and his humiliation that he reveals what God is like*, and it is through his taking the form of a slave that we see 'the form of God'.[21]

Similarly Colin Gunton affirms that

it seems . . . not inappropriate to speak of a self-emptying of God, but only if it is understood in such a way as to be an *expression* rather than a 'retraction' of his deity. The self-emptying is part of God's fullness, for the heart of what it means to be God is that he is able to empty himself on behalf of that which is not himself. In other words, it is part of his love, through which he comes among us in our time and history to transform our existence from within.[22]

Amazing love! How can it be that thou, my God, shouldst die for me?

Some have claimed that the phrase 'even death on a cross' in Phil. 2.8 is a clumsy addition to the Christ-hymn which disturbs its poetic shape and form. Such 'trouble in the text' is probably more imagined than real, implying a need for rigid adherence to inflexible laws of poetry. It seems more reasonable to suggest that whether the apostle Paul added these words, or found them in a pre-existent hymn, in their current context they actually function as the climax of the story of Christ's humiliation. The one who did not regard his position of 'equality with God' as something to be exploited, for his own benefit, embarked on a journey of self-humiliation on behalf of others, which led to his death on a cross. Crucifixion was a shameful form of execution, reserved for runaway slaves and rebels against the state. The journey which Christ takes, from the glory of heaven to the ignominy of the cross, turns human ideas about status and position upside down.

Brian Peterson reports that questions about status were high on the agenda of people in the Roman colony of Philippi. In such a city, seeking for status and position was high on the agenda for all self-respecting citizens. In stark contrast to that eager pursuit of status, Paul tells the shocking story of one who had the ultimate status, nothing less than equality with God; who freely chose to make himself nothing, ending up on a criminal's cross. In the Philippian context, this was the most strikingly counter-cultural message.

Peterson asserts that the story of Christ's humiliation and obedience, rightly understood, challenges and threatens the contemporary status quo in equally shocking ways:

> The world we live in is no more welcoming of this story, no more open to this 'mind' than was Roman Philippi. We are inundated with narratives that promise life found in superior force, in acquiring the best looks, the best bank accounts, the best weapons, the best 'stuff'. We are told that life is secured by our winning—socially, economically, politically, religiously—and everyone else losing. There is little room for the claim that the obedient death and resurrection of Jesus is the story of God's ultimate loving victory, the defining reality for all the world.[23]

The sermon by Michael Quicke which follows later in this chapter explores some of these ideas about status and position by using the image of the 'escalator of life'. The Christ-hymn is indeed troubling in the sense that it disturbs and provokes us into asking, Have we bought in too easily to the prevailing culture that assumes that life is about 'going up' and getting to the top?

Kenōsis—Bad news for women?

It seems clear that the apostle Paul is using this hymn pastorally and ethically, urging his readers to follow the self-giving example of Christ. However, Daphne Hampson argues that this is not good news for women today. She asserts that clearly *kenōsis* is indeed a critique of patriarchy. . . . It may well be a model which men need to appropriate and which may helpfully be built into the male understanding of God. But as we have said in our discussion of what salvation might be for women, the theme of self-emptying and self-abnegation is far from helpful as a paradigm. *Kenōsis* is a counter-theme within male thought. It does not build what might be said to be specifically feminist values into our understanding of God.[24]

In response, Sarah Coakley argues that Hampson's critique of *kenōsis* only applies to certain understandings of *kenōsis* which assume that Christ had to shed various powers during the incarnation. If, as we have argued, the *kenōsis* of Christ is more about revealing the nature and power of God in a surprisingly new light, then *kenōsis* presents a view of power through vulnerability which challenges both male and female understandings of power. For 'only', she suggests, 'by facing—and giving new expression to—the paradox of "losing one's life in order to save it", can feminists hope to construct a vision of the Christic "self" that transcends the gender stereotypes we are seeking to up-end'.[25]

Therefore God also highly exalted him

Some years ago a representative of the Jehovah's Witnesses knocked on my door. After a brief conversation on our doorstep, I agreed to visit him in his home to carry on our conversation. At one point I suggested that we turn to Phil. 2.9–11, and then I invited him to read this in the light of Isa. 45.23:

> By myself I have sworn,
>> from my mouth has gone forth in righteousness
>> a word that shall not return.
> 'To me every knee shall bow,
>> every tongue shall swear'.

Those words come from a passage where YHWH speaks through the prophet, affirming that he alone is God. When I pointed out that the apostle Paul was applying that Old Testament language about Almighty God to Jesus Christ in Phil. 2.9–11, I was told in no uncertain terms that I was guilty of 'twisting the Scriptures'. For that gentleman, the juxtaposition of those two biblical passages posed an uncomfortable challenge to the Arian-like beliefs of the Jehovah's Witnesses that 'in the beginning was the Word and the Word was a god'.

YHWH—the name that is above all names

Perhaps many believers in mainstream Christian churches would also find this direct identification of Jesus Christ with YHWH something of a shock. For a closer look at Phil. 2.9–11 reveals that some startling things are being claimed for the Jesus we are called to proclaim. Bauckham convincingly argues that

> there can be no doubt that 'the name that is above every name' (v. 9) is YHWH: it is inconceivable that any Jewish writer could use this phrase for a name other than God's own unique name. Contrary to much comment on this passage the name itself is not 'Lord' (*kurios*: v. 11), which is not the divine name nor even a Greek translation of the name, but a conventional reverential *substitute* for the name. . . . Jesus is given the divine name because he participates in the divine sovereignty. Thus, confession 'that Jesus Christ is Lord' (v. 11) is both a surrogate for calling on him by his name, YHWH, and also a confession of his lordship.[26]

Bauckham goes on to show that in exalting Jesus to the place of highest honour, he was not being exalted to a status which he had not previously enjoyed; but that God had 'exalted him to a higher status than that of anyone or anything else, i.e. to the pre-eminent position in the whole cosmos'.[27] This Jesus shares in the unique divine identity and in YHWH's sovereignty over all creation. Another aspect of this christology of divine identity is that Jesus is included in the worship that Jewish monotheistic faith reserved for YHWH. 'Since he does so as the Son of the Father, sharing, not rivalling or usurping, his Father's sovereignty, worship of Jesus is also worship of his Father, but it is nonetheless really worship of Jesus'.[28]

Many Christians describe the beginnings of their spiritual journey in terms of accepting Jesus Christ as Lord. Reading Phil. 2.9–11 with passages such as Isa. 45.23 in mind suggests that messages about personal commitment to Christ barely scratch the surface of this amazing passage. The call to personal discipleship is a valid and important message which needs to be proclaimed, but our preaching must not stop there. Somehow we must find the language to herald the good news of the eternal Son of God who has the 'pre-eminent position in the whole cosmos'.

At a time when many people have become more aware of living in a religiously-plural world, some Christians may find this stress upon the supremacy and universality of Christ somewhat uncomfortable. Rediscovering something of this passage's stress upon the universal lordship of Christ need not lead to Christian witness characterized by imperial arrogance, but calls instead for 'mission in bold humility'.[29]

Lesslie Newbigin challenged the Church to continue to make public the surprising truths at the heart of the Christian faith in a humble but confident way:

> If, in fact, it is true that almighty God, creator and sustainer of all that exists in heaven and earth, has—at a known time and place in human history—so humbled himself as to become part of our sinful humanity and to suffer and die a shameful death to take away our sin and to rise from the dead as the first-fruit of a new creation, if this is a fact, then to affirm it is not arrogance. To remain quiet about it is treason to our fellow human beings.[30]

Speaking provocatively

In the first-century world, Roman emperors with delusions of grandeur were fond of declaring that 'Caesar is lord'. In such a context the apostle Paul was broadcasting a dangerous story by declaring that there was only one Lord: Jesus Christ. For as Bauckham argues, Paul's christological monotheism 'must have had anti-imperial force and' Phil. 2.9–11 'is a key passage for recognizing that'.[31]

Back in 1612 the English Baptist pioneer Thomas Helwys published an apology for religious freedom with a snappy title: *A Short Declaration of the Mistery of Iniquity*.[32] The book represents the first plea for religious liberty in the English language, and the author dedicated the book respectfully to King James I. Whilst the language strikes us as archaic, it was provocative, explosive speech in a society where those in authority still believed in the divine right of kings. For Helwys was pleading for religious liberty, and it is significant that his request went far beyond simply asking for religious freedom for Baptist Christians:

> For mens religion to God is betwixt God and themselves; the King shall not answer for it, neither may the King be judg betwene God and man. Let them be heretikes, Turks, Jewes, or whatsoever, it apperteynes not to the earthly power to punish them in the least measure.[33]

By writing such a book, Thomas Helwys was spelling out some of the practical implications of his firm belief that Jesus Christ is Lord. His prophetic plea for tolerance was dangerous stuff; and Helwys ended up not with the Nobel Prize for Literature or Peace, but with a term in prison, where he died. In the seventeenth century, as in the first, proclaiming Jesus Christ as Lord was a dangerous thing to do.

If we believe that Jesus Christ is Lord, then our preaching will have a much larger agenda than simply commenting on 'my spiritual life' or 'the life of the church'. If Jesus is Lord over all, then there can be no division between sacred and secular. Something of the vast agenda the lordship of Christ sets for preaching was expressed back in the 1880s by the Dutch Christian leader Abraham Kuyper, who affirmed: 'There is not one inch in the entire area of human life about which Christ who is Sovereign of all does not cry out "Mine!"'

Practical theology

Some today, like Richard Dawkins, see theology as something inherently dangerous,[34] but probably many more people believe that theology is abstract speculation which is irrelevant to real life. As a former Bishop of Durham, Ian Ramsey, once put it: 'Theology seems often to the outsider just so much word-spinning, air-borne discourse which never touches down except disastrously'.[35]

In contrast to the troubling idea that theology is abstract and irrelevant, what we see in Philippians 2 is profound theology being used for a very practical purpose. For Paul did not set out to teach the church at Philippi abstract lessons about christology. He certainly does offer them an inspiring picture of the person of Christ; but that theology is a practical and pastoral response to down-to-earth situations within the life of the church. At this point in the letter, it is clear that he is urging them to be united, to be of one mind, so that together they will be able to stand firm and hold forth the word of life to a bleak and fearful world. Theology and ethics are inextricably woven together here in Philippians 2, where the person and work of Christ provide an ethical example and an inspiration for a new way of life. This chapter demonstrates that theology is important, because what you believe shapes what you do and affects how you treat others. That link between worship and life is clear in one of the hymns inspired by this passage:

In your hearts enthrone Him;
   There let Him subdue
All that is not holy,
   All that is not true;
Crown Him as your captain
   In temptation's hour,
Let His will enfold you
   In its light and power.[36]

The church near Oxford which commended me for Baptist Ministry presented me with a book of *Orders and Prayers for Church Worship*. Inside the front cover someone had written the biblical reference '2 Corinthians 4:5'. It is a good motto for Christian ministry: 'We do not proclaim ourselves; we proclaim Jesus Christ as Lord and ourselves as your servants for Jesus' sake'. Preaching involves resisting the temptation to preach ourselves, so that we can proclaim Jesus Christ as Lord; and Philippians 2 offers us rich resources for such proclamation.

Now if people learn theology from hymns, then this hymn to Christ as God in Philippians 2 is one that's worth paying attention to, for it is chock-a-block full of theology. There is plenty more worth exploring here, but rather than dissecting the passage to bits, it is worth following the advice of Hans Urs von Balthasar, who encourages us to let the words of this hymn speak for themselves. He says,

> If we look back from the mature Christology of Ephesus and Chalcedon to the hymn of Philippians 2 and do so with the intention of not exaggerating its capacity for 'dogmatic' assertiveness, we can hardly help registering a 'plus factor' in its archaic language—stammering out the mystery as this does—to which the established formulae of the unchangeability of God do not really do justice.[37]

'Stammering out the mystery': not a bad description for the work of preaching the good news of Jesus Christ as Lord from this rich passage.

Trouble in the text

There is a touch of hyperbole in the claim that this passage is 'one of the most difficult and provocative sections in the Christian Scriptures'.[38] The real difficulty in Philippians 2 does not relate to the exegetical difficulty of translating rare Greek words. The real trouble in this text is that it provokes and rebukes us for all too often preaching a domesticated, small-scale version of the Christian message.

Sermon: Going up? Going down?*

Michael Quicke

If I say the word 'escalator', you'll picture something. I think of the London Tube—the underground railway system, with escalators, some of them steep and long, going way down. Sometimes you have to take two or three escalators to get down to the trains. Others may think of shopping malls. In popular culture there's a phrase from a 1980s Robert Hazard song, set in a shopping mall:

> We're dancing on the escalator of life.
>> Won't be happy 'til we have it all.

'Escalator of life' is a strong metaphor. Because escalators convey people together, they're people movers. In the United States, in 2004, apparently 30,000 escalators moved 9 billion people. But escalators also have their own momentum. Once you are on them, you are moving. Of course if there's a break, you can get off. But if you want to arrive, then you stay on. And if you want to arrive faster, you muscle your way through.

But is the 'escalator of life' going up or down? The world says 'Up', of course. That's the popular mass direction. Everything important is about moving up. You start at the bottom and move up to the top, or at least as high as you can. At the bottom you may be nothing, a nobody, but as you go up, you become somebody. Increasing significance, status, power and, maybe, wealth. Ever since Adam, that's how human life works.

And you know about all that here at university. You come in at the bottom as freshmen and women and then, relieved, move up into sophomore year, then junior and senior, . . . then onwards and upwards as graduate students. You know just where you belong—and you're moving up! It's the same direction for careers, relationships. And even in the Church. The escalator of life moves up, often with pushing and shoving. Because the higher up we go, the more pride, power, status, significance we have. Ever since Adam, that's how human life works.

The moving-up creed chants: 'Do everything out of selfish ambition and vain conceit and in pride consider others worse than yourselves. Each of you should look only to your own interests'. Each step up you can look down

---

*Preached by Michael J. Quicke at University Baptist Church, University of Illinois, on Sunday, 6 April 2008. Dr Quicke is the Charles W. Koller Professor of Preaching and Communication at Northern Seminary in Lombard, Illinois.

and say, 'I don't need to be as humble'. At the bottom, humility is necessary; you can't throw your weight around. But going up, you can dispense with humility. And at the top, you can throw your weight around, because you've arrived. You're a winner. The world applauds you. Ever since Adam, that's how human life works.

But could there be any other way of living? Is a different direction possible?

Sometime after the first Easter someone, maybe it was the apostle Paul, wrote a hymn. A hymn to make you think hard as well as to celebrate. Studdert Kennedy, an unusual preacher in the First World War, used to say that 'Christianity is meant to give you peace in the heart and pain in the head'. Well, this hymn gives a migraine! Philippians 2.6–11 is rightly set out as a hymn in our translations and brings together some extraordinary claims about the person of Jesus. It speaks of his incarnation, literally, his 'enfleshing'.

Who 'being in the very nature God' (some translate as 'form of God'). What, the *creator* God? Who in the beginning made everything and without him nothing was made that has been made? What—the *holy* God? Who meets Moses on the mountain and says: 'Take off your sandals. I AM WHO I AM. Don't let others touch this holy mountain'. What—the *awesome* God of might, whose right hand divides the sea and brings a new people to birth? What—the God whom David praises: 'Yours, O LORD, are the greatness, the power, the glory, the victory, and the majesty; for all that is in the heavens and on the earth is yours' (1 Chr. 29.11)?

Jesus is in very nature God? Charles Wesley could only stammer out the lines

> Our God contracted to a span,
> Incomprehensibly made man.

Incomprehensibly? Could Jesus ever say, 'I and the Father are one'? Could he claim to exist before Bethlehem? 'Truly, I tell you, before Abraham was I am'. And when he did make that claim (Jn. 8.58), 'they picked up stones to throw at him' (v. 59). Of course they certainly did. How dare he? Some have described him as 100% God, 100% man. Well, you can't have 200% of anything. It's incomprehensible. Oh, yes it is! Jesus is Son of God and Son of Man.

And by his incarnation, Jesus reverses the direction of human life. Ever since Adam, getting to the top, with pride and power, was *the* way to live. But Jesus reverses the direction. He chooses to go down, with humility and service. To show humans a new way of living.

Being in very nature God, he did not consider equality with God something to be grasped, but made himself nothing (Phil. 2:6 NIV). Jesus is in very nature, form, God, and nothing can destroy that. We gain glimpses of his divinity at the transfiguration and in his miracles. Yet he refuses to use his power, status and glory to benefit himself. 'Grasp' has the sense that it's always within his reach. The NRSV translates 'did not regard equality with God as something to be exploited, but emptied himself'. It was always possible, every day of his life, for him to assert himself. But, incomprehensibly, he doesn't. He goes down, down, down.

With Mary and at Bethlehem, he goes down to nothing. A nobody girl, with a nine-months pregnancy (no short cuts here), a birth in an outhouse on the margins of significance, power, wealth. Yes, shepherds and wise men enter the story, but they are followed by thirty years of rural living in de-spised Nazareth. Whenever we see faces of poor, displaced nobodies in the television news, we remember that our Lord began like this.

Taking the very nature of a servant (v. 7 NIV). Consciously he chooses to serve. With each step he says: 'I choose to be humble. I need to look to oth-ers' needs'. *Being made in human likeness, and being found in appearance as a man* underlines the extraordinary paradox of what Jesus chooses to be and to do: *he humbled himself* (vv. 7–8 NIV). Instead of looking down on people, he treats them with significance, even looking up at them while on his knees, washing dirty feet.

Can you find any moment in his story, any single time, when he asserts himself over ordinary people? During Holy Week some of us surely long for him to confront those who treat him like trash, looking down on him with pride and power. Pilate, Herod, the high priest and the council. Why doesn't Jesus just once assert himself? But he never does . . . he never does. His is a new way of living.

And when you think it couldn't get worse, *he humbled himself and became obedient to death—even death on a cross!'* (v. 8 NIV). Some scholars see this last phrase, 'even death on a cross', as out of step with the hymn's lyrical qual-ity. It's jarring. Mention death if you must . . . but on a cross? This is the worst form of execution. The Romans didn't use it for their own citizens no matter how grave their crimes, for it was far too degrading and barbaric. And Jesus knew that, and the cost of bearing sin upon it. That's why in the garden of Gethsemane he pleads for this cup of wrath to be taken away. 'I don't want to drink it. I don't want to go to the cross'. Three times he pleads with the Father. Yet each time he wrestles through: 'Not my will but yours be done'. Jesus goes down even to death.

Of course the hymn goes on to finish gloriously and triumphantly. Because he has gone to the cross, *therefore God exalted him to the highest place and gave him the name that is above every name, that at the name of Jesus every knee should bow in heaven and on earth and under the earth, and every tongue confess that Jesus Christ is Lord, to the glory of God the Father* (vv. 9–10 NIV).

This is a wonderful conclusion. But, actually, the apostle Paul is using this hymn, with its profound theology, to challenge how the Philippian church is living—and how we should live too. He focuses on the hymn's first part: downward humble service. Jesus reverses the world's practice of power by his ethic of humble service. Are you going up with pride and power, or down with humble service?

I blog sermon preparation (on michaelquicke.blogspot.com) so that friends can share in my preaching journey. Last week I mentioned the possibility of using the escalator metaphor. A lawyer, who works in downtown Chicago, commented:

> It's a great mental picture. I see an escalator going up full of hurried people with their Starbuck coffee cups, brief cases and tailored suits, talking on their cell phones about their most recent successful investments. Next to them is the down escalator with only one person on it. He looks different as he politely smiles to everyone, making serious eye contact. In their minds, they can't figure out why he's going down. Their world is up.

I like that picture. But look further and you will see others coming down behind Jesus. His people are joining him in his new community, living a new way. Living counter-culturally. Stepping off the world's escalator of life, on to a new way of living with Jesus. Reversing the world's creed. *Do nothing out of selfish ambition or vain conceit, but in humility consider others better than yourselves. Each of you should look not only to your own interests, but also to the interests of others. Your attitude should be the same as that of Christ Jesus* (Phil. 2:3–4).

The old way upwards of pride and power comes naturally. The new way of humility and service comes supernaturally. The old way has momentum built into fallen humankind's DNA. The new way needs Christ's grace and power among his people to stand a chance. Because it affects everything about our attitudes and behaviour, including how we treat those sitting next to us right now. Little steps as well as bigger ones.

For *little steps*, look to the interests of others around us. On Wednesday near the seminary, I had a lunch meeting with a church leader in a restaurant called Sweet Tomatoes. Lining up for soup and salad, we were greeted by a church family: a mother with her two children already eating lunch. Later, as they were leaving, the teenage son dashed across and asked me, 'Will you be using Sweet Tomatoes in your next sermon?' That's a bizarre question, I thought, but I suppose he remembered that everyday events do creep into my sermons. And even a salad and soup matter to God! But then his mother came over. And she *apologized*. 'I hope you didn't mind us interrupting'. Ah! So did she sense that we were higher up, and above them? That they didn't count? Of course , we can insensitively interrupt others. But we can also allow the church to become an organization where certain people rise higher, so that they don't need to take notice and serve others. Leaders up here— the rest down there? No! Jesus wants to make us into a new community of brothers and sisters who relate not in the world's way, but in his way.

But reversing direction with Jesus brings far more radical steps. He goes down and down with us. Paul is a seminary student at Northern. He spends much of his spare time working as a volunteer at a homeless shelter, and in the Christmas break he decided to stay overnight at the shelter. He spoke in chapel a few weeks ago:

> Prior to lying on the cot the first night, I never understood the full significance of God sending his Son Jesus into the world in the form of a man, dwelling among us as a lower-class citizen. Lying in my bed, surrounded by 25- to 75-year-old men, men who did not have a home and had to stay in temporary shelters to get out of the cold, I realized why Jesus did what He did. You see, staying at the shelter as a guest put me at a level with the men that I didn't have as a volunteer, who after serving goes back to my bed in the suburbs.
>
> How do we, in following the example of Christ, leave our positions of wealth and privilege to minister to those who are less fortunate than us?
>
> What about our churches? Do they look like places of sacrifice and service, or comfort and consumerism? I want to encourage each of you to follow the example of Christ and get uncomfortable for a change.

We did feel uncomfortable. Because journeying down with Jesus takes us to places we don't want to go. Yet, together with Him, radical things can happen. We can go beyond little steps.

When I was pastor in Cambridge, homeless people used to beg on the church steps after worship. Some in the church pushed us to offer food and drink. But others said we should do more and open up our main hall to sleep them during the cold winter months. Choosing to say yes was extremely uncomfortable, messy and demanding. Yet together, over several winters, we knew something of belonging to the Lord who made himself nothing in order to serve. We discovered deeper places of travelling down with Jesus.

Jesus reverses the world's practice of power by his ethic of humble service. Bluntly he asks: Are you going up with pride and power? Or, by little steps and bigger ones, are you joining me going down with humble service? Going up or going down?

Sermon commentary

Working with students, I often find it helpful to point to Richard Jensen's suggestions about some key characteristics in literate and oral cultures (Table 8.1).[39] No doubt his twofold analysis simplifies a very complex and fast-changing situation, but it helps explain some of the dynamics between two different ways of approaching the preaching task.

Table 8.1 Preaching in different cultures

In a literate culture	*In an oral culture*
1. Linear development of ideas	1. Stitching stories together
2. Structure ideas in space	2. Use of repetition
3. Propositions as the main points	3. Situational versus abstraction
4. Analytical in nature	4. A tone of conflict
5. Left Brain communication	5. Right Brain communication
6. Metaphors of illustration	6. Metaphors of participation
7. Thinking in ideas	7. Thinking in pictures

To some extent these two sets of characteristics highlight the contrast between an 'old homiletic' and the 'new homiletic'. As Michael Quicke explains, '"New" relates to postmodernity, secondary orality and electronic literacy, whereas "old" is connected to modernity and literacy'.[40] His sermon on Philippians 2 exemplifies the approach which Jensen suggests is best suited for 'Preaching in an oral culture'.

For example, it is clear that this preacher is someone who is 'thinking in pictures' and images. For this engaging sermon is held together not so much by a 'big idea', but by the vivid image of the escalator going up and down. It is hard to disagree with Michael Quicke when he says that the general cultural consensus is about seeking to move up the escalator of life as high as possible. Even if a financial downturn means austere times which make that upward journey harder than usual, the prevailing narrative is that moving up is our natural goal.

Another way in which this preacher helps his listeners to stay tuned in to the message is by the 'use of repetition'. So, for example, in the opening sections of the sermon we regularly hear the refrain that 'ever since Adam, that's how human life works'.

The sermon appeals to the hearers' imaginations with its central image and with the three stories that come in the final stages of the sermon. We see the preacher 'stitching stories together' as we hear about an encounter in the Sweet Potatoes restaurant, about the student volunteer at the shelter for the homeless, and about the congregation risking opening its premises to homeless people. It is the cumulative impact of those stories which appeals to the hearts and minds of the congregation.

In preparing this sermon, Quicke followed Thomas Long's suggestions about writing Focus and Function statements.[41] In his blog written a few days before preaching the sermon, he outlined his emerging ideas about what the sermon would aim to Say (Focus) and Do (Function):

> At the moment I sum up this passage's main impact: by God's grace what my sermon will SAY is: As Jesus refused to use his divine power, but humbly became nothing—a servant prepared to die for his mission—so those united with him should follow his way of humility.
>
> And by God's grace, what my sermon will DO: challenge us together to join with him in his downward movement of humility.[42]

The preacher's aim is to challenge people to join with Jesus in this downward movement of humility and service, and the powerful emotional impact created by 'stitching stories together' makes it more likely that people will be moved to respond and the sermon's 'Function' will be achieved.

Later in the sermon the main image of the escalator is developed further: we have the picture of a crowd of people going up, and one person (Jesus) going down in the opposite direction. This is further expanded into a picture of the people of God joining Jesus in this downward movement of humility and service.

It would be wrong to imagine that this sermon is just about stories and images which stir people's emotions, because a carefully reasoned argument is also being advanced. There is 'a tone of conflict' because the preacher advances the argument that Christians all too often conform to the values of this world, and that we need to turn around and join with Jesus in travelling in a different direction.

The sermon is firmly rooted in the biblical text, and the preacher uses a lot of material from this passage in a creative way. For example, I like the way in which the change of one word highlights the choice that needs to be made. There is a sharp contrast between 'the moving-up creed' which 'chants, *Do everything out of selfish ambition and vain conceit*', and the Word of God which says, *Do nothing out of selfish ambition and vain conceit.*

Here we have a preacher who has confidence in the power of the Bible to speak for itself without excessive explanation. The preacher is well aware of the textual problems in the passage but does not dump all of that technical knowledge upon his unsuspecting hearers. The aim here is to draw people into the text, so that they can begin to indwell it for themselves.

Through his blog, Michael Quicke invites friends to share in his preaching journey, and this sermon has clearly been enriched by this wider listening to the text. Preachers are often encouraged to find ways of involving others in the sermon preparation process, and it is interesting to catch a glimpse of one way of doing that. I am left wondering in what ways it might be possible to encourage others to share in my preparation for preaching.

9

God's true image
COLOSSIANS 1.15–20

The situation in Colossae

The letter to the Colossians contains one of the most awe-inspiring descriptions of 'the son God loves' in the whole of the New Testament: the passage that begins in 1.15 with the words 'He is the image of the invisible God'.

These words are most commonly interpreted as introducing a series of assertions about the pre-existent Son, the second person of the Trinity. Yet if we take the statement this way, we are faced with an interesting puzzle. Paul[1] seems to say nothing about the actual process of this Son becoming human, but jumps straight from the heavenly Christ (vv. 15–17) to the cross, resurrection and Church (vv. 18–20), with no intervening stage. Even v. 19, 'In him all the fullness of God was pleased to dwell', on this reading would clearly refer to the pre-existent Son, not to his incarnation.

The Fathers, however, were divided on the meaning of the clause 'He is the image of the invisible God'.[2] Some did indeed take it as referring to the heavenly, pre-existent Christ, the *invisible* image of the *invisible* God. Others, however, including Irenaeus, linked it to the claim of Gen. 1.26–28 that *men and women* were created in God's image. They thus took it as a statement about the human Jesus of Nazareth, the *incarnate* Son, in whom the invisible God became visible. For this second group, also, the *process* of incarnation is not mentioned here, but *that is because all along it is the human Jesus about whom Paul is talking.*

In this chapter I take this latter view: that when Paul says, 'He is the image of the invisible God' (Col. 1.15), 'he' refers not to the one whom later theology was to identify as the eternal pre-existent Word, but to the human Jesus of Nazareth. But this is not a 'low' form of christology that falls short of asserting Jesus' divinity. On the contrary, Paul shares the widespread belief in early Christianity that Jesus was to be identified with Yahweh himself, the God of Israel.[3] The 'he' of v. 15 is this already divinely-identified Jesus. But v. 15 is an *assertion* not of Jesus' divinity, but of his fulfilling the destiny of the human race. 'He is the image of the invisible God' means that *Jesus Christ is the end-time fulfilment of humanity's destiny to rule over the earth.* This provides us with a fresh perspective on the incarnation. Paul tells the story not, like John, by recounting the journey of the eternal Word to his human dwelling place (Jn. 1.1–14), but by harking back to the original creation of humanity and showing how it has reached its divine fulfilment.

Such christology does not arise out of nowhere. It is formulated in response to the situation of a church which, despite its grounding in true Christian faith, hope and love (1.4–5), is threatened by views which in some way deny the unique authority of Christ. They are in danger of being taken captive by systems of thought that exercise sway without reference to Christ (2.8). They are being tempted to accord to other spiritual beings the honour due to Christ alone, and to submit themselves to forms of religious observance instead of the one to whom these forms are meant to point (2.15–17). Thus they need to be faced with the stunning majesty of Christ's true identity, the extent of his achievement and the scope of his authority. He is the true human ruler, the one on whom all humans are to model themselves.

We may profitably reflect on what contemporary situations are in some way analogous to that in Colossae, and the direction in which Paul's words may point today. George Caird aptly comments:

> It would appear that Paul's opponents accepted Christ and claimed to be Christians, but held that there were considerable tracts of human behaviour which could not be subsumed under his rule, but must continue to be governed by other manifestations of divine authority. If this be so, then their nearest modern counterparts are those theologians and philosophers who have insisted that the ethics of the gospel cannot be applied to the corporate life of society.[4]

We might extend his point further. It is not only 'the corporate life of society' that is sometimes excluded (by Christians!) from the domain of Christ, but aspects of the everyday life of believers. Christ is acclaimed as Lord, yet in practice other 'lords' are granted independent validity and status over aspects of life. We are not thinking here of the obviously competing authorities of materialism, consumerism, sexual licence and the like (though such things may indeed still exercise sway over the Christian, and their corresponding desires thus need to be 'put to death': Col. 3.5–9). It is the subtler, less obvious appeal of apparently harmless religious practices or philosophical ideas that is Paul's primary concern in Colossians. Individual Christians and churches need to think carefully about what practices and ideas today might correspond to the 'worship of angels' (2.18) or the 'hollow and deceptive philosophy' (2.8 NIV) in the air at Colossae. Perhaps the independent, almost religious authority accorded to ideals like 'choice' and 'freedom'—within the Church as well as beyond it—fit the bill.

What, though, are the implications of the fact that it is not simply the pre-existent or the exalted Christ, but the *human* Christ, who possesses this universal authority to which we are called to submit? At this point we need to turn to a more detailed examination of Paul's argument in our central verses, 1.15–20, setting them in the context of the surrounding passage.

Paul's argument

Prayer and thanksgiving (Col. 1.3–12)

Paul's exposition of the nature of Christ arises out of his concern and prayer for the Colossian Christians. The account of his prayer serves not only to assure them of his care and remind them of his vision, but also to encourage them to appropriate the blessings for which he thanks God, and fully to embrace the way of life which he longs for them to follow. An expression of prayerful concern thus shades into doxological teaching about Christ.

New land, new freedom, new king (Col. 1.12–14)

Paul begins his account of what God has done in Christ by evoking the powerful Old Testament symbol of the promised land (v. 12). He asserts that God has made the (mainly Gentile) Colossian Christians co-inheritors with historical Israel. All the inexhaustible wealth stored up for these 'saints in light' is for them too. The 'promised land' itself surely evokes the gift of the earth to humanity. Israel's calling in Canaan was no more, and no less, than to fulfil the stewardship to which Adam and Eve were summoned in Eden. This gift and duty has now, says Paul, become the inheritance of all who are in Christ. In Christ the particular calling of Israel is fulfilled, and humanity as a whole is enabled to enjoy and care for God's earth.

The territorial imagery is strengthened in v. 13, where Paul writes of the 'transfer' of Christians from one regime to another. In Christ, Paul

says, we are no longer in bondage to the 'power of darkness', to alienation, negativity and death, obliged to satisfy their demands and feed their
inflated self-importance. Like Israel in the first flush of her freedom from
Egypt, we have entered into a new allegiance, and our ruler is none other
than 'God's own Son'—by which Paul certainly means Jesus of Nazareth.
That which he has rescued us *from* is no mere Pharaoh or Nebuchadnez-
zar; it is nothing less than the 'sins' which have kept Jew and Gentile at
loggerheads with God, their fellow-humans and their vocation on earth
since the dawn of time.

Jesus, the image of God (Col. 1.15–20)

Three clues may help us grasp the meaning of Paul's striking claim that
Jesus of Nazareth is 'the image of the invisible God' (v. 15).

First, this is a continuation of the themes of inheritance and allegiance
from vv. 12–14. In the ancient world, rulers set up images of themselves
in far-flung parts of their territory, so the inhabitants would be left in no
doubt who was in charge.[5] As God's 'image', therefore, Jesus expresses to
us God's lordship over his world and constantly calls us to place ourselves
under it. Then we will be able to enjoy our inheritance.

Second, this is an echo of Gen. 1.27–28, which tells of how God created *humanity*, male and female, 'in his own image' (NIV).[6] Jesus is seen
as the quintessential expression of this truth.[7] It seems highly unlikely that
Paul would have wished his readers to block out this creation narrative
from their minds and think instead of 'the image of God' purely as some
pre-existent divine being. Surely his point is precisely that Jesus expresses
the identity and fulfils the calling given to humanity by divine decree at
creation. It may be that by saying 'He *is* the image of the invisible God',
Paul is deliberately, at the same time, marking off Jesus' *distinction* from
the mass of humanity, who were said only to be created '*in*' God's image
and '*according to*' his likeness. But whatever may have been Paul's precise
intention here, Genesis 1 is surely by implication being read as a prophetic
narrative, speaking not merely of a past event, but also of a future destiny
for the human race.[8]

Putting these two points together, we can say that Paul sees Jesus as the
true human being who exercises God's rule over all his creation. But there
is a third illuminating clue to this verse. In roughly-contemporary Jewish
literature, such as the book of Wisdom and the works of Philo, divine
Wisdom is regarded as the 'image of God'.[9] Wisdom (and the closely-
related 'Logos') 'thus become ways of safeguarding the unknowability of

God by providing a mode of speaking of the invisible God's self-revelatory action . . . by means of which he may nevertheless be known'.[10] Such a way of speaking would have appealed both to the Jewish mindset, with its abhorrence of idolatry yet belief in God's self-disclosure, and to the Hellenistic culture with which Jews and Christians were surrounded in the centuries immediately before and after the time of Christ, with its Platonic distinction between the world of invisible 'ideas' and the world of sense-perception.[11] There is actually a further key link to be made here. Jewish thinkers had identified divine Wisdom with Torah, God's 'law' or 'teaching'.[12]

Scholars such as Dunn see this association of Christ with Wisdom as evidence of a stage in the progression to the full recognition of Jesus' divinity. It is better, however, to assume that Paul already recognizes this and is asserting that Jesus is the human embodiment of divine wisdom, the mediation of his invisible being to the visible world. To speak of the human Jesus as 'the image of the invisible God' is, indeed, a startling claim; but it is no more startling than the analogous, and only slightly less exalted claim of Gen. 1.26–27—that humanity itself is created 'in' God's image. Moreover, it must be stressed again that when Paul thinks of Jesus, he is not thinking of some static, unchanging personage, as it were the rock-carved image of a distant overlord. He is thinking of the career of an individual of recent memory: of his striking character, provocative teaching, powerful deeds, shameful death and risen life. It is *this Jesus* who is the image of the invisible God. If we wish to see God as he is, we must look to Jesus. If we wish to see humanity in its ideal form, we must look to Jesus. Thus reading v. 15 as if Paul has suddenly taken his eyes off the earthly Jesus on to an invisible divine being is to miss the force of what he is saying.[13]

The subsequent assertions unfold Paul's claim. 'The firstborn of all creation' (v. 15) was a rabbinic title for the Messiah, based on Ps. 89.27; so this is another way of speaking of Jesus as the divinely-appointed regent of the world.[14] The language of v. 16a, 'in him all things . . . were created', also echoes Jewish belief, this time about the Torah. God's word and wisdom were seen as being at the heart and goal of his created world: this place of pre-eminence Paul assigns to Jesus himself.[15] Included in 'all things' are both the seen and unseen realms and, explicitly, all those authorities to which human beings are tempted to ascribe independent agency and validity. Paul refers to the cosmology of his time, which saw spiritual agencies lying behind earthly powers. The key thing to notice here is that not only does he not deny the existence of these 'thrones or dominions or rulers or powers'. He also asserts that they have a role and function oriented towards Jesus, the supreme authority.

Two points of grammar are worthy of note in v. 16. First, the prepositions. At the beginning of the verse, Paul states that all things were created
'in him' (Jesus); this is taken up at the end of the verse and rephrased—
'through him and for him'. It would be unwise to draw over-neat distinctions between these different phrases, and still less wise to try to imagine
too literally a Jesus-figure involved as a kind of foreman in God's factory.[16]
Through piling up the prepositions, Paul seems to be straining to express
his conviction that Jesus fills the roles assigned to both Messiah and Torah in Jewish belief. They convey a strong sense of Jewish teleology—that
creation is driven forward from origin to goal by an overriding divine
purpose: and that purpose, for Paul, can be defined in one word: Jesus.

Second, the tenses. At the beginning of the verse, Paul uses the aorist—
the tense of definite, completed action: 'in him all things *were* created'.
At the end of the verse he uses the perfect—the tense which speaks of the
past's ongoing, present implications: 'all things *have been* created through
him and for him'.[17] This combination of expressions speaks both of the
firmness of God's work and the fact that it calls for continuing recognition
and response.

Verses 17 and 18 each begin with an emphatic 'he', *autos*. The expression 'before all things', following on from Paul's assertions about Christ's
pivotal role in the creation, has naturally been used to claim Pauline
support for the doctrine of Christ's 'pre-existence', which emerges more
clearly in John and Hebrews. Undeniably, neither Paul nor we can escape
temporal language when making the claims we want to make about the
unique identity and role of Jesus. But again, it is a mistake to read back
later debates into this passage. The preposition 'before' (*pro*) can itself be
used in non-temporal ways and does not have to be taken in a temporal
sense here. Paul's concern is not (or at least not so much) with Jesus' pre-
natal history, but with his supreme authority. It is better, once more, to
see Paul as piling up phrases to express what is beyond expression, phrases
not themselves sharply differentiated from each other. To say that 'in him
all things hold together' is not essentially different from saying that 'he is
before all things' (v. 17): both point to aspects of the same truth, that only
in Jesus can we see the meaning of the universe. 'He is the very centre and
crown of creation, because he is man as God from the beginning designed
man to be'.[18] Caird, again, offers an apt interpretation of Paul's thrust:
only 'in unity with "the proper man" could the universe be brought to
its destined coherence'.[19] Dunn notes that the assertion is made in 'the
language . . . of poetic imagination, precisely the medium where a quan-
tum leap across disparate categories can be achieved by use of unexpected
metaphor'.[20] He goes on:

Paradoxical as it may seem, the wisdom which holds the universe together is most clearly to be recognized in its distinctive character by reference to Christ. This will mean, among other things, that the fundamental rationale of the world is 'caught' more in the generous outpouring of sacrificial, redemptive love (1.14) than in the greed and grasping more characteristic of 'the authority of darkness' [1.13].[21]

When Paul says, 'And he is the head of the body, the church' (v. 18 NIV), we are reminded that he has not been indulging in rarefied or abstract speculation, but speaking of a real human being who has left behind a real human community. The picture of the 'head' is the most intimately organic way of expressing the relationship of Jesus to his followers, yet in the context it is probably, yet again, the idea of Jesus' authority that is uppermost here. The Church is introduced into Paul's presentation here because it is the visible demonstration of what he has been saying about Jesus. It is the community in which the reality of Jesus' rule over creation is being shown.

The next clause, too, leaves us in no doubt that the story of the human Jesus of Nazareth remains in Paul's sights. 'He is the beginning, the firstborn from the dead, so that he might come to have first place in everything' (v. 18). The resurrection of Jesus is the sign that a new order has begun.[22] Just as physical death was always a sign of something far more painful and serious, the alienation of human beings from their creator and from one another, so Jesus' physical resurrection is a sign of something far more wonderful than the possibility of endless physical life: the restoration of human beings to their creator and to one another. But this is as yet an incomplete process, as shown by Paul's wording 'so that he might come . . . ' (v. 18). Again, the appeal Paul makes explicit elsewhere is implicit here. We are to be active players in seeing that Jesus does indeed 'have first place in everything'.

Verses 19 and 20 complete the picture—at least as far as we can trace it here. Verse 19 says literally that 'all the fullness was pleased to dwell in him' (NIV). 'The fullness' was a term for God's nature that was later to be picked up in Gnostic thought.[23] The significance of Paul's usage here is probably that the Colossians were being tempted to think of Jesus as an insufficient revelation of God, and to look to other 'authorities' as a way of filling out their spiritual experience. The expression reminds us once more that the purpose of God is not to be worked out in some ethereal realm, but on the solid ground of human history. Broken relationships are to be overcome; peace is to be made. And it is to happen 'through the blood of his cross', through the poured-out life of a human being, which ended in loneliness, ignominy and terror. The following verses remind the readers how they themselves have come into the enjoyment of this peace and exhort them not to shift from the hope held out in this good news of Jesus (vv. 21–23).

As we reflect on Paul's doxological description of Jesus, three things perhaps stand out above all.

First, it is hard to imagine any higher accolades that Paul might have given to Jesus. Over and over again, his ultimate, supreme authority is asserted, and so is his unique relationship to God. Yet Paul does so in ways which should not be expected to fit neatly with the later categories of doctrinal debate. He draws, rather, on the Jewish categories of Messiahship, Torah and Wisdom, which lie close to hand. It is clear that the man Jesus is the subject of his meditations throughout.[24] Equally, it is clear that this Jesus is no alien intruder into God's world. 'Redemption is not an invasion from a different or a hostile realm. The Lord of this world has come to claim his rightful possession'.[25]

Second, the accolades here given to Jesus reflect their glory on to humanity as a whole. By calling Jesus 'the image of the invisible God', so clearly picking up the language of Gen. 1.26–27, Paul hints at the restoration of lost splendour for the entire race. It was not until this image of God was put to this shameful death that it could be clearly demonstrated *what* kind of human life it was that would endure (the Jesus kind!) and *that* this kind of human life would indeed endure (God raised him!)

Third, the scope of Jesus' significance and authority is universal. Like bookends for our passage, both vv. 15 and 20 stress that it is all things both 'on earth' and 'in heaven' that find their original purpose and their ultimate reconciliation in Christ. This human being is not merely the founder of a human community, or the saviour of men and women. He is also the pivot and restorer of the cosmos itself.[26] In being reconciled to God, 'all things' wonderfully become reconciled to one another too.

Preaching the incarnation from Colossians 1.15–20

Our reading of these verses underlines that they are indeed, centrally, about the incarnation, and that Paul understands that truth in a more radical way than some interpretations have suggested. For if the 'he' and 'him' refer to a pre-existent divine being, an invisible 'second person of the Trinity', the effect is to shift the weight of vv. 15–17 and 19: they become more about the nature of the divine economy, and less immediately about the identity of Jesus of Nazareth. To be sure, even on this reading, incarnation is implied, not least by the references to the crucifixion, resurrection and Church in vv. 18 and 20. On my reading, however, there is no escaping full-blooded incarnation all the way through. *Jesus of Nazareth*, a man of flesh and blood, is 'the image of the invisible God', for whom all things were created. In *him* all the fullness of God was pleased to dwell. Irenaeus' famous doctrine of 'recapitulation' is thus seen to be a valid exposition of the canonical witness:

When [the Son of God] was incarnate and made man, he recapitulated [or summed up] in himself the long line of the human race, procuring for us salvation thus summarily, so that what we had lost in Adam, that is, the being in the image and likeness of God, that we should regain in Christ Jesus.[27]

Further, Gen. 1.26–27 is seen to point to the consistency of the incarnation with God's earlier revelation, just as, we argued in Chapters 1 and 2, do Exod. 3.1–15 and Proverbs 8. It was no strange thing for a humanity created 'in' God's own image one day to play host to a man who *was* God's own image.

How, though, is it that the incarnation of God in this man—even a man thus crucified and raised—should have the cosmic effects Paul ascribes to it? The answer lies, surely, close to hand. The human Jesus is not alone: he is the head of a body; he is the firstborn from the dead, not the only-born (v. 18). He is not an isolated glimmer of hope, an ideal figure whom we might (or might not) be able to imitate, the sign of a future that we might (or might not) be enabled to share. He is the embodiment and enabler of a new human solidarity. Behind Paul's words here surely lies the kind of Adam-christology expressed in Rom. 5.12–21 and 1 Cor. 15.42–50. Jesus is the new representative of the race. He has set it on a new trajectory. As the 'image of the invisible God', in Paul's thinking he thus takes on a 'corporate identity'.

Paul's message about the incarnation is great good news, therefore, not only for what it says about God but also for what it says about humanity. In the thesaurus of faith available to him, there could be no more stunning way of affirming either the radical humility of God or the radical glory of humanity. In Jesus, God shows *his* very being and character, but also *our* very purpose and destiny—a destiny to which the very future of the cosmos is inextricably attached.

How then do human beings become sharers in this new solidarity of the race? Paul clearly assumes that baptism and the complete reorientation it symbolizes are foundational (2.12); yet he spends much of the letter urging the already-baptized, in a variety of ways, to hold on to and live out the new identity they have discovered in Christ. Whatever this corporate solidarity means, it does not entail sitting back in smug satisfaction. It is about continuing in 'faith' and 'hope' (1.23). It is about growth into maturity 'in Christ' (1.28). It is about living *in* Christ, 'rooted and built up in him' (2.7). It is about seeking the things that are above, putting to death an old life, and putting on a new life (3.1–17).

In all this, the preacher surely recognizes the familiar two sides of the gospel, indicative and imperative. The particular focus of the 'indicative' in this case is the identity of Jesus as the one in whom God's authority over his universe is vested, and the extraordinary implications that has for the identity and future of humanity and the cosmos. Once that vision has been glimpsed, obedience to the consequent 'imperatives' will seem natural. No human wisdom, no practices of human devotion and self-development, no powerful ideas or political and spiritual forces—none of these are in principle without value, irredeemable or worthless.[28] Equally, if any of these things are allowed to eclipse the glory of the one true image of the invisible God, their pretensions must be exposed, for by themselves they will only enslave those destined for freedom in Christ.[29] It is therefore a prime task of the preacher to seek to identify and name the particular 'authorities' which may hold sway in the society and era in which one preaches. There must be an appropriate tentativeness here, but simply raising the questions for congregations will alert them to the need to use their own God-given wisdom and discernment. The call to speak a living word from God does not allow us to retreat from such prophetic engagement and questioning.

Bishop Handley Moule offers poetic and homiletic inspiration for preaching on this passage:

> No surer test, according to the Holy Scriptures, can be applied to anything claiming to be Christian teaching, than this: Where does it put Jesus Christ? Is He something in it, or is He all? Is He the Sun of the true solar system, so that every planet gets its place and its light from Him? Or is He at best a sort of Ptolemaic sun, rolling together with other luminaries around an earthly centre—whether that centre take the form of an observance, a constitution, or a philosophy?[30]

And again, on the way in which Paul paints the cosmic significance of Jesus Christ:

> How much it has to say to us! For one thing, it binds both 'worlds', the seen and unseen, the material and the spiritual, into one, under one Head. . . . For another thing, it sanctifies 'Nature' to us, and makes its immeasurable heights and depths at once safe and radiant with the Name of Jesus Christ. It connects the remotest aeon of the past

with Him. It connects the remotest star detected by the photographic plate with Him. It bids us, when we feel as if lost in the enormity of space and time, fall back upon the Centre of both—for that centre is our Lord Jesus Christ, who died for us. In Him they hold together. . . . With His Name the traveller can rejoice in the glories of mountain, forest, and flood, worshipping not Nature but Christ its Cause and End; Artificer of the landscape, while He is Saviour of the soul. With that same dear Name the explorer of physical secrets can consecrate his laboratory, remembering that Christ is the ultimate Law of compound and cohesion, while He is the Saviour of the soul.[31]

Finally, with especial pertinence to the preacher, Moule comments on the *mode* of Paul's writing. Here we recall the hymnic quality of Paul's words. Moule says that the Bible is full of 'articulate and reasoned statements of eternal verities',[32] yet

the dogmatic predication is shaped in the very soul, usually the suffering soul, of the seer who utters it. The dogmatic exposition is written down by a teacher who as it were writes upon his knees, and looks up continually from his argument to worship the Subject of it, with love, and joy, and tears. . . . All is oracle. But the human heart, new-created by the Lord, and filled with Him, is the temple where this oracle is delivered. And we who so receive our oracles of eternal truth and life are bound to carry them away and use them in a spirit worthy of their origin. Our creed is never to be a mere code of propositions in the abstract. It is to breathe and glow, even where it is most systematic, with the Christian's own experience of worship, rest, and joy, in full sight of the glory of Him who has loved him and has died for him.[33]

Moule thus encourages us to preach in the same spirit in which Paul writes. It is a vision which makes at least this preacher feel his great inadequacy, but which nonetheless remains heart-warming.

Sermon: Images and the image of God*

Stephen Wright

They stared out at you from walls and screens wherever you looked: smiling images of the great Ruler, the benevolent Leader, the one who was guiding your nation on its onward march to prosperity and victory. Saddam's Iraq, Mao's China, Stalin's Russia: and for all I know, it is still a common tactic in

*Preached by Dr Stephen I. Wright at St Swithun's Church, Purley, UK, on Sunday, 25 November 2007.

various one-party states around the world. I don't know if you've ever tried to imagine what it must be like to live in a state like that. George Orwell's *1984* got uncomfortably close to the mark with its portrayal of the figure of 'Big Brother, black-haired, black-moustachio'd, full of power and mysterious calm, and so vast that it almost filled up the screen'.[34] The image of the dictator could, I would think, be both alarming and reassuring at different times. It would make you very scared to step out of line. And yet people get used to it. At least you know where you stand. And after a while, people can start to believe the propaganda. The image is everywhere; the image orients your life.

Of course, it's not like that here. The prime minister doesn't have his face plastered on every public building. People can put up pictures of the royals in their homes and offices if they like; or they can have pictures of Keira Knightley or David Beckham, Britney Spears or Brad Pitt. Every week on our bus shelters there are new attractive models, enticing us into a fresh era of moisturizing or mobile telephony. And the buildings themselves shout loudly about the range of choices, the multiple powers that jockey for position in orienting our lives. Go to a high spot near here, and you'll see the great Wembley arc, the temple of sport. Go down to the main road, and you'll see the reassuring red bricks of Tesco, the cathedral of consumption. Take a bus into town, and you're surrounded by towering icons. Nestlé, shrine to big business; Croydon College, where 'you know you can do it'; Fairfield, cultural home to everything from Mozart to wrestling. We don't have one image, but many. And I'm glad about that. That's better than having the dictator smiling down at us all the time. But the images are confusing and distracting and disturbing as well as alluring, reassuring, powerful, dazzling. So much freedom, but in the conflict of images and all they represent, maybe not much peace. They struggle with each other to orient our lives, and often end up pulling them apart.

In the ancient world, some things weren't much different. Because travel was harder, it was especially important that rulers should be able to remind subjects in far-flung parts of their territory who was really in charge. And so they had massive images carved and sculpted in strategic places. In the thirteenth century BC, one of the Egyptian Pharaohs, Rameses II, had a great image of himself carved out of the rock on the Mediterranean coast, north of Beirut in Lebanon. The image was meant to orient his subjects' lives.

But the Jewish people had come to a very different view of the world. It was radical, subversive, exhilarating and wonderfully simple. There was only one real king—the invisible God. And where was his image? Astonishingly, it was nothing other than the human race itself! That's what they claimed in Genesis. God created humanity in his own image, male and female. Human beings, women and men, you and I: *we* are God's chosen means of claiming and exercising his authority in the world, of reminding the world who is in charge. We aren't meant to domineer *over each other:* we are meant to rule the world wisely, in submission to God. So all the dictators in history are put decisively in their place—from ancient Babylon to modern Iraq or Burma and beyond. Human beings don't need to be afraid of them. We can all celebrate the dignity that God has given to each one of us. We need be slaves of no-one. We *are* the image, meant to orient the life of the world.

But something has gone wrong. Instead of a world running smoothly, with order and freedom, we see a world that's cracked and groaning, with brokenness in the midst of its beauty, chaos in the midst of its creativity. What has happened to the image? We *were* the image. What has happened to us?

All this is the background of the wonderful words we have heard this morning. *He is the image of the invisible God.*

There is one who has come to rescue us from the chaos and slavery, to restore us to our rightful role in the cosmos, our dignity as the image of God the King.

He is one from whose eyes God himself in all his glory shines out.

He is one who is putting the broken pieces of the universe back together again.

He is the image to orient our lives.

Yet all these other images around are at once so dazzling, so enticing, or so oppressive. And the great temptation for Christians in our day in the western world may well be quite similar to the great temptation that seems to have faced the people of Colossae to whom Paul was writing. It was not the temptation to reject Jesus Christ. Of course not! It was the temptation to have a lifestyle that we might describe as 'Christ plus'. We'll have our bit of Jesus, and then we'll have our bit of everything else. We'll have our bit of consumerist indulgence, and our bit of self-help therapy, and our bit of big business, and our sporting or cultural 'fix', and so on. And the message of Paul is not that food and drink and self-help wisdom and money and pleasure and so on are wrong or to be avoided. Of course not! This is God's world, created for us to enjoy and use wisely. No—the message is that *Christ is the image of God on whom we must take our bearings and orient our lives.* He's not just another hobby or activity or interest. Without him, our lives remain fragmented, enslaved, chaotic. With him, they come together: they find focus, direction, purpose.

How then can we do this? After all, we can't see him. How can we orient our lives on him? Remember first that he is not somewhere 'out there', apart from us, like a Big Brother on the screen, or the forbidding image of a Pharaoh on the rock face. We are organically related to him. Paul says, 'He is the head of the body, the church'. Our baptism is the sign that we are joined to him; that all his dignity as God's image is now shared with us; that we, together, can shine again with God's glory in the world, if we will.

Remember then the story of his life and death. The peace he made, Paul says, was through the blood of his cross. Look in your mind's eye at *this* image: a young man, of Middle Eastern appearance, somewhat haggard beyond his years, elevated a few feet above the ground, between two others; gasping words of forgiveness from lungs already breathless; ignoring taunts and promising paradise; a rough inscription pinned to the wood on which he hung: 'This is the king of the Jews'. Look at *this* image, the image of Christ, your king and mine. See there the mercy, the love, the courage to take violence rather than to give it. Let *this* be the image that orients your life, that gives you both your freedom and your peace: the image of God himself.

Sermon commentary

This sermon was preached in an Anglican church with which I was not familiar. However, it is not far from where I live in the southern suburbs of London, and it was easy to find at least some common ground via the references to particular 'images' in the locality—not dissimilar to the kind of 'images' to be found in most western or westernized cities. I wanted the sermon to contribute to the worship of God's people in this particular eucharistic service by focusing on Paul's remarkable claim that Jesus 'is the image of the invisible God'. The epistle reading was Col. 1.11–20, and the Gospel which followed was Lk. 23.32–43, both pointing in striking ways to the nature of 'Christ the King'. This is a designation for the last Sunday of the Christian year, an opportunity to celebrate the victory of Christ before taking up again the mood of expectation and longing which marks the season of Advent.

The Colossians passage is so rich that there would have been a serious danger either of indigestibility or of superficiality if I had tried to cover it all. I chose rather to focus on the single assertion at the beginning of 1.15. This gave me the opportunity to unpack its background in more depth, as well as to set the context in the overall thrust of Paul's letter. It also seemed to me to get to the heart of Paul's message. His appeal to the Colossians is based on the assertion of the ultimate, God-given authority of Jesus Christ. Paul's words about Jesus being the head of the body (v. 18) provided a necessary means of drawing out the implications, but I felt that the omission of detailed reference to other parts of the text was a justifiable and indeed a necessary exercise of interpretative selectivity, which did not do violence to the passage.

The sermon sought to proclaim the incarnation by highlighting the remarkable dignity bestowed on the human race by the particular way in which God has chosen to exercise his authority over us. It aimed to catch people up into the excitement of this by reminding them of their organic relationship to Christ, inspiring them to worship, and also to warn of the threats which continue to surround us from attractive alternative 'authorities' and 'images' claiming more for themselves than they should.

Within David Schlafer's triad of 'image, story, argument', mentioned in Chapter 5,[35] my tendency is to gravitate to image or argument. This sermon's shaping principle was clearly the 'image' of 'image' itself. The idea of an image's 'orienting' power was a connecting refrain (though the word 'orient' seemed to me rather weak for what I wanted to say). I find this a powerful and helpful symbolic connecting-point between the world of Scripture and the world of today. Observers have often noted the dominance of images in contemporary western culture, and their perplexing and often competing allure. Brian Walsh and Sylvia Keesmaat, discussing Col. 1.15, make the link between the numerous imperial images in Roman society and those of consumer affluence that surround us today.[36] Jean Baudrillard has even proposed that the images around us are so powerful that we tend to lose our grip on what is reality and what is reflection or representation.[37] Though in this form this may be a typical manifestation of 'postmodernity', the power of images to shape people's consciousness and even allegiances seems to be an enduring feature of human life. It is easy to trace the continuity with the Bible's warnings against idolatry.

Although Schlafer is no doubt right that in any one sermon, just one of the three 'modes' of image, story and argument must form the central strategy,[38] I believe that a weakness of this sermon was the absence of concrete stories. Narrative examples of being beguiled by one or more 'images', and of discovering or rediscovering the priority of Jesus in their midst, would have helped to flesh out the message, contributing a sense of dynamism and movement, and also communicating something of my own story, indicating—even indirectly—the influence of the message on my own life.

I reflected on these things before preaching a variant of this sermon in a Baptist church some months later, as part of an Easter series on some great christological passages. I adjusted the 'local' references slightly, and (having more time) included a more discursive section in the middle, stressing the significance of its being a *human* figure about whom these exalted claims were made (a paradox too easily forgotten, I suggested, in much contemporary praise of Jesus). In keeping with the Easter season, I also stressed the phrase 'firstborn from the dead' (v. 18), and what it implies about Jesus being the founder of a new humanity.

In addition, I took the opportunity to include a personal story in the closing stages. This concerned the way in which I had benefited greatly from a particular kind of psychological therapy, but had also discovered in practice that no such treatment can replace the need to look outside ourselves to Christ, the image of God, who is to be the orienting centre of our lives. He does not drive out other forms of human wisdom but enables us to see them in their true light. Interestingly (and typically), it was this step of self-disclosure which particularly drew appreciative comment afterwards.

No sermon should be seen as a static, finished product. Furthermore, the occasion and situation of the hearers must rightly exercise considerable sway over what is said and how. This 'repeat' of a sermon was therefore an exercise in seeing how a sermon might 'grow up'[39] between one context and another. Another time, I hope it would grow up further still.

10

Able to help

HEBREWS 2.5–18

Our Lord Jesus Christ . . . truly God

Some years ago I helped plan a weekend exhibition for a church anniversary. It celebrated the congregation's journey of faith, which had been under way for over 190 years. Through the exhibition local people could explore something of the church's story and sample some of the things the church was currently doing. The overarching theme chosen for the weekend was the text from Hebrews which declares that 'Jesus Christ is the same yesterday and today and forever'.[1]

On the Sunday morning the guest preacher 'upset the equilibrium': he started his sermon by saying that for some people talk of Jesus Christ being the 'same' conveyed the impression of a Christ who was old, passé and out of date. In a fast-changing, fluid world, something which stays the 'same' may appeal to nostalgia buffs, but it looks less attractive to most of our contemporaries.

For the fearful group of disciples addressed by the author of Hebrews, the message that Christ is the 'same' was far from irrelevant. They were 'resident aliens' in a society which was becoming increasingly hostile to Christian faith and, without the help of their founding fathers, it was an uphill struggle to keep going. For those besieged believers, the message that the living Christ was the 'same yesterday and today and forever' was a lifeline. Like everything in the letter to the Hebrews, the description of Christ as the 'same yesterday and today and forever' was a dose of practical theology, delivering encouragement to disciples who were being tempted to abandon the race of faith.

The language of Heb. 13.8 directly echoes ch. 1, where verses from Psalm 102 are applied to Jesus.[2] The psalmist affirms that YHWH is the one who remains the 'same' even if the heavens wear out and fade away; Hebrews declares that Jesus Christ is the 'same': that he is the one whose 'years will never end' (Ps. 102.25–27; Heb. 1.10–12). As Richard Bauckham puts it,

> The scriptural words [from Psalm 102] are used to attribute to the Son precisely what distinguishes the one God from all creation: the full eternity that God alone possesses, by contrast with the createdness, mutability and transience of all created things. Left to themselves all things perish, but God alone, here including Christ, has in himself the indestructible life that makes it possible for the psalmist to say, 'You are the same', i.e. eternally.[3]

Whilst some feel that the stress in Heb. 13.8 is primarily pastoral,[4] Bauckham is sure that

> this description of Jesus constitutes a much more emphatic assertion of the full divine eternity of Jesus Christ than has usually been supposed. . . . Jesus, in his participation in the unique divine identity, remains eternally the 'same', that is, his identity is unchanged. He remains himself eternally and can, therefore, be trusted in the present and the future just as he was in the past.[5]

This portrayal, at the beginning and end of this letter (1.12; 13.8), of Jesus as the one who is eternally the 'same', alerts readers to the fact that from start to finish, Hebrews affirms the full divinity of the Lord. It exemplifies the 'Christology of divine identity', which Bauckham argues is woven throughout the warp and weft of the New Testament.[6] For any preacher wishing to explore the doctrine of the incarnation, the opening chapter of Hebrews offers rich resources for celebrating and proclaiming the full divinity of the Son of God.

For example, although many commentators suggest that the 'more excellent' name mentioned in Heb. 1.4 is probably 'the Son', Bauckham makes a convincing case for saying that 'the name that is so much more excellent than those of the angels must be the Hebrew divine name, the Tetragrammaton [YHWH], which is also said to be conferred on Jesus at his exaltation in Phil. 2.9 ("the name that is above every name")'.[7] Seen against the monotheism of those early converts from Judaism, the assertion that Jesus has been given the name YHWH is mind-blowing. It is another piece of evidence showing that 'the earliest Christology was already *in nuce* the highest Christology'.[8]

Many years would pass before Church leaders would agree on a formal definition about 'our Lord Jesus Christ, at once complete in Godhead and complete in manhood, truly God and truly man'.[9] Yet this does not mean that recognition of the full divinity of the Son of God was a much-later development. Hebrews 1 is just part of the evidence showing how those earliest believers were led by their experience to include Jesus Christ in the unique identity of the one God of Israel.

Whether they prefer singing traditional hymns or charismatic songs, most worshippers are familiar with this high view of the person of Christ. Even if many believers might find it difficult to offer precise definitions of christology, anyone frequenting mainstream Christian worship on a regular basis soon begins to imbibe language expressing belief in the eternal Son of God.

Living as 'resident aliens' in a society questioning traditional views of faith, it is vital that the Church continues confidently to proclaim the full divinity of the Son of God. This message is essential because Jesus Christ can only fully reveal the truth about God if he is fully divine. Similarly, if Jesus Christ is not fully divine, then he would be unable to rescue fallen humanity from the sorry mess we had gotten ourselves into.

The steady procession of biblical quotations in Hebrews 1 functions as a fanfare of tributes celebrating the full divinity of Christ. Building on that confession of faith in the eternal Son of God, the next section of Hebrews focuses upon the less familiar, but no less important, story about the humanity of Christ. So we find that the opening chapters of this epistle make it clear that telling the truth about our Lord Jesus Christ means confessing him *truly God and truly man*.

Our Lord Jesus Christ . . . truly man

The cartoons our grandchildren now enjoy employ more spectacular special effects than the ones our children watched a generation earlier: but the stories still follow a very similar plot. Some good people get into trouble, and it sure looks as if the powers of evil will be victorious. But then the cartoon superhero appears, and using a secret source of power, our hero rises up to defeat the villains. Disaster is averted, and everyone lives happily ever after. Well, maybe not for ever after, but at least until the next episode, when evil raises its ugly head all over again.

My sneaking suspicion is that many Christians view Jesus as a sort of cartoon superhero. They happily believe 'that the Word became flesh and dwelt among us' (Jn. 1:14 NKJV). At the same time, however, they sense that when things got difficult and evil launched its attacks, Jesus was somehow able to switch on a secret, invisible power supply to help him out of trouble. This cartoon theology is another version of the problem of Docetism that has dogged the Church over the years: the belief that our Lord Jesus Christ only seemed to be fully human.

This is an understandable desire to keep Jesus at a safe distance from the unholy mess that is human life as we know it, but it has disastrous theological consequences. For as Thomas F. Torrance used to explain to his students,

> any docetic view of the humanity of Christ would mean that God only appears to act within our human existence. . . . Atonement is real and actual only if and as the mediator acts fully from the side of man as man, as well as from the side of God as God. If the humanity of Christ is imperfect, atonement is imperfect, and we would then still be in our sins.[10]

From its earliest times the Church has acknowledged that if the Lord Jesus Christ was not 'truly man', then 'what he has not assumed he has not healed', the hopeless result being that our fallen sinful humanity remains diseased and disordered.[11]

In sharp contrast to any suggestion that Jesus Christ only seemed to be truly human, George Caird points out that 'in outlining their understanding of the humanity of Jesus, the New Testament writers make three rather dramatic claims. Jesus is fully human, perfectly human, and he identifies fully with sinful humanity in its need'.[12] Whilst the author of Hebrews may not use those precise terms, Heb. 2.5–18 clearly focuses upon the humanity of Christ and supplies the preacher with ample resources for preaching the incarnation.

Restoring the divine image: Hebrews 2.5–9

Christians agree that we have been created in the image of God (Gen. 1.26–28), and that this bestows dignity and value upon each and every individual. Disagreement arises over attempts to define the essence of that divine image. For example, does it mainly consist of the ability to think and act rationally, or does it refer to the capacity to enter into relationship with God?

Some argue that humanity's fall into sin has left the divine image so defaced and damaged that people are so depraved as to be incapable of any genuine good. A more balanced theological perspective says that whilst every aspect of human existence is damaged and distorted by sin, the divine image still remains intact.

Perhaps part of the difficulty here is doing theology back to front. Speculation about how much of the divine image was lost as a result of the fall assumes an ability to resolve those complex disputes as to the essence of the original divine image. It may be better to interpret the divine image eschatologically, as the goal for which human beings were created: something which becomes visible fully for the first time in the person of Jesus Christ. It is he who provides the gold standard judged against which all of us 'fall' short.

An important element of God's intention was to create human beings in the divine image, who would exercise dominion over creation. For 'humanity was put on earth with a mission—to rule over, to keep and to care for the rest of creation'.[13] That mission, entrusted to humanity in Gen. 1.26–28, was reaffirmed in Ps. 8.6–8.

In the christological exegesis of Psalm 8 which unfolds in Hebrews 2, the author sadly observes that in spite of this divine plan, 'we do not yet see everything in subjection to them'.[14] In other words, the chaos and decay visible to all of us are signs that human beings have fallen short of God's intention for them. Mercifully all is not lost, because while everything is clearly not in harmony under the caring control of human beings, 'we do see Jesus, . . . crowned with glory and honor'. Lane explains that 'in Jesus we see exhibited humanity's true vocation. In an extraordinary way he fulfills God's design for all creation and displays what had always been intended for all humankind, according to Ps. 8. He is the one in whom primal glory and sovereignty are restored'.[15]

The doctrines of the person and work of Christ are inseparable

He might taste death for everyone

Whilst the focus in this book is on the incarnation, we have been conscious throughout that it is impossible to keep separate the doctrines of the person and work of Christ. Their co-inherence is evident in Hebrews 2, where the author not only reminds his fearful friends of the one who is truly God and truly man, but also recalls what the God-man has done for them. For a little while, during his incarnation, Christ was 'made lower than the angels' so that he could 'taste death for everyone' (2.9).

Almost two hundred years ago a young minister, starting work in his first parish, was troubled by what he found. In 1825 as John McLeod Campbell visited his parishioners in the village of Rhu, on the shores of the Gareloch, he was disturbed by 'the want of living religion'. In part, the low level of spiritual life in the parish was the result of a preaching tradition which stressed how Christ died only for the elect, an emphasis which left people uncertain as to whether or not they were included within that select group. Searching within for evidences of election did not bring people the assurance of salvation they craved. Campbell was clear that the only secure foundation for Christian assurance was the knowledge that Christ died for all, that he had tasted death for everyone.[16]

Campbell paid a high price for proclaiming that Christ died for all, for he was evicted from the ministry of the Kirk in 1831. The message that Christ tasted 'death for everyone' may be less controversial today, but it is still urgently needed for other reasons. In societies where people place such a high value on feeling and experience, it is important to underline that salvation is based not on how I happen to feel, but on something objective: the cross where Christ tasted death for everyone.

Dying apart from God?

Standard translations of v. 9 state that it was 'by the grace of God', *chariti theou*, that Christ tasted death for everyone. The emphasis upon the grace or generosity of God is important. It stresses that God is not under obligation to satisfy an external law of justice, but that Christ's atoning work is motivated by 'sheer love': by grace.

Some early Greek manuscripts contain the alternative reading 'apart from God', *chōris theou*, which conveys a complementary perspective on Christ's death. This reading, which has a distinguished textual pedigree, provides an echo of Jesus' cry of dereliction from the cross (Mk. 15.34). To acknowledge the profound abandonment experienced by Jesus on the cross does not lead automatically to punitive understandings of atonement, as some may fear, but underscores the profound cost of our salvation.[17]

It is not difficult to imagine that the phrase *chōris theou* could have been changed to *chariti theou* as scribes copied manuscripts by hand. If we follow the principle that the harder text is more likely to be the original one, it may lead us to conclude that the original text may have spoken of Christ dying 'apart from God'.[18] On the other hand, Lane argues that 'it is probable . . . that the reading *chōris theou* originated as a marginal gloss (suggested by 1 Cor. 15.27) to explain that 'everything' (*ta panta*) which is made subject to the Son (cf. Heb. 2:8) does not include God'.[19]

With honourable scholars lining up in support of both translations of

Heb. 2.9, preachers can legitimately exploit the homiletical potential of both approaches. With the passion narrative in mind, to say that it was 'apart from God' that Christ tasted death for everyone points to the Son of God plumbing the depths of abandonment, which cause so many people to cry: My God, why have you abandoned me? Far from contradicting the notion that Christ died for us 'by the grace of God', this intensifies our wonder at the love evident in the cross, highlighting the lengths to which God was willing to go to rescue us from self-destruction.

A sacrifice of atonement

The connections between christology and soteriology are also visible towards the end of Hebrews 2, which portrays Jesus Christ as 'a merciful and faithful high priest', who makes 'a sacrifice of atonement for the sins of the people' (v. 17). This is the first occasion where Jesus is described as a 'high priest', and this theme is explored at length as the letter unfolds.[20]

The refrain 'once for all' (Heb. 7.26; 9.12, 26, 28; 10.10) declares that the perfect sacrifice of obedience has been offered by this high priest, and that this represents the only permanent solution to the problems of sin, guilt and forgiveness. Talk about priests and sacrifice is not abstract, theoretical discussion but something serving the practical purpose of appealing to believers being tempted to abandon their Christian faith. If Christ has offered the perfect sacrifice 'once for all', it would surely be folly to turn away from him.

A friend at hand to share my pain

For the First Sunday of Christmas in Year A, the designers of the Revised Common Lectionary have chosen to place Heb. 2.10–18, which speaks of the one made 'perfect through sufferings', alongside the Gospel reading about Herod's slaughter of the innocents (Mt. 2.13–23).[21] Lest we be tempted to spend too long cooing at the baby in the manger, the Gospel reading shocks and awakens us to realize that the Word entered fully into a brutal, violent world, where innocents are still being slaughtered by war, poverty and preventable disease. Faced with the realities of that world, the preacher is called to point to the pioneer of our salvation who was made 'perfect through sufferings' (Heb. 2.10).

The pioneer of salvation

A few months ago I was leading a study day for a group of preachers in the west of England. During a lull in the proceedings, one lady asked if she could pose a question that had always puzzled her. 'What does it mean when it says in Hebrews that Jesus was made perfect? Wasn't he perfect already?' It is a reasonable question, given that Heb. 2.10 says that Jesus, the pioneer of salvation, was made 'perfect through suffering'.

One response to that question would be to note Craddock's observation that 'in the LXX, "to perfect" is used to describe the consecration of the priest (Exod. 29.9; Lev. 16.32; Num. 3.3), and in view of the movement toward the presentation of Jesus as high priest, the cultic use of the term in the LXX must lie close to the writer's intention'.[22] So while there is no sense here that Jesus was in any way imperfect to begin with, his experiences of pain and suffering acted as a process preparing and consecrating him for the work of high priest.

The title 'pioneer' translates the word *archēgos*, which can carry the idea of someone who blazes a trail for others to follow, and may also convey the idea of a champion fighting on behalf of others. In the sermon that follows later in this chapter, the figure of the pioneer as the trailblazer introduces the idea that Jesus has shared the pain and the suffering which is our default experience. 'It was fitting' (Heb. 2.10) for this to happen, for as Montefiore comments, 'it was appropriate that the action taken to help man should include suffering, since suffering is mankind's common lot'.[23] By virtue of his experience of suffering, Jesus becomes perfectly qualified to be the one who blazes a trail in and through suffering which others can follow.

The language may be a little old-fashioned, but Calvin's comments on Heb. 2.17 helpfully convey the idea that the sufferings and testing which Jesus experienced fully equipped him to help us face whatever trials life throws at us. According to Calvin, it was not that God in any way needed some additional experiences in order to know exactly what we face, but that Jesus Christ willingly endured these sufferings to persuade us that he was truly trustworthy.

It was not because the Son of God needed to experience it to become accustomed to the emotion of mercy, but because He could not persuade us that He is kind and ready to help us, unless He had been tested by our misfortunes: and this like other things He has given us. Whenever, therefore, all kinds of evils press upon us, let this be our immediate consolation, that nothing befalls us which the Son of God has not experienced Himself, so that He can sympathize with us; and let us not doubt that He is in it with us as if He were distressed along with us.[24]

Who do you think you are?[25]

Perhaps it is a function of growing older, but I find myself becoming more interested in tracing bits of our family history. Judging from the magazines, websites and TV programmes devoted to tracing the ancestors, it seems that lots of others share that interest.

There are many interesting people it would be nice to be related to, but Hebrews 2 makes the startling claim that, by virtue of the incarnation, Jesus Christ has adopted me into his family. What an encouraging message for those first-century Christians fearing persecution and possible death to know that the living Christ gladly acknowledges them as his family and stands with them in their predicament. He announces his solidarity with this small faithful remnant, who are facing such difficulties, and proudly declares, 'Here am I and the children whom God has given me' (Heb. 2.13).

The fact that Christ has identified fully 'with sinful humanity in its need'[26] comes across clearly in the declaration that Christ 'had to become like his brothers and sisters in every respect' (2.17). This language expresses the idea that Christ has assumed our fallen human nature and not some sanitized version of it. It is because he has become like us 'in every respect' that he is able to experience and endure the full power of the tests and temptations which everyone faces. Referring to Jesus' plumbing the depths of our human condition in order to redeem it, Pope Benedict says that 'the Letter to the Hebrews is particularly eloquent in stressing that Jesus' mission, the solidarity with all of us that he manifested beforehand in his Baptism, includes exposure to the risks and perils of human existence'.[27]

Tested as we are, . . . yet without sin

As a result of sharing our fallen humanity, Jesus Christ is exposed to the 'risks and perils of human existence', but as Heb. 4.15 declares, while he was tested in every respect as we are, the miracle is that he was 'without sin'. Once again, it is important to avoid lapsing into the cartoon theology mentioned earlier. As Ivor Davidson puts it,

> Son though he is, he *learns* obedience through what he suffers (Heb. 5.7–10). His human career has a moral and spiritual history, and involves real challenges, trials and frustrations; it is not an untroubled existence in which humanity is somehow calmly steered through the world by divine autopilot, or in which there is serene constancy of insights into what lies around the corner.[28]

Enabled not to sin

Colin Gunton expresses disquiet with some of the traditional ways of explaining how Jesus could be exposed to real temptations and remain 'without sin'. The idea that 'he was *unable* to sin' (*non potuit peccare*) runs the risk of undermining Jesus' full humanity by implying that he was 'automatically immune' to temptation. Similarly the notion that 'he *was able* not to sin' (*potuit non peccare*) might suggest that this human being, even without God's help, had the power to do God's will.

Gunton claims that 'if this man is truly to be the author and pioneer of our faith, [we need] a stronger sense of the fact that the incarnate Word is like us in requiring divine enabling if he is to remain faithfully human. Must we not say rather . . . that 'He *was enabled* not to sin', enabled, that is, by the Spirit, the mediator of all God's perfecting action?'[29] Although the Holy Spirit's role is not explained in great detail in Hebrews, the stress on Christ's offering the sacrifice of perfect obedience 'through the eternal Spirit' (9.14) implies that it was through his reliance on the Spirit that the incarnate Son fulfilled his mission. So we see Jesus full of the Spirit, learning obedience through what he suffered, resisting temptation and offering himself to God upon the cross.

An elder brother

One of the joys of living in the global city of London is the diversity of its peoples. For the last twenty years, my Christian experience has been deepened in all sorts of ways through belonging to congregations made up of people from many tribes and nations.

One of my West African friends is the senior brother of an extended family with several branches in different parts of the city. Being the senior brother of an African diaspora family in London means that he has a responsibility to come to the aid of any members of the family who are in need. So if a nephew ends up in trouble late at night in another part of the city, it is his responsibility as the senior brother to drop whatever he is doing and go to help sort things out. Within the extended family, which still functions in many parts of the world, the elder brother plays a strategic role, intervening on behalf of those facing difficulties.

Knowing that, it comes as no surprise to me that when Diane Stinton asked African Christians about their understanding of Christ, she discovered that one popular image of Jesus was as the elder brother. For 'the image of Jesus as brother is said to communicate his humanity in a meaningful way, incorporating notions of intimacy and solidarity, contemporary presence and availability, protection from harm, and peace amid the hostilities of divided humanity'.[30]

This is the kind of worldview we see in Hebrews 2. Jesus has adopted us into his family, and as our elder brother he has taken upon himself the task of rescuing us from the tyrants of sin, evil and death which oppress us. The good news we are called to proclaim is that whatever our family background, there is an unbroken family bond with this elder brother, who is fully committed to helping us.

Breaking death's grip

It was a bit surprising to hear a minister saying that lots of Christians tell him that they have never heard a sermon about death and dying. Then again, thinking about the sermons I have preached and listened to over the last few years, maybe it is not so surprising.

Perhaps our reluctance to preach about death, apart from rather briefly at funerals, is partly a reaction against a manipulative style of preaching which used the fear of death as a way of frightening people into the kingdom. Another factor could be the popularity of pragmatic approaches to preaching which offer five steps to successful living, or several keys to healthy relationships.

With characteristic candour, Tony Campolo argues that the major emphasis of evangelical Christianity has become 'self-centredness'. If we doubt his analysis, he advises us to

> go to the Christian bookstores and see how many of the books are concentrated on how you can become more Christian, more spiritual, more holy, more sanctified, more joyful and so on. It is totally self-centred, and the fact that you put Jesus into it doesn't change a thing. In the end, Jesus is only a means for you to become 'all that you can be'.[31]

Whatever the causes, there is a low level of theological literacy and a lot of confusion amongst Christians about orthodox beliefs about death and eternal life.[32] Not surprisingly, that confusion is similarly visible in surveys of public opinion. In 2009 a research project on death and dying in the UK reported that '50% of Britons admit to fearing the process of dying. . . . In the poll of over 1,000 adults undertaken for Theos by ComRes, 20% admit to fearing both the way they will die and death itself. 30% say that they fear the way they will die but not death itself. 25% claim to fear neither death nor the way they will die'.

Paul Woolley, director of Theos, commented on the research findings: 'The proportion of people fearing death in society could be explained by the breakdown of an overarching religious narrative in the culture. It might also have something to do with the lack of experience people have in dealing with death'.[33]

The first readers of Hebrews did not lack experience in dealing with death. The comment in Heb. 12.4, that they had 'not yet resisted to the point of shedding [their] blood', implies not only that they had already experienced persecution, but also that there was a real fear of martyrdom for those remaining faithful to Christ. For people facing such perilous times, the message that Jesus has broken the power of death was desperately-needed good news.

The passage does not offer a detailed explanation about how Christ broke 'the power of death' (2.14), but it seems content simply and confidently to proclaim it. This passage lends support to the *Christus Victor* model of atonement, which sees the work of Christ in terms of victory over sin, death and evil.[34] Although Christ's resurrection is not mentioned here, it is surely implicit in any claim to have destroyed the one who 'has the power of death' (Heb. 2.14–15).

The language used in Hebrews 2 is reminiscent of Sir. 40.1–5a, which declares that the reality of death means that rich and poor alike experience anxiety.

> Perplexities and fear of heart are theirs,
> and anxious thought of the day of their death. (40.2)

Even if most of the time our material comforts succeed in distracting us from that anxiety about our own mortality, that 'fear of heart' still lingers on beneath the surface, making its painful presence felt from time to time. This underlines the constant need to proclaim the good news that the one who is truly God and truly man is the pioneer who has blazed a trail 'through the valley of the shadow of death' (Ps. 23.4 KJV).

Now perhaps some may fear that encouraging preachers to put death back on the agenda means reverting to sermons playing on people's fears. Or they may be fearful that it represents yet another appeal to self-centredness, encouraging people to be concerned about their own survival beyond death above all other concerns. There are, however, good grounds for suggesting that the opposite can be the case, that a lively theology of hope can inspire people to forget their own comfort in order to seek first the kingdom of God.

Richard Bauckham and Trevor Hart suggest that most people in richer nations live in societies where 'the fear of death and loss hold the majority subconsciously in its grip'. Their argument is that 'we struggle for more, because we are afraid that this is all there is'; but since there is never enough to go around, an aggressive competitiveness for scarce resources develops. It is only when the fear of death is removed that we can be 'set free from the security blanket which our earthly possessions become, and then we can give away what we have for the common good . . . without fearing that we shall lose out in doing so'.[35]

In other words, without a clear future hope of sharing in God's eternal kingdom, we are tempted to play safe and look after number one. The absence of a living hope means that people are less likely to commit themselves to seeking the common good and 'building for the kingdom'.[36] The good news of the pioneer of our salvation, who has broken death's grip by his death and resurrection, provides the foundation for Christian hope. Biblical hope is practical eschatology which inspires people to serve God and others here and now. Exploring that living hope further, however, must be left for another day or for another book!

The sermon which follows deliberately did not try to cover all of these topics but seeks to convey something of this less-familiar story about the humanity of Jesus.

Sermon: Living well . . . in suffering*

Peter Stevenson

[*The church building is located at the One Mile mark for the London Marathon. One Sunday morning each year, thousands of runners come past the church. The sermon started with two pictures of competitors from the marathon streaming past the church.*]

Last Sunday we mentioned the church's location at the One Mile mark for the London Marathon and talked about *all the saints*, about all of God's people who're running the race of faith and encouraging others to run the race of faith. And when there are 35,000 brave souls *running the race* in the London marathon, trying to keep going for 26 miles and 385 yards, I suspect that along the way some of those runners fall by the wayside.

*Preached by Dr Peter Stevenson at Blackheath and Charlton Baptist Church, London, on Sunday, 9 November 2008.

And that image of *running the race* is a well-known image for the Christian life. For the race of faith is not some 100-metre sprint—it's a lifelong marathon, *running with perseverance* the race marked out for us, with our eyes firmly fixed on Jesus, the pioneer and perfecter of our faith.

Some people in church this morning have been running the race of faith for many years, and others here are at the earlier stages of their Christian journey. I've been running the race of faith for over thirty years; during that time it's been sad to notice how some people have dropped out of the race, and appear to've dropped out of Christian faith. And the letter to the Hebrews was addressed to believers who were having a hard time. It's addressed to Christians who're being tempted to drop out of the race of faith.

But why is it that some people drop out of the race of faith?

A little while ago I received a letter telling me about a friend whose faith in God has been sorely tested by the great wave of suffering and death caused by the tsunami on Boxing Day 2004. And for some people it's the problem of pain and suffering which causes them to falter.

But I suspect that far more people fall by the wayside in terms of Christian faith because they've been treated badly, treated in an unloving way by their fellow Christians.

Others stumble and fall because they've only ever been offered a small-scale, diluted, domesticated version of Christianity that just isn't strong enough to cope with the pressures that a fast-changing world brings.

One preacher suggests that the Christians who first read the letter to the Hebrews were simply exhausted:

> They are tired—tired of serving the world, tired of worship, tired of Christian education, tired of being peculiar and whispered about in society, tired of the spiritual struggle, tired of trying to keep their prayer life going, tired even of Jesus. . . . Tired of walking the walk, many of them are considering taking a walk, leaving the community and falling away from faith.[37]

And how does this Christian pastor who wrote the letter to the Hebrews respond to this problem? Well, . . . the short answer is that he responds to this pastoral crisis by encouraging them to do some serious theology. And so in chapter 1 of this letter, he reminds them that Jesus Christ is fully divine.

[*At this point we read Heb. 1.1–3*]

And then in chapter 2 the emphasis switches to declare that Jesus Christ is not just fully divine; but he's also fully human. He's not just the image of the invisible God who reveals what God is like; but he's also the image of the invisible God who shows us what it means to be fully human.

And this Jesus, who's fully human as well as fully divine, is the one who's perfectly qualified, who's perfectly able to help them face these challenging times. '*Because [Jesus] himself suffered when he was tempted, he is able to help those who are being tempted*'—which really means '*those who are being tempted to give up*' (2.18 NIV).

Our reading this morning highlights a number of reasons why this Jesus is perfectly qualified to help us to live well even in the midst of suffering.

First, we see that Jesus is perfectly qualified to help us live well in suffering because he's shared our humanity to the full.

In Hebrews 2.14 we hear that '*since the children have flesh and blood, Jesus too shared in their humanity*' (NIV); and in verse 17 we hear that Jesus had to be '*made like his brothers and sisters in every way*' (TNIV).

Now perhaps in church we're more familiar with affirming and defending the fact that Jesus Christ truly is the Son of God—and that's clearly vital and important. But alongside that we also need to affirm that Jesus Christ was fully human. That when God came to earth in the person of his Son, Jesus Christ, he didn't become almost human—or just like a human being.

When God came to earth in the person of his Son, the miracle and the wonder of it was that

the Word became flesh;
    the Son of God took our human nature.
        He shared our humanity to the full.

Listen to how the great Reformer Martin Luther put it:

Christ became a mortal like any other human being of flesh and blood. He did not flutter about like a spirit, but he dwelt among human beings. He had eyes, ears, mouth, nose, chest, stomach, hands and feet, just as you and I do. He took the breast. His mother nursed him as any other child is nursed.[38]

So when we celebrate that '*the Word became flesh and dwelt among us*' (Jn. 1:14 NKJV), and when we say with Hebrews 2 that Jesus Christ had to be '*made like his brothers and sisters in every way*', we're saying something absolutely amazing because we're saying that God loved the world so much that he sent his Son

• to share our life to the full.
• to share our humanity.
• to share in the whole range of experiences from birth to death.

1. Jesus is perfectly qualified to help us live well in suffering because
2. he's shared our humanity to the full.

Jesus is perfectly qualified to help us live well in suffering because he's shared the suffering which all of us must face.

Many years ago at university, every Saturday night I attended meetings of the Christian Union. And one night a husband and wife came to give the Bible exposition. The husband taught at the local theological college and was no doubt used to addressing large congregations; but it's what his wife said that made the biggest impact.

This lady looked at all these young men and women on the threshold of life and said something like this: 'I don't know exactly what the future holds for you. You have all sorts of hopes and plans. But one thing I can guarantee is that you will encounter suffering'.

And she was absolutely right: suffering's an inevitable ingredient of life in this fragile, damaged world. And the good news is that God came in the person of his Son to share in the pain and suffering that causes people to cry out, 'My God, my God, why have you forsaken me?' (Mk. 15.34). And that's what's in mind here in Hebrews 2.10, where we read: 'In bringing many sons and daughters to glory, it was fitting that God, for whom and through whom everything exists, should make the author of their salvation perfect through suffering' (TNIV).

It's not that Jesus Christ was in any way imperfect before, but by passing through the pain and suffering that everyone must face, Jesus Christ was perfectly equipped and perfectly qualified to help us and save us.

A Sri Lankan preacher puts it like this:

> The incarnation speaks of a God who is entangled with our world, who immerses himself in our tragic history, who embraces our humanity with all its vulnerability, pain and confusion, including our evil and our death. God is neither absent from nor irrelevant in our age, because he knows for himself the experience of unjust suffering and death. Here is a God who comes to us . . . to suffer brualization and dehumanization at the hands of his creatures.[39]

Because this Jesus has shared in our humanity and shared in the pain and suffering that we all must face, he's uniquely qualified to be the Pioneer of our Salvation:

1. Jesus is perfectly qualified to help us live well in suffering because he's shared our humanity to the full.

2. And second, Jesus is perfectly qualified to help us live well in suffering because he's shared the suffering which all of us must face.
3. And third, Jesus is perfectly qualified to help us live well in suffering because he's experienced and overcome death.

The big news this last week has certainly been the historic election of Barack Obama as the next, forty-fourth, president of the United States. From whatever angle you look at it, his election is remarkable: he's not been active in politics very long, and yet he's been elected to the most powerful post in the world.

He's broken through the 'bitter legacy of slavery and bigotry'.[40] He's broken through barriers of racism and prejudice in a land where rigid segregation between black and white was still in place in the South back in the 1950s and 1960s. On Tuesday night one lady at the big celebration rally in Grant Park in Chicago said, *'I am 63 years old. I marched with Dr King in Selma, Alabama, and I never thought this day would come. . . . The day has come when anybody in America can be who they want to be'.*[41]

'The day has come when anybody in America can be who they want to be'.
Well, it may not be quite as simple as that, but what's clearly true is that

Barack Obama's a pioneer;
    he's a trailblazer;
        he's overcome obstacles;
            he's broken through barriers; and
                he's blazed a trail so that others can follow in his path.

Now when Hebrews 2 describes Jesus as the *author* of their salvation, the word *author* carries with it the sense of the *pioneer* or the *trailblazer*. For Jesus Christ is someone who's blazed a trail for us to follow—and in his case it's an even more amazing story than the story of Barack Obama because Jesus has blazed a trail through suffering and death. He's pioneered a way through suffering and death that leads to God and leads to eternal life.

[*At this point we read Heb. 2.14–15.*]

Jesus the Pioneer, the Trailblazer, has endured death for us, and in that way he's broken the power of death so that everyone could be free from the fear of death. Jesus is the pioneer of salvation who's blasted a pathway through death that leads to eternal life.

One preacher sums it up like this:

Jesus bears the scars of the cross, the scars of human suffering and death, and he was 'tested by what he suffered' (2.18). For all of us who must still face suffering, for all of us who must still trudge to the cemetery in sorrow, we are not without comfort and help, for the great high priest who sits on the throne of glory has been there too. He bears the scars of his testing and 'he is able to help those who are tested'.[42]

Each year Remembrance Sunday reminds me of my late father, because one of the most important experiences of his life was his wartime service during the Second World War. Now one legacy of that time was that my father came back from the war with a serious disability: one of his legs had to be amputated after he was hit by mortar fire as his regiment was advancing into Germany. About twenty years ago Dad wrote down some memoirs, and at one point he wrote about coming home from the war: coming home and starting to come to terms with losing a leg. It was a very painful time. Let me read you a little of what he said:

I was at home. . . . I was still on crutches—awaiting the time when I would be fitted with an artificial limb. In those early days, I was in much more pain than I would ever admit. The . . . pains were severe. One day I had more pain than usual, and I did not know which way to turn in bed to get ease.

It was morning. I can remember seeing Jesus, standing at the door looking at me. . . . I felt then that I had a FRIEND at hand to share my pain.

'*A vision of Jesus—a FRIEND at hand to share my pain*'. Now I'm undoubtedly somewhat biased, but it seems to me that the description of Jesus as 'a friend at hand to share my pain' is a pretty good summary of these verses from Hebrews 2 that we've been looking at this morning. For those verses tell us that Jesus Christ is uniquely qualified to be *a friend at hand to share our pain* and to share our lives.

Jesus Christ is uniquely qualified to be a friend at hand to share our pain and our lives because he was fully human: he shared in our humanity. He's uniquely qualified to be a friend at hand to share our pain because he shared in the pain and suffering and death which we all must face.

And Jesus is uniquely qualified to be *a friend at hand to share our pain* because he rose again from the grave and is alive for evermore. And it's because Christ is alive today and for evermore that he's always able to be *a friend at hand to share our pain*, that he's always able to help us to live well even when we face suffering.

In our Old Testament reading this morning we encountered a believer called Job, who was up to his neck in suffering. And in the verses we read, we feel his pain and despair—and the thing that's led to Job's despair is that he doesn't know where on earth to turn to find God so that he can ask God some questions.

[At this point we read Job 23.1–5 and 8–9.]

We understand his pain, but the good news is that we don't have to hunt high and low to find some elusive God. The good news is that God has come to find us—in the person of his Son, Jesus Christ, God has come to share in our pain and suffering. In Jesus Christ we have a friend at hand to share our pain.

So even in suffering, it's possible to live well because the living Christ is with us to sustain us and help us. *'Because he himself suffered when he was tempted, he is able to help those who are being tempted and tested'* (cf. Heb. 2:18 NIV).

Conclusion

Last year Barack Obama published a book called *The Audacity of Hope*, and people voted for someone who offered them hope and the promise of change. Now he carries on his shoulders not only the hopes of millions of Americans, but also the hopes of billions of others around the world. And you know as well as I do that no human being, however brilliant, will be able to live up to that level of expectation: he won't be able to fulfil everybody's hopes.

But we're here this morning because we believe that there is someone who can give hope to us—and to everyone else living on this planet. Faced with a dangerous, violent and volatile world, we proclaim that there is hope, because

- in Jesus Christ we have one who is able to help us to live well.
- in Jesus Christ we have one who is able to help us to live well in good times and in the not-so-good times.
- in Jesus Christ we have one *who is able to help us to live well even when suffering* casts its shadow over life.

For Jesus is the one

- who's shared our humanity to the full.

- who's shared in the suffering that we all have to face.
- who's pioneered and blasted a way through death that leads to eternal life.

[*The sermon concluded by reading Heb. 2.14–18.*]

Sermon commentary

Some years ago Thomas Long suggested that 'good preaching is now much more local'.[43] Another way of saying that would be to suggest that good preaching must be relevant to its immediate context.

For some people it is important that preaching is strong in terms of its 'application'. Maybe I am just not very good at 'application', but I find it hard to legislate in detail for how my sermon might 'apply' to the many different kinds of people in the congregation. It seems to me more helpful to ask questions about the sermon's relevance to its context in the life of a particular congregation. So in assessing students' sermons, I am more likely to ask, 'To what extent did the sermon proclaim a Christian faith that is relevant today? Was the sermon appropriate to the context of the worship and the hearers' local context?' Reflecting on this sermon with that in mind, it is clear that it only makes sense when we take into account the different contexts which helped to shape it.

In terms of liturgy, it was preached in the context of a Remembrance Sunday service which included the annual Act of Remembrance for all those affected by war. With wars being fought in Iraq and Afghanistan, such acts of remembrance still touch many raw nerves.

Within the life of the local church, the sermon formed part of a series exploring some biblical perspectives on what it means to 'live well', and this sermon asked questions about what could help people to 'live well' when life brings so much in terms of suffering.

The sermon also stands in a particular historical context, coming just a few days after the historic election of Barack Obama. It affirms that Obama can be seen as a trailblazer, but contrasts him with the different ways in which Jesus, the pioneer of salvation, blazes a trail through suffering and death for others to follow.

On this occasion, the structure leans more in the direction of a traditional three-point sermon than would usually be the case. In earlier stages of my preaching career, I would have used this format much more often. Currently I am more attracted to sermons shaped by narrative or held together by a dominant image. However, on this occasion being sensitive to the form of the biblical material suggested that a more traditional format might be appropriate. Hebrews is an exhortation directed to weary disciples, but it is a closely-argued piece of writing. This suggested that a clearly-structured sermon would be a form-sensitive and suitable way of helping hearers connect with the material.

Kenton Anderson suggests a map of homiletical structures illustrating the different strategies employed by preachers.[44] He advocates 'the Integrative Sermon', which draws on the strengths of the following four approaches:

- Declarative Sermon *Make an argument*
- Pragmatic Sermon *Solve a mystery*
- Narrative Sermon *Tell a story*
- Visionary Sermon *Paint a picture*

In terms of his analysis, the sermon on Heb. 2.5–18 integrates at least three of the four approaches. It has some features of the *declarative* sermon in the sense that it unashamedly seeks to teach people about the humanity of Christ. The sermon is trying to construct arguments that will appeal to both head and heart. It employs some *narrative* techniques by telling a story about a disabled soldier finding comfort in a vision of Jesus. The sermon also seeks to be a *visionary* sermon in the sense that there are images and pictures to appeal to the imagination (e.g. running the race, the trailblazer).

If the *pragmatic* approach requires the preacher to offer practical steps for dealing with problems, then the sermon falls short on that count. However, there was an opportunity after the sermon for people to respond through silence and prayer. I am quite content to give my hearers their share of the responsibility for working out the practical implications of God's Word for their own lives.

Conclusion

Twice a year, we welcome prospective students to college open days. On such occasions our college principal enjoys reading out some words from our founder, C. H. Spurgeon. At the opening of the Metropolitan Tabernacle in London, the Prince of Preachers offered his personal credo:

> I would propose that the subject of the ministry in this house, as long as this platform shall stand, and as long as this house shall be frequented by worshippers, shall be the person of Jesus Christ. . . . If I am asked what is my creed, I reply, 'It is Jesus Christ'. My venerated predecessor, Dr Gill, has left a body of divinity, admirable and excellent in its way; but the body of divinity to which I would pin and bind myself for ever, God helping me, is not his system, or any other human treatise; but Christ Jesus, who is the sum and substance of the gospel, who is in himself all theology, the incarnation of every precious truth, the all-glorious personal embodiment of the way, the truth and the life.[1]

In writing this book, we have not sought to impose a particular theological system. Our approach has been to engage with a variety of texts and to see what they contribute to our understanding of the person of Christ. Our understanding of incarnation has been enriched by listening to insights from different parts of the Christian family.

In the course of our explorations, we have discovered something of what Spurgeon had in mind when he talked about Christ Jesus, 'who is in himself all theology'. All the major doctrines of Christian faith are interrelated; and by exploring christology, we have been forced into thinking about other great themes, such as the work of Christ and the trinitarian nature of God.

At the end of *Preaching the Incarnation*, our hope is that there are enough resources here to provoke you into exploring further both the biblical texts and the theological themes. The sermons we have included do not represent the only ways of preaching the incarnation from these texts, yet we hope that they will stimulate you to proclaim the miracle of incarnation in your own preaching voice.

Focusing on incarnation does not solve all theological problems, but it does take us closer to the heart and centre of Christian faith.

Bibliography

Adams, Samuel L, 'Servant Leadership and the Earth: Philippians 2:1–13', *Journal for Preachers* 31.4 (2008), pp. 29–33.

Anderson, Kenton C., *Choosing to Preach: A Comprehensive Introduction to Sermon Options and Structures* (Grand Rapids, MI: Zondervan, 2006).

Auerbach, Erich, *Mimesis: The Representation of Reality in Western Literature* (trans. Willard R. Trask; Princeton, NJ: Princeton University Press, 1953).

Backhouse, Robert (ed.), *The Autobiography of C. H. Spurgeon: Compiled by His Wife and Private Secretary* (London: Hodder & Stoughton, 1993).

Balthasar, Hans Urs von, *Mysterium Paschale* (Edinburgh: T&T Clark, 1990).

Barrett, C. K., *A Commentary on the Epistle to the Romans* (London: A & C Black, 1971).

Barth, K., *Church Dogmatics*, vol. I, *The Doctrine of the Word of God*, part 2 (Edinburgh: T&T Clark, 1956).

—— *Church Dogmatics*, vol. IV, *The Doctrine of Reconciliation*, part 1 (Edinburgh: T&T Clark, 1956).

—— *Church Dogmatics*, vol. IV, *The Doctrine of Reconciliation*, part 2 (Edinburgh: T&T Clark, 1958).

Bartholomew, Craig, *Reading Proverbs with Integrity* (GBS 22; Cambridge: Grove, 2001).

Bauckham, Richard, *Jesus and the God of Israel: God Crucified and Other Studies on the New Testament's Christology of Divine Identity* (Milton Keynes and Colorado Springs: Paternoster, 2008).

Bauckham, Richard, and Trevor Hart, *Hope Against Hope: Christian Eschatology in Contemporary Context* (London: Darton, Longman & Todd, 1999).

Baudrillard, Jean, *Simulations* (trans. Paul Foss, Paul Patton and Philip Bleitchman; New York: Semiotext, 1983).

Beasley-Murray, Paul, *Joy to the World: Preaching the Christmas Story* (Leicester: Inter-Varsity Press, 2005).

Bettenson, Henry (ed.), *Documents of the Christian Church* (Oxford: Oxford University Press, 2nd edn, 1963).

—— (ed.), *The Early Church Fathers: A Selection from the Writings of the Fathers from St. Clement of Rome to St. Athanasius* (Oxford: Oxford University Press, 1956).

Bloom, Harold, and David Rosenberg, *The Book of J* (New York: Vintage, 1991).

The Book of Common Prayer with the Additions and Deviations Proposed in 1928 (Oxford: Oxford University Press, 1928).

Borg, Marcus J., and J. Dominic Crossan, *The First Christmas: What the Gospels Really Teach about Jesus's Birth* (London: SPCK, 2008).

Bonhoeffer, Dietrich, *The Cost of Discipleship* (London: SCM Press, 1959).

Bosch, D. J., K. Kritzinger, W. Saayman, and J. J. Kritzinger (eds.), *Mission in Bold Humility: David Bosch's Work Considered* (Maryknoll, NY: Orbis Books, 1996).

Bowman, Robert M., Jr, and J. Ed Komoszewski, *Putting Jesus in His Place: The Case for the Deity of Christ* (Grand Rapids, MI: Kregel, 2007).

Branick, Vincent P., 'The Sinful Flesh of the Son of God (Rom 8:3): A Key Image of Pauline Theology', *CBQ* 47.2 (1985), pp. 246–62.

Briggs, Richard S., *One God Among Many?* (GBS 42; Cambridge: Grove, 2006).

Brooks, Phillips, 'The First Sunday in Advent', in Ellen Wilbur (ed.), *The Consolations of God: Great Sermons of Phillips Brooks* (Grand Rapids, MI: Eerdmans, 2003), pp. 11–22.

Brown, R. E., *The Birth of the Messiah: A Commentary on the Infancy Narratives in Matthew and Luke* (ABRL; London: Geoffrey Chapman, new edn, 1993).

—— *Jesus: God and Man: Modern Biblical Reflections* (London: Geoffrey Chapman, 1968).

Browne, R. E. C., *The Ministry of the Word* (London: SCM Press, 1958, reissued 1976/1994).

Buechner, Frederick, *Wishful Thinking: A Theological ABC* (New York: Harper & Row, 1973).

Butterfield, Herbert, *Christianity and History* (London: Collins, 1957).

Buttrick, David, *Homiletic: Moves and Structures* (Philadelphia: Fortress Press, 1987).

Caird, G. B., *New Testament Theology* (ed. L. D. Hurst; Oxford: Clarendon Press, 1994).

—— *Paul's Letters from Prison* (New Clarendon Bible; Oxford: Oxford University Press, 1976).

—— *Saint Luke* (Harmondsworth: Penguin Books, 1963).

Calvin, J., *The Epistle of Paul the Apostle to the Hebrews and the First and Second Epistles of St. Peter* (CNTC 12; Grand Rapids, MI: Eerdmans, 1963).

—— *A Harmony of the Gospels: Matthew, Mark and Luke; and James and Jude* (CNTC 3; Grand Rapids, MI: Eerdmans, 1972).

—— *Institutes of the Christian Religion* (ed. J. T. McNeill; Philadelphia: Westminster Press, 1960).

Campbell, John McLeod, *The Nature of the Atonement*, with new Introduction by James B. Torrance (Carberry, UK: Handsel Press, reprint edn, 1996 [1856]).

—— *Notes of Sermons by the Rev. J. McL. Campbell, Taken in Short Hand*, 3 vols. (Paisley: J. Vallance, 1831–32).

—— *Sermons and Lectures, Taken in Short Hand*, vol. II (Greenock: R. B. Lusk, 1832).

Campbell, John McLeod, et al., *Fragments of Expositions of Scripture* (London: J. Wright & Co, 1843).

Campolo, Tony, 'Preaching to the Culture of Narcissism', in Michael P. Knowles (ed.), *The Folly of Preaching: Models and Methods* (Grand Rapids, MI: Eerdmans, 2007), pp. 29–42.

Carmody, John, *Cancer and Faith: Reflections on Living with a Terminal Illness* (Mystic, CT: Twenty-Third Publications, 1994).

Childs, Brevard S., *Exodus: A Commentary* (OTL; London: SCM Press, 1974).

Collins, Adela Yarbro, 'Psalms, Philippians 2:6–11, and the Origins of Christology', *BibInt* 11 (2003), pp. 361–72.

Colwell, John E., *The Rhythm of Doctrine* (Milton Keynes and Colorado Springs: Paternoster, 2007).

Cotes, Mary, 'Standing in the Stable', in Heather Walton and Susan Durber (eds.), *Silence in Heaven: A Book of Women's Preaching* (London: SCM Press, 1994), pp. 4–8.

Craddock, Fred B., *As One Without Authority* (St. Louis: Chalice Press, rev. edn, 2001).

—— 'The Letter to the Hebrews', in Leander E. Keck (ed.), *NIB*, vol. XII (Nashville: Abingdon Press, 1998), pp. 1–173.

Cranfield, C. E. B., *Romans: A Shorter Commentary* (Edinburgh: T&T Clark, 1985).

Crisp, Oliver, 'Did Christ Have *a Fallen* Human Nature?' *IJST* 6.3 (2004), pp. 270–88.

Culpepper, Alan, 'The Gospel of Luke', in *NIB*, vol. IX (Nashville: Abingdon, 1995), 1–490.

Davidson, Ivor J., 'Pondering the Sinlessness of Jesus Christ: Moral Christologies and the Witness of Scripture', *IJST* 10.4 (2008), pp. 385–86.

Dawkins, Richard, *The God Delusion* (London and Toronto: Bantam Press, 2006).

Day, David, *Embodying the Word: A Preacher's Guide* (London: SPCK, 2005).

Dearman, J. Andrew, 'Theophany, Anthropomorphism and the *Imago Dei*: Some Observations about the Incarnation in the Light of the Old Testament', in Stephen T. Davis, Daniel Kendall, SJ, and Gerald O'Collins, SJ (eds.), *The Incarnation: A Symposium* (Oxford: Oxford University Press, 2002), pp. 31–46.

Dorries, David W., 'Nineteenth Century British Christological Controversy, Centring upon Edward Irving's Doctrine of Christ's Human Nature' (PhD. diss., Aberdeen University, 1987).

Dunn, J. D. G., *Christology in the Making: An Inquiry into the Origins of the Doctrine of the Incarnation* (London: SCM Press, 1980; 2nd edn, 1989).

—— *The Epistles to the Colossians and to Philemon: A Commentary on the Greek Text* (NIGTC; Grand Rapids, MI: Eerdmans; Carlisle, UK: Paternoster, 1996).

—— 'Paul's Understanding of the Death of Jesus as Sacrifice', in S. W. Sykes (ed.), *Sacrifice and Redemption: Durham Essays in Theology* (Cambridge: Cambridge University Press, 1991).

—— 'Prayer', in Joel B. Green, Scot McKnight and I. Howard Marshall (eds.), *Dictionary of Jesus and the Gospels* (Downers Grove, IL: InterVarsity, 2002), pp. 617–25.

—— *Romans 1–8* (WBC 38A; Dallas: Word, 2002).

—— *The Theology of Paul the Apostle* (Edinburgh: T&T Clark, 1998).

Dyrness, William A., and Veli-Matti Kärkkäinen, (eds.), *Global Dictionary of Theology* (eds.), (Downers Grove, IL: InterVarsity Press; Nottingham: Inter-Varsity Press, 2008).

Fee, Gordon D., 'St Paul and the Incarnation: A Reassessment of the Data', in Stephen T. Davis, Daniel Kendall, SJ, and Gerald O'Collins, SJ (eds.), *The Incarnation: A Symposium* (Oxford: Oxford University Press, 2002), pp. 62–92.

Fitzmyer, Joseph A., *Romans* (AB 33; Garden City, NY: Doubleday, 1993).

Florence, Anna Carter, *Preaching as Testimony* (Louisville, KY: Westminster John Knox Press, 2007).

France, R. T., *The Gospel of Mark: A Commentary on the Greek Text* (NIGTC; Grand Rapids, MI: Eerdmans, 2002).

Fretheim, Terence E., *Exodus* (IBC; Louisville, KY: John Knox Press, 1991).

Gillman, Florence Morgan, 'Another Look at Romans 8:3: "'In the Likeness of Sinful Flesh"', *CBQ* 49.4 (1987), pp. 597–604.

Gordon, Robert P., 'A Warranted Version of Historical Biblical Criticism? A Response to Alvin Plantinga', in Craig Bartholomew, C. Stephen Evans, Mary Healy and Murray Rae (eds.), *Behind the Text: History and Biblical Interpretation*, Scripture and Hermeneutics Series 4 (Carlisle, UK: Paternoster; Grand Rapids, MI: Zondervan, 2003), pp. 79–91.

Green, Joel B., 'Gethsemane', in Joel B. Green, Scot McKnight and I. Howard Marshall (eds.), *Dictionary of Jesus and the Gospels* (Downers Grove, IL: InterVarsity Press, 2002), pp. 265–68.

—— *The Gospel of Luke* (NICNT; Grand Rapids, MI: Eerdmans, 1997).

Green, Joel B., Scot McKnight and I. Howard Marshall (eds.), *Dictionary of Jesus and the Gospels* (Downers Grove, IL: InterVarsity Press, 2002).

Greidanus, Sidney P., *The Modern Preacher and the Ancient Text: Interpreting and Preaching Biblical Literature* (Grand Rapids, MI: Eerdmans, 1988).

Gunton, Colin E., *The Christian Faith: An Introduction to Christian Doctrine* (Oxford: Blackwell Publishing, 2002).

—— *Theology Through the Theologians: Selected Essays 1972–1995* (Edinburgh: T&T Clark, 1996).

—— *Yesterday and Today: A Study of Continuities in Christology* (London: SPCK, 2nd edn, 1997).

Halpern, Baruch, 'Monotheism', in Bruce M. Metzger and Michael D. Coogan (eds.), *The Oxford Companion to the Bible* (Oxford: Oxford University Press, 1993), pp. 524–27.

Hampson, Daphne (ed.), *Swallowing a Fishbone? Feminist Theologians Debate Christianity* (London: SPCK, 1996).

—— *Theology and Feminism* (Oxford: Basil Blackwell, 1990).

Hanson, Anthony Tyrrell, *Grace and Truth: A Study in the Doctrine of the Incarnation* (London: SPCK, 1975).

—— *The Image of the Invisible God* (London: SCM Press, 1982).

Harmon, Steven R., 'Hebrews 2:10–18', *Int* 59 (2005), pp. 404–6.

Hawthorne, Gerald F., *Philippians* (WBC 43; Milton Keynes: Word [UK], 1983).

Helwys, Thomas, *A Short Declaration of the Mistery of Iniquity* ([Amsterdam?], 1612), in H. Leon McBeth, *A Sourcebook for Baptist Heritage* (Nashville: Broadman Press, 1990), 70–72.

Hooker, Morna D., *The Gospel According to Saint Mark*, Black's New Testament Commentaries (Peabody, MA: Hendrickson Publishers, 1991).

——— 'Letter to the Philippians', in Leander E. Keck (ed.), *NIB*, vol. XI (Nashville: Abingdon Press, 2000), pp. 467–549.

Hunter, Alastair, *Wisdom Literature* (SCM Core Text; London: SCM Press, 2006).

Hurtado, Larry W., *Lord Jesus Christ: Devotion to Jesus in Earliest Christianity* (Grand Rapids, MI: Eerdmans, 2003).

Jensen, Richard A., *Thinking in Story: Preaching in a Post-Literate Age* (Lima, OH: CSS Publishing, 1994).

Kapic, Kelly M., 'The Son's Assumption of a Human Nature: A Call for Clarity', *IJST* 3 (2001), pp. 154–66.

Kidner, Derek, *Proverbs: An Introduction and Commentary* (TOTC; Leicester: Inter-Varsity Press, 1964).

Lane, William L., *Hebrews 1–8* (WBC 47A; Dallas: Word, 1991).

——— *Hebrews 9–13* (WBC 47B; Dallas: Word, 1991).

Levison, J., and P. Pope-Levison, 'The New Contextual Christologies: Liberation and Inculturation', in William A. Dyrness and Veli-Matti Kärkkäinen (eds.), *Global Dictionary of Theology* (Downers Grove, IL: InterVarsity Press; Nottingham: Inter-Varsity Press, 2008).

Lewis, C. S., 'Deeper Magic Conquers Death and the Powers of Evil', in Mark D. Baker (ed.), *Proclaiming the Scandal of the Cross: Contemporary Images of the Atonement* (Grand Rapids, MI: Baker Academic, 2006).

——— *Mere Christianity* (London: Collins, 1955 [1952]).

——— *Miracles* (London: Collins, 1960 [1947]).

——— *The Problem of Pain* (Glasgow: Collins, 1977 [1940]).

Long, Thomas G., *Hebrews* (IBC; Louisville, KY: John Knox Press, 1997).

——— *The Witness of Preaching* (Louisville, KY: Westminster John Knox Press, 2nd edn, 2005).

Lowry, Eugene, *The Homiletical Plot: The Sermon as Narrative Art Form* (Atlanta: John Knox Press, 1980).

——— 'Surviving the Sermon Preparation Process', *Journal for Preachers* 24.3 (2001), pp. 28–32.

MacFarland, Ian A., 'Fallen or Unfallen? Christ's Human Nature and the Ontology of Human Sinfulness', *IJST* 10.4 (2008), pp. 399–415.

Marshall, I. Howard, *The Gospel of Luke: A Commentary on the Greek Text* (NIGTC; Exeter: Paternoster, 1978).

Martin, Ralph P., *Carmen Christi: Philippians 2:5–11 in Recent Interpretation and in the Setting of Early Christian Worship* (Cambridge: Cambridge University Press, 1967).

—— *Mark: Evangelist and Theologian* (Exeter: Paternoster, 1972).

McGrath, Alister E. (ed.), *The Christian Theology Reader* (Oxford: Blackwell Publishing, 2nd edn, 2001).

McKane, William, *Proverbs: A New Approach* (OTL; London: SCM Press, 1970).

Middleton, J. Richard, *The Liberating Image: The 'Imago Dei' in Genesis 1* (Grand Rapids, MI: Brazos Press, 2005).

Migliore, Daniel L., *Faith Seeking Understanding: An Introduction to Christian Doctrine* (Grand Rapids, MI: Eerdmans, 2nd edn, 2004).

Montefiore, Hugh, *A Commentary on the Epistle to the Hebrews* (BNTC; London: A & C Black, 1964).

Morgan, D. Densil, *The Humble God: A Basic Course in Christian Doctrine* (London: SPCK, 2006).

Moule, Handley C. G., *Colossian Studies* (London: Hodder, 1898).

Murray, Stuart, 'Interactive Preaching', *Evangel* 17.2 (Summer 1999), pp. 53–57.

Musk, Bill, *Kissing Cousins? Christians and Muslims Face to Face* (Oxford: Monarch Books; Grand Rapids, MI: Kregel Publications, 2005).

Newbigin, Lesslie, 'A Sermon Preached at the Thanksgiving Service for the Fiftieth Anniversary of the Tambaram Conference of the International Missionary Council', *International Review of Mission* 77 (1988), pp. 325–31.

Norris, Kathleen, 'A Word Made Flesh: Incarnational Language and the Writer', in Stephen T. Davis, Daniel Kendall, SJ, and Gerald O'Collins, SJ (eds.), *The Incarnation: A Symposium* (Oxford: Oxford University Press, 2002), pp. 303–12.

O'Collins, Gerald, 'The Incarnation: The Critical Issues', in Stephen T. Davis, Daniel Kendall, SJ, and Gerald O'Collins, SJ (eds.), *The Incarnation: A Symposium* (Oxford: Oxford University Press, 2002), pp. 1–27.

Orwell, George, *Nineteen Eighty-Four* (Harmondsworth: Penguin Books, 1949).

Pannenberg, Wolfhart, *Jesus, God and Man* (Philadelphia: Westminster Press, 1968).

Peskett, H., and V. Ramachrandra, *The Message of Mission* (Leicester: Inter-Varsity Press, 2003).

Peterson, Brian K., 'Philippians 2:5–11', *Int* 58 (2004), pp. 178–80.

Quicke, Michael J., *360-Degree Preaching: Hearing, Speaking, and Living the Word* (Grand Rapids, MI: Baker Academic, 2003).

Rae, Murray A., *History and Hermeneutics* (London: T&T Clark, 2005).

Rahner, Karl, *Theological Investigations*, vol. 5 (London: Darton, Longman & Todd; New York: Crossroad, 1966).

Ramsey, Ian, *Models of Divine Activity* (London: SCM Press, 1973).

Randall, Ian M., *Communities of Conviction: Baptist Beginnings in Europe* (Schwarzenfeld: Neufeld Verlag, 2009).

Ratzinger, Joseph, Pope Benedict XVI, *Jesus of Nazareth: From the Baptism in the Jordan to the Transfiguration* (London and New York: Bloomsbury, 2007).

Robinson, John A. T., *The Body: A Study in Pauline Theology* (London: SCM Press, 1952).

Rogerson, John W., 'Made in the Image and Likeness of God', in Jean Mayland (ed.), *Growing into God: Exploring Our Call to Grow into God's Image and Likeness* (London: Churches Together in Britain and Ireland, 2003), pp. 25–30.

Rowell, Geoffrey, Kenneth Stevenson and Rowan Williams (eds.), *Love's Redeeming Work: The Anglican Quest for Holiness* (Oxford: Oxford University Press, 2001).

Rowling, J. K., *Harry Potter and the Half-Blood Prince* (London: Bloomsbury, 2005).

Schaberg, Jane, *The Illegitimacy of Jesus* (Sheffield: Sheffield Academic Press, 1987).

Schlafer, David J., *Playing with Fire: Preaching Work as Kindling Art* (Cambridge, MA: Cowley Publications, 2004).

—— *Surviving the Sermon: A Guide to Preaching for Those Who Have to Listen* (Boston: Cowley Publications, 1992).

Shuster, Marguerite, 'The Incarnation in Selected Christmas Sermons', in Stephen T. Davis, Daniel Kendall, SJ, and Gerald O'Collins, SJ (eds.) *The Incarnation: A Symposium* (Oxford: Oxford University Press, 2002), pp. 373–96.

Spina, Frank Anthony, *The Faith of the Outsider* (Grand Rapids, MI: Eerdmans, 2005).

Stackhouse, Ian, *The Day Is Yours: Slow Spirituality in a Fast-Moving World* (Milton Keynes and Colorado Springs: Paternoster, 2008).

Sternberg, Meir, *The Poetics of Biblical Narrative: Ideological Literature and the Drama of Reading* (Bloomington: Indiana University Press, 1985).

Stevenson, Peter K., *God in Our Nature: The Incarnational Theology of John McLeod Campbell* (Carlisle, UK, and Waynesboro, GA: Paternoster, 2004).

Stevenson, Peter K., and Stephen I. Wright, *Preaching the Atonement* (Louisville, KY: Westminster John Knox Press, 2009).

Stinton, Diane B., *Jesus of Africa: Voices of Contemporary African Christology* (Maryknoll, NY: Orbis Books, 2004).

Tennent, Timothy C., *Theology in the Context of World Christianity: How the Global Church Is Influencing the Way We Think About and Discuss Theology* (Grand Rapids, MI: Zondervan, 2007).

Thompson, James W., *Preaching Like Paul: Homiletical Wisdom for Today* (Louisville, KY: Westminster John Knox Press, 2001).

Thompson, Marianne Meye, *Colossians and Philemon* (Two Horizons New Testament Commentary; Grand Rapids, MI: Eerdmans, 2005).

Torrance, James B., 'The Contribution of McLeod Campbell to Scottish Theology', *SJT* 26 (1973), pp. 295–311.

—— *Worship, Community and the Triune God of Grace* (Carlisle: Paternoster, 1996).

Torrance, Thomas F., *Incarnation: The Person and Life of Christ* (ed. Robert T. Walker; Milton Keynes: Paternoster; Downers Grove, IL: Inter-Varsity Press, 2008).

—— *Scottish Theology from John Knox to John McLeod Campbell* (Edinburgh: T&T Clark, 1996).

—— *Space, Time and Incarnation* (Oxford: Oxford University Press, 1969).

Underhill, Evelyn, *Collected Papers* (ed. Lucy Menzies; London: Longmans, Green & Co., 1946).

Van Dyk, Leanne, *The Desire of Divine Love: John McLeod Campbell's Doctrine of the Atonement* (New York: P. Lang, 1995).

Vanstone, W. H., *Love's Endeavour, Love's Expense: The Response of Being to the Love of God* (London: Darton, Longman & Todd, 1977).

Wainwright, Geoffrey, *For Our Salvation: Two Approaches to the Work of Christ* (Grand Rapids, MI: Eerdmans, 1997).

Walsh, Brian J., and Sylvia C. Keesmaat, *Colossians Remixed: Subverting the Empire* (Milton Keynes: Paternoster, 2005).

Waruta, Douglas W., 'Who Is Jesus Christ for Africans Today? Prophet, Priest, Potentate', in Robert Schreiter (ed.), *Faces of Jesus in Africa* (Maryknoll, NY: Orbis Books, 1991).

Wegener, Mark I., 'Philippians 2:6–11—Paul's (Revised) Hymn to Jesus', *CurTM* 25 (1998), pp. 507–17.

Weinandy, Thomas G., *Does God Suffer?* (Edinburgh: T&T Clark, 2000).

—— *In the Likeness of Sinful Flesh: An Essay on the Humanity of Christ* (Edinburgh: T&T Clark, 1993).

Westcott, Brooke Foss, *The Epistles of St John: The Greek Text with Notes and Essays* (London: MacMillan & Co., 1883).

Wilson, R. McL., *Colossians and Philemon* (ICC; London and New York: T&T Clark International, 2005).

Witherington, Ben, with Darlene Hyatt, *Paul's Letter to the Romans: A Socio-Rhetorical Commentary* (Grand Rapids, MI: Eerdmans, 2004).

Wright, Christopher J. H., *The Mission of God: Unlocking the Bible's Grand Narrative* (Nottingham: Inter-Varsity Press, 2006).

Wright, N. T., *The Challenge of Jesus* (London: SPCK, 2000).

—— *Colossians and Philemon* (TNTC; Leicester: Inter-Varsity Press; Grand Rapids, MI: Eerdmans, 1986).

—— *Jesus and the Victory of God* (London: SPCK, 1996).

—— 'Jesus' Self-Understanding', in Stephen T. Davis, Daniel Kendall, SJ, and Gerald O'Collins, SJ (eds.), *The Incarnation: A Symposium* (Oxford: Oxford University Press, 2002), pp. 47–61.

—— 'The Letter to the Romans', in Leander E. Keck (ed.), *NIB*, vol. X (Nashville: Abingdon Press, 2002), pp. 393–770.

—— 'Poetry and Theology in Colossians 1:15–20', in *The Climax of the Covenant: Christ and the Law in Pauline Theology* (Edinburgh: T&T Clark, 1992), pp. 99–119.

—— *Surprised by Hope* (London: SPCK, 2007).

Wright, Nigel G., *The Real Godsend: Preaching the Birth Narratives in Matthew and Luke* (Oxford: Bible Reading Fellowship, 2009).

Wright, Stephen I., 'The Phrase "Image of God" in the New Testament', in Jean Mayland (ed.), *Growing into God: Exploring Our Call to Grow into God's Image and Likeness* (London: Churches Together in Britain and Ireland, 2003), pp. 31–44.

Yenson, Mark L., 'Battered Hearts and the Trinity of Compassion: Women, the Cross and Kenosis', *The Way*, January 2006, pp. 51–65.

Zagzebski, Linda, 'The Incarnation and Virtue Ethics', in Stephen T. Davis, Daniel Kendall, SJ, and Gerald O'Collins, SJ (eds.), *The Incarnation: A Symposium* (Oxford: Oxford University Press, 2002), pp. 313–31.

Ziesler, John, *Paul's Letter to the Romans* (Valley Forge, PA: Trinity Press International, 1989).

Notes

Introduction

[1] Dr John Colwell; see John E. Colwell, *Promise and Presence: An Exploration of Sacramental Theology* (Waynesboro: Paternoster, 2005), p. 1.

[2] C. S. Lewis, *The Problem of Pain* (Glasgow: Collins, 1977 [1940]), p. 13. I do not take 'male' as a reflection of the sexism of Lewis' age, but as a label for 'hard-edged', perhaps even 'invasive' (language Lewis uses elsewhere of the incarnation)—certainly dominant characteristics of maleness through much of history. I have always taken Lewis' phrase as a powerful encapsulation of the way in which the truth of God in Jesus impresses itself upon us, rather than in any way suggesting aggressiveness in the person of Jesus (still less the 'maleness' of God himself).

[3] From the Nicene Creed in the translation used in the Anglican Common Worship service of Holy Communion: http://www.cofe.anglican.org/worship/liturgy/common worship/texts/hc/orderone.html#creed.

[4] Gerald O'Collins, 'The Incarnation: The Critical Issues,' in Stephen T. Davis, Daniel Kendall, SJ, and Gerald O'Collins, SJ (eds.), *The Incarnation* (Oxford: Oxford University Press, 2002), pp. 1–27, here p. 19.

[5] http://www.cofe.anglican.org/worship/liturgy/commonworship/texts/hc/orderone .html#creed.

[6] Peter K. Stevenson and Stephen I. Wright, *Preaching the Atonement* (Louisville, KY: Westminster John Knox Press, 2009). The close connection between the doctrines of incarnation and atonement is illustrated in Ch. 6 of that book, which shows how John 1—the classic biblical account of the incarnation—and Athanasius' *De Incarnatio Verbi Dei*—the classic patristic one—are also, in fact, accounts of the atonement.

[7] For this see Davis et al. (eds.), *The Incarnation*.

[8] Jean-François Lyotard, *The Postmodern Condition: A Report on Knowledge* (Manchester: Manchester University Press, 1984).

[9] See Stuart Murray, 'Interactive Preaching', in *Evangel* 17.2 (Summer 1999), pp. 53–57.

[10] On this theme see David Day, *Embodying the Word: A Preacher's Guide* (London: SPCK, 2005); Geoffrey Stevenson and Stephen Wright, *Preaching with Humanity: A Practical Guide for Today's Church* (London: Church House Publishing, 2008).

[11] See the comment in note 6 above.

[12] See Paul Beasley-Murray, *Joy to the World: Preaching the Christmas Story* (Leicester: Inter-Varsity Press, 2005); Marcus J. Borg and John Dominic Crossan, *The First Christmas:*

What the Gospels Really Teach about Jesus's Birth (London: SPCK, 2008); Nigel G. Wright, *The Real Godsend: Preaching the Birth Narratives in Matthew and Luke* (Oxford: Bible Reading Fellowship, 2009).

13 C. S. Lewis, *Miracles* (London: Collins, 1960 [1947]), pp. 115–16.

Chapter 1: The involved 'I am': Exodus 3:1–15

1 On this analogy, see especially the work of Karl Rahner, *Theological Investigations*, vol. 5 (London: Darton, Longman & Todd; New York: Crossroad, 1966), pp. 115–34; cited in Alister E. McGrath (ed.), *The Christian Theology Reader* (Oxford: Blackwell Publishing, 2nd edn, 2001). Space unfortunately forbids detailed treatment of this important topic. I use quote marks round 'God' *not* to imply that the claims of other faiths are inevitably flawed, but as a reminder of how contentious a matter is the nature of God. We should not assume *a priori* that we know the content or supposed referent of the word 'God' in any situation. See further below.

2 The point is well made by Lewis, *Miracles*, p. 118. Strict monotheism, asserting the absolute authority of a single god, Yahweh, who is the creator of the whole world, appears only in later parts of the OT (particularly Isa. 40–55 and some of the Psalms). Many OT expressions of faith in Yahweh do not deny the existence of other gods, merely denying their potency and right to claim Israel's allegiance. Yet even 'strict' monotheism, which is undoubtedly the background against which the claims made by and for Jesus are to be understood, continued to allow for the ideas of a heavenly court, of angels and of Satan (see e.g. John 10.34–36). See Baruch Halpern, 'Monotheism', in Bruce M. Metzger and Michael D. Coogan (eds.), *The Oxford Companion to the Bible* (Oxford: Oxford University Press, 1993), pp. 524–27; Richard S. Briggs, *One God among Many?* (GBS 42; Cambridge: Grove, 2006).

3 Cf. John E. Colwell, *The Rhythm of Doctrine* (Milton Keynes: Paternoster, 2007), p. 31.

4 On the relevance of 'anthropomorphism' and theophanies in the OT for understanding the incarnation, see J. Andrew Dearman, 'Theophany, Anthropomorphism and the *Imago Dei*: Some Observations about the Incarnation in the Light of the Old Testament', in Davis et al. (eds.), *The Incarnation*, pp. 31–46.

5 Terence E. Fretheim, *Exodus* (IBC; Louisville, KY: John Knox Press, 1991), p. 54.

6 There is a long tradition of seeing the 'pre-existent Christ' in such 'human' manifestations of Yahweh. Anthony Tyrrell Hanson finds this in Paul: 'according to Paul the pre-existent Christ whenever he revealed himself appeared in human form': *The Image of the Invisible God* (London: SCM Press, 1982), p. 80.

7 Brevard S. Childs reads the Hebrew preposition *b* here as 'as' (grammatically termed *beth essentiae*) rather than 'in': *Exodus: A Commentary* (OTL; London: SCM Press, 1974), pp. 47, 50.

8 Colwell, *Rhythm of Doctrine*, pp. 32–37; see further his comments on the Exod. 3 story on pp. 16–17.

9 Cf. W. H. Vanstone, *Love's Endeavour, Love's Expense: The Response of Being to the Love of God* (London: Darton, Longman & Todd, 1977), pp. 57–74.

10 Fretheim, *Exodus*, p. 53.

11 The location of Jesus' *resurrected* body has always been a contentious matter for theologians. For a summary and critique of traditional views, see Hanson, *Image*, pp. 24–58.

12 Exodus language and imagery pervade the entire NT (e.g. redemption, the Lamb, blood, deliverance, bondage/freedom, land).

[13] Cf. Joel B. Green, *The Gospel of Luke* (NICNT; Grand Rapids, MI: Eerdmans, 1997), p. 158.

[14] Here, like a string of other OT figures, Moses forms a contrast with the career of Jesus, though in other respects they may display similarities. From the start Jesus was obedient to the will of God, though it did not, to be sure, come easily (Mt. 4.1–11; 26.36–46).

[15] The fact that Yahweh displays emotions so freely is another point of significance in considering the consistency of the incarnation with earlier revelations of God. It both contradicts notions of 'divine impassibility' that were popular among some early Christian thinkers, and also confirms the importance of emotions in understanding human personality and relationships.

[16] See Childs, *Exodus*, p. 75.

[17] Fretheim, *Exodus*, p. 63.

[18] Childs, *Exodus*, 85; Colwell, *Rhythm of Doctrine*, pp. 16–17.

[19] Harold Bloom and David Rosenberg, *The Book of J* (New York: Vintage, 1991), p. 294.

[20] Fretheim, *Exodus*, p. 63.

[21] Fretheim, *Exodus*, p. 65.

[22] On the identification of Jesus with Yahweh, see further the discussion of Phil. 2.5–11 in Ch. 8 below.

[23] Childs, *Exodus*, 84, citing Eusebius, *Praep. Ev.* XI.9ff.; Justin, *Trypho*, 59–60; Irenaeus, *Adv. Haer.* III.6; IV.110; Ambrose, *De Fide* I.13.

[24] See Halpern, 'Monotheism'.

[25] Hanson makes the important point that if the idea of the first Christians *recognizing* God in Christ makes any sense at all, it must imply the necessity of some prior apprehension of who this 'God' was. Acknowledging that different kinds of non-Christian religious experience may certainly be a means of encountering God in Christ, he rightly emphasizes that, nevertheless, 'anyone who comes to recognize God in Christ by such means must then be introduced to the Old Testament. . . . For the Christian the Old Testament must be the normative, regular way by which we recognize God in Christ': Anthony Tyrrell Hanson, *Grace and Truth: A Study in the Doctrine of the Incarnation* (London: SPCK, 1975), p. 79.

[26] Cf. Hanson, *Image*, p. 140: 'We must thus regard the language which the New Testament writers use about Jesus Christ as forming a sort of climax or culmination of what was already known about God in Israel. The incarnation was not the irruption of something entirely new. It was more the full revelation of what was always there, about which the greatest spirits in Israel already knew something'.

[27] On this, see Herbert Butterfield, *Christianity and History* (London: Collins, 1957), esp. pp. 9–12; Meir Sternberg, *The Poetics of Biblical Narrative: Ideological Literature and the Drama of Reading* (Bloomington: Indiana University Press, 1985), passim; Murray A. Rae, *History and Hermeneutics* (London: T&T Clark, 2005), passim.

[28] Frank Anthony Spina traces a fascinating series of episodes in which 'the outsider' is seen as exemplary of true faith in Yahweh, in *The Faith of the Outsider* (Grand Rapids, MI: Eerdmans, 2005).

[29] Elizabeth Barrett Browning, *Aurora Leigh*, bk. vii, lines 820–21.

[30] Hanson, *Image*, p. 142.

[31] Here it will be seen that I tend to side with the 'Antiochene' emphasis in early Christian interpretation (seeing the OT in primarily historical-typological terms) rather than the 'Alexandrian' (seeing it in primarily 'allegorical' or 'spiritualizing' terms).

[32] Dick Cavett, 'Memo to Pretraeus and Crocker: More Laughs, Please', NYTimes

.com, 11 April 2008, http://cavett.blogs.nytimes.com/2008/04/11/memo-to-petraeus-crocker-more-laughs-please/.

33 Cavett, 'Memo to Pretraeus and Crocker'.

34 'Online', lyric by Chris Dubois, Kelley Lovelace, and Brad Paisley (New York: EMI Music Publishing, 2007).

35 Fretheim, *Exodus*, p. 63.

36 Frederick Buechner, *Wishful Thinking: A Theological ABC* (New York: Harper & Row, 1973), pp. 96–97.

37 Buechner, *Wishful Thinking*, p. 97.

38 John Carmody, *Cancer and Faith: Reflections on Living with a Terminal Illness* (Mystic, CT: Twenty-Third Publications, 1994), p. 54.

39 Fred B. Craddock, *As One without Authority* (rev. ed.; St Louis: Chalice Press, 2001), pp. 79–94.

40 Cf. Sidney P. Greidanus, *The Modern Preacher and the Ancient Text: Interpreting and Preaching Biblical Literature* (Grand Rapids, MI: Eerdmans, 1988), p. 199.

Chapter 2: Embodied Wisdom: Proverbs 8 and John 1:1–14

1 See Larry W. Hurtado, *Lord Jesus Christ: Devotion to Jesus in Earliest Christianity* (Grand Rapids, MI: Eerdmans, 2003). Matthew (28.17) and John (20.28) testify that at least some disciples had reached this point before Jesus finally disappeared from their sight.

2 James D. G. Dunn, *Christology in the Making: An Inquiry into the Origins of the Doctrine of the Incarnation* (London: SCM Press, 1980), pp. 168–76.

3 See, for example, the discussion by Gordon D. Fee of the figure of Wisdom as putative background for Paul's understanding of Jesus: 'St Paul and the Incarnation: A Reassessment of the Data', in Davis et al. (eds.), *The Incarnation*, pp. 62–92. Fee seeks to demonstrate that the correspondence between Paul's statements about Christ and Jewish assertions about Wisdom is more tenuous than often proposed.

4 See N. T. Wright, *The Challenge of Jesus* (London: SPCK, 2000), pp. 70–93.

5 No doubt scholars will continue to debate whether the Jewish or Greek connotations are uppermost in John's use of *logos*, though the Jewishness of John's Gospel now tends to be emphasized more strongly than its indebtedness to wider Hellenistic thought. Perhaps this is an example of how too narrow a focus on the intention of the human author can skew a healthy appraisal of a text's significance. Whatever may have been the dominant resonance for John and his first readers, there is surely no doubt that his great Prologue (Jn. 1.1–18) would early on have spoken in a polyvalent way to people of different cultures, as it continues to do today. In the background is the quest of Philo of Alexandria in the first century CE to interpret the Scriptures in terms accessible to Greek thought.

6 A similar, shorter appeal is made by Wisdom in Prov. 1.20–33.

7 'The increasing boldness of the thought, culminating in [Prov. 8.]22–31, is not designed to preoccupy the reader with metaphysics but stir him to decision': Derek Kidner, *Proverbs: An Introduction and Commentary* (TOTC; Leicester: Inter-Varsity Press, 1964), p. 76.

8 There is debate among OT scholars about the sense of this word. William McKane prefers 'confidant': *Proverbs: A New Approach* (OTL; London: SCM Press, 1970), pp. 223, 356–58. But see Alastair Hunter, *Wisdom Literature* (SCM Core Text; London: SCM Press, 2006), p. 103: 'There are mysteries here. Is Wisdom God's consort, or daughter,

or simply a skilled cosmic worker? Along with the uncertainty surrounding v. 22, there is further ambiguity in v. 30. The word translated as "master worker" might also mean "child" or "one who is in a close trusting relationship"—these alternatives clearly match the choices we are offered in v. 22'. Similarity has been noted between Proverbs' portrayal of Wisdom here, and the Egyptian fertility deity Ma'at (see Hunter, *Wisdom Literature*, pp. 101–2). As always with such comparisons, it is important to highlight what is distinctive in the biblical picture as well as what is shared with other cultures: in this case, above all, what marks out Wisdom in Proverbs is her inseparability from Yahweh.

9   Craig Bartholomew, *Reading Proverbs with Integrity* (GBS 22; Cambridge: Grove, 2001), p. 9.

10   For a fuller discussion, see Robert M. Bowman Jr and J. Ed Komoszewski, *Putting Jesus in His Place: The Case for the Deity of Christ* (Grand Rapids, MI: Kregel, 2007), p. 107.

11   Kidner, *Proverbs*, p. 79. See also the discussion of Col. 1.15–16 in Ch. 9 below.

12   Bowman and Komoszewski, *Putting Jesus in His Place*, p. 107.

13   But see n. 3 above.

14   For further discussion of this passage in the light of what it contributes to our understanding of *atonement*, in particular, see Peter K. Stevenson and Stephen I. Wright, *Preaching the Atonement* (Louisville: Westminster John Knox Press, 2009), Ch. 6.

15   'Wisdom' in Proverbs is a female personification, yet the 'Word' in John is a masculine noun. Although translators normally stick to 'he', it should be obvious that in speaking of such divine manifestations, we are moving beyond the realms in which our human gender language is adequate.

16   The text is Prov. 8.1–4, 22–31, one of those set for Trinity Sunday, Year C in the Common Lectionary.

17   McKane, *Proverbs*, p. 342.

18   The first stage of Lowry's 'homiletical plot': Eugene Lowry, *The Homiletical Plot: The Sermon as Narrative Art Form* (Atlanta: John Knox Press, 1980), pp. 28–35.

19   See the rich and evocative treatment of this subject in Day, *Embodying the Word*.

20   On 'instances', see Day, *Embodying the Word*, pp. 74–82.

21   For this way of thinking about preaching, see especially R. E. C. Browne, *The Ministry of the Word* (London: SCM Press, 1958, reissued 1976/1994).

Chapter 3: 'God with us': Matthew 1:1–25 and Luke 1:26–2:21

1   For helpful treatments of these passages with an eye to preaching, see Beasley-Murray, *Joy to the World: Preaching the Christmas Story*; and N. G. Wright, *The Real Godsend*.

2   Mary Cotes, 'Standing in the Stable', in Heather Walton and Susan Durber (eds.), *Silence in Heaven: A Book of Women's Preaching* (London: SCM Press, 1994), pp. 4–8.

3   Preached at St Martin's and broadcast on BBC Radio 4 on 1 May 2008, http://www2 .stmartin-in-the-fields.org/uploadpdfs/sermon/May%201%2008%20GF.pdf.

4   Thomas F. Torrance, *Space, Time and Incarnation* (Oxford: Oxford University Press, 1969), p. 53. Large theological debates have arisen from the question of what happened to Jesus' human flesh when he was no longer visible on earth. On this see T. F. Torrance, *Space*, passim; and Hanson, *Image*, passim.

5   Hence comes the Marxist aversion to the dematerialized version of Christianity propounded by nineteenth-century liberalism, which preached 'a Gospel of timeless events in which there is merely a tangential or paradoxical relation between history and the Kingdom of God' (T. F. Torrance, *Space*, p. 47).

6   As in the so-called 'Athanasian Creed', *Quicunque Vult*: 'Who although he be God and
     man: yet he is not two, but is one Christ. . . . One altogether: not by confusion of
     substance, but by unity of person': from the revised translation in *The Book of Common
     Prayer with the Additions and Deviations Proposed in 1928* (Oxford: Oxford University
     Press, 1928), p. 114.

7   Cf. the view of Wolfhart Pannenberg: 'In its content, the legend of Jesus' virgin birth
     stands in an irreconcilable contradiction to the Christology of the incarnation of the
     preexistent Son of God found in Paul and John': *Jesus, God and Man* (ET, Philadelphia:
     Westminster Press, 1968), p. 143; cited and discussed in R. E. Brown, *The Birth of the
     Messiah: A Commentary on the Infancy Narratives in Matthew and Luke* (ABRL; London:
     Geoffrey Chapman, new edn, 1993), pp. 529–31. My thanks to John Colwell for draw-
     ing my attention to Pannenberg's view.

8   One reason for doubting Jesus' Messiahship, from a Jewish point of view, was his known
     upbringing in the non-royal town of Nazareth. Hence comes Matthew's emphasis on his
     birth in Bethlehem, the city of David (2.1), and how he eventually came to Nazareth
     (2.23). See Richard T. France, *The Gospel of Matthew* (NICNT; Grand Rapids, MI:
     Eerdmans, 2007), pp. 41–42.

9   France, *The Gospel of Matthew*, p. 48.

10   See Borg and Crossan, *The First Christmas*, pp. 103–4. They argue here that 'the earlier
     Christian claim of divine conception led to an anti-Christian accusation of adultery'
     rather than the other way round. However, on the other side, see the careful discussion
     in Jane Schaberg, *The Illegitimacy of Jesus* (Sheffield: Sheffield Academic Press, 1987),
     pp. 157–58, 160–64. Her tentative thesis is that Celsus was right, and that Mary was
     the victim of a rape by a Roman soldier, a historical event given delicate theological
     interpretation by the Evangelists.

11   Schaberg, *Illegitimacy*, passim.

12   Hanson, *Image*, p. 113.

13   If we read the texts in Schaberg's sense, as indicating a 'natural' conception caught up
     into a unique purpose of God, the issue of the different resonances of *'almah* and *parthe-
     nos* becomes less significant. On this view, Matthew reads Isaiah's 'sign' as being simply
     that one who was *now* a young unmarried woman would become pregnant (in the
     normal way) and have a child named 'Emmanuel'; Schaberg believes that this applied
     to Mary too. Schaberg finds an allusion to the law in Deut. 22.23–27 concerning the
     rape of a betrothed virgin. See *Illegitimacy*, 68–73. France thinks the semantic distinc-
     tion between *'almah* and *parthenos* is not as clear-cut as often assumed (*The Gospel of
     Matthew*, p. 56).

14   The echoes of the story of Moses in the early chapters of Matthew are also a part of this
     picture. See Borg and Crossan, *First Christmas*, pp. 105–10.

15   See Robert P. Gordon, 'A Warranted Version of Historical Biblical Criticism? A Re-
     sponse to Alvin Plantinga', in Craig Bartholomew, C. Stephen Evans, Mary Healy and
     Murray Rae (eds.), *Behind the Text: History and Biblical Interpretation* (Scripture and
     Hermeneutics Series 4; Carlisle: Paternoster; Grand Rapids, MI: Zondervan, 2003), pp.
     79–91, here 86; Borg and Crossan, *First Christmas*, pp. 112–13, 202–5.

16   See the excellent treatment in Green, *Luke*, pp. 47–158.

17   For detailed comparison between Matthew's and Luke's infancy narratives, see Borg and
     Crossan, *First Christmas*; Brown, *Birth*; Schaberg, *Illegitimacy*.

18   Cf. Schaberg, *Illegitimacy*, pp. 78–144.

19   Green, *Luke*, p. 133. Cf. the very lucid treatment of the Roman background in Borg
     and Crossan, *First Christmas*, here pp. 159–61.

20 'Those whom he favours' should not be taken as indicating a (perhaps arbitrary) choice by God of a select number on whom to display 'favouritism'. Rather, it is a typically Jewish way of expressing the truth that no good thing happens to humans unless it comes ultimately from God (cf. Jas. 1.17).

21 The phrase (but not the application to these particular stories) is from Erich Auerbach, *Mimesis: The Representation of Reality in Western Literature* (trans. Willard R. Trask; Princeton, NJ: Princeton University Press, 1953), p. 12.

22 Borg and Crossan, *First Christmas*, pp. 25–53.

23 As given, for instance, in Schaberg, *Illegitimacy*.

24 As given, for instance, in Borg and Crossan, *First Christmas*.

25 Cf. Schaberg, *Illegitimacy*, pp. 121, 124.

26 Thomas F. Torrance, *Incarnation: The Person and Life of Christ* (ed. Robert T. Walker; Milton Keynes: Paternoster; Downers Grove, IL: InterVarsity Press, 2008), pp. 98–99, claiming that 'the doctrine of the virgin birth was inserted into the creed partly in order to combat Docetism'.

27 The phrase was used by the Prime Minister Gordon Brown, defending his 'serious' character as suitable for leading the country through the difficult financial crisis that erupted in September 2008.

28 I first heard this phrase from Revd Ian Paton.

29 On the incarnation as 'the end of creation from the beginning', see Brook Foss Westcott, *The Epistles of St John: Greek Text with Notes and Essays* (London: MacMillan & Co., 1883), pp. 274–75; cited in Geoffrey Rowell, Kenneth Stevenson and Rowan Williams (eds.), *Love's Redeeming Work: The Anglican Quest for Holiness* (Oxford: Oxford University Press, 2001), 457.

Chapter 4: From infant to adolescent: Luke 2:21–52

1 Gregory Thaumaturgus, *Twelve Topics on the Faith*, 'Topic XII', in *Ante-Nicene Christian Fathers*, vol. 6, http://en.wikisource.org/wiki/Ante-Nicene_Fathers/Volume_VI/Gregory _Thaumaturgus/Dubious_or_Spurious_Writings/Twelve_Topics_on_the_Faith/ Topic_XII.

2 *Council of Chalcedon*, Actio V, Mansi, vii.116–17; cited in Henry Bettenson (ed.), *Documents of the Christian Church* (London: Oxford University Press, 1943), p. 73.

3 Hanson, *Grace*, pp. 97–98.

4 Hanson, *Image*, p. 96. See also Hanson's discussion of Barth in *Grace*, pp. 100–103; and N. T. Wright, 'Jesus' Self-Understanding', in Stephen T. Davis et al. (eds.), *The Incarnation*, pp. 47–61.

5 Hanson, *Grace*, p. 3.

6 Hanson, *Grace*, p. 19.

7 See Ch. 2 above; and N. T. Wright, *Challenge*, pp. 82–93.

8 N. T. Wright, 'Jesus' Self-Understanding', p. 51.

9 Dunn, *Christology in the Making*.

10 Such poetry may sadly be lacking all too often in contemporary worship and preaching, in which 'mere words' provide a thin substitute for a truly incarnated 'word'. Kathleen Norris makes this point in penetrating fashion: 'People come to church to be reminded of God's presence, to have the hope they know in Jesus Christ reincarnated in their lives. . . . They come seeking language in a world of verbiage, language that will make them more fully present to God, and to each other. And that is a real trick in today's

talk culture': 'A Word Made Flesh: Incarnational Language and the Writer', in Davis et al. (eds.), *The Incarnation*, pp. 303–12, 309.

[11] Richard Crashaw, 'An Hymne of the Nativity, sung as by the Shepheards', in Helen Gardner (ed.), *The Metaphysical Poets* (rev. ed.; Harmondsworth: Penguin, 1972), p. 207, with original spelling.

[12] John Donne, 'Nativitie', in Herbert J. C. Grierson (ed.), *Donne: Poetical Works* (Oxford: Oxford University Press, 1971), p. 290, with original spelling.

[13] Evelyn Underhill makes this point, writing about 'The Distinctive Character of Christian Mysticism': '[Christian mysticism] is different [from other forms of mysticism] because it is based on the Incarnation. . . . The Christian mystic tries to continue in his own life Christ's balanced life of ceaseless communion with the Father and homely service to the crowd. . . . The more profound his contemplation of God, the more he loves the world and tries to serve it as a tool of the divine creative love': from Lucy Menzies (ed.), *Collected Papers of Evelyn Underhill* (London: Longmans, Green & Co., 1946), pp. 114–16; cited in Rowell et al., *Love's Redeeming Work*, p. 570.

[14] Irenaeus, *Adv. Haer.* V.16.2; cited in Linda Zagzebski, 'The Incarnation and Virtue Ethics', in Davis et al. (eds.), *The Incarnation*, pp. 313–31, 317.

[15] See further Green, *Luke*, p. 141.

[16] George B. Caird, *Saint Luke* (Harmondsworth: Penguin Books, 1963), p. 63.

[17] Green, *Luke*, p. 146.

[18] Cf. Brown, *Birth*, p. 461. Brown notes that the child Immanuel from the same section of Isaiah (7.14) is called a 'sign' to the house of David.

[19] Here I take those 'falling' and 'rising' to be different groups of people (so Brown, *Birth*, p. 461). Caird offers another interpretation, perhaps not completely incompatible with this: that Israel as a whole must 'fall and rise', and Jesus their Messiah must lead the way (*Luke*, p. 64).

[20] Green, *Luke*, p. 149.

[21] Green, *Luke*, pp. 148–49, citing Exod. 10.21; Ps. 36.9; Isa. 10.17; 51.4.

[22] For further discussion of Luke's portrayal of disciples, see P. K. Stevenson and S. I. Wright, *Preaching the Atonement* (2005), pp. 76–82.

[23] Acts 3.15; 5.31; the same word is used in Heb. 2:10; 12.2. See Ch. 10 below.

[24] *Adv. Haer.* II.22.4; cited in Bettenson (ed.), *Documents of the Christian Church* (Oxford: Oxford University Press, 2nd edn, 1963), p. 30.

[25] On the high doctrine of incarnation and creation in nineteenth-century Anglicanism, see Rowell et al. (eds.), *Love's Redeeming Work*, p. 370.

[26] Phillips Brooks, 'The First Sunday in Advent', in Ellen Wilbur (ed.), *The Consolations of God: Great Sermons of Phillips Brooks* (Grand Rapids, MI: Eerdmans, 2003), pp. 11–22.

[27] In the twentieth century, Harry Emerson Fosdick was a prominent preacher for whom the incarnation seemed mostly to concern human potential rather than unique divine gift. See the examples in Marguerite Shuster, 'The Incarnation in Selected Christmas Sermons', in Davis et al. (eds.), *The Incarnation*, pp. 373–96, 377, 380–81. T. F. Torrance traces the way in which such an approach was influenced by the Lutheran idea of Christ's humanity as something 'finite with a capacity for infinity' (*finitum capax infiniti*), logically extended by his theological successors to humanity as a whole, contributing thus to the rationalistic idea of 'the capacity of the human spirit for the eternal and necessary truths of the reason': *Space*, p. 41.

[28] Brooks, 'The First Sunday in Advent', p. 22.

[29] I was thinking especially of J. K. Rowling, *Harry Potter and the Half-Blood Prince* (London: Bloomsbury, 2005), e.g. pp. 187–200. The 'Pensieve' is a shallow stone basin

allowing one to immerse oneself in an occasion in the life of one whose thoughts, extracted magically as a silvery substance from the head, have been poured into it.

30 Mal. 3.1–2.

31 Mal. 3.2–5.

32 A common stereotypical designation in the UK referring to the major left-leaning newspaper.

33 See Thomas G. Long, *The Witness of Preaching* (Louisville, KY: Westminster John Knox Press, 2nd edn, 2005), Ch. 4, pp. 99–116.

Chapter 5: 'Who do you say that I am?' Luke 9:18–27

1 Alan Culpepper, 'The Gospel of Luke', in *NIB*, vol. IX (Nashville: Abingdon, 1995), p. 199.

2 N. T. Wright, *Jesus and the Victory of God* (London: SPCK, 1996), pp. 152–53. He is referring here to the work of Robert L. Webb, *John the Baptizer and Prophet: A Socio-Historical Study* (JSNTSup 62; Sheffield: Sheffield Academic Press, 1991).

3 See e.g. Luke 4.24.

4 Kevin Keegan's second spell as manager of Newcastle United Football Club in January 2008 was hailed by the Newcastle fans as the 'return of the Messiah', but in September 2008, he handed in his resignation for a second time.

5 N. T. Wright, *Jesus and the Victory of God*, pp. 482–83.

6 Bill Musk, *Kissing Cousins: Christians and Muslims Face to Face* (Oxford: Monarch Books; Grand Rapids, MI: Kregel Publications, 2005), p. 355.

7 Culpepper, 'Luke', in *NIB*, vol. IX, pp. 18–19.

8 N. T. Wright, *Jesus and the Victory of God*, p. 518.

9 I. Howard Marshall, *The Gospel of Luke: A commentary on the Greek Text* (Exeter: Paternoster, 1978), p. 369.

10 C. S. Lewis, 'Deeper Magic Conquers Death and the Powers of Evil', in Mark D. Baker (ed.), *Proclaiming the Scandal of the Cross: Contemporary Images of the Atonement* (Grand Rapids, MI: Baker Academic, 2006), pp. 37–41.

11 Richard Dawkins, *The God Delusion* (London and Toronto: Bantam Press, 2006), p. 252.

12 This idea is explored more fully in P. K. Stevenson and S. I. Wright, *Preaching the Atonement*, Ch. 6, esp. pp. 92–95.

13 Daniel L. Migliore, *Faith Seeking Understanding: An Introduction to Christian Theology* (Grand Rapids, MI, and Cambridge: Eerdmans, 2nd edn, 2004), p. 168.

14 C. S. Lewis, *Mere Christianity* (London: Collins, 1952), pp. 52–53.

15 Dawkins, *The God Delusion*, p. 92.

16 Musk, *Kissing Cousins*, pp. 340–41; see e.g. Ch. 11, 'Made-up Messiah'.

17 See e.g. N. T. Wright, *Jesus and the Victory of God*, pp. 651–52.

18 N. T. Wright, *Jesus and the Victory of God*, pp. 652–53.

19 Migliore, *Faith Seeking Understanding* (2004), p. 169.

20 Timothy C. Tennent, *Theology in the Context of World Christianity: How the Global Church Is Influencing the Way We Think About and Discuss Theology* (Grand Rapids, MI: Zondervan, 2007), p. 109.

21 Douglas W. Waruta, 'Who Is Jesus Christ for Africans Today? Prophet, Priest, Potentate', in Robert Schreiter (ed.), *Faces of Jesus in Africa* (Maryknoll, NY: Orbis Books, 1991), pp. 52–53.

22 See, for example, the pictures produced in Cameroon to assist the work of local cate-
    chists: http://www.jesusmafa.com/anglais/accueil.htm. The work of the Chinese Christ-
    ian artist He Qi is increasingly well known: see http://www.heqigallery.com/comment
    .htm.

23 See Diane B. Stinton, *Jesus of Africa: Voices of Contemporary African Christology* (Mary-
    knoll, NY: Orbis Books, 2004). The picture of Jesus as the Elder Brother is discussed
    later in this book, as part of the exploration of Heb. 2 in Ch. 10 below.

24 Tennent, *Theology in the Context of World Christianity*, p. 109.

25 Tennent, *Theology in the Context of World Christianity*, pp. 116–17.

26 Dietrich Bonhoeffer, *The Cost of Discipleship* (London: SCM Press, 1948, 1959).

27 Culpepper, 'Luke', in *NIB*, vol. IX, p. 203.

28 Ian Stackhouse, *The Day Is Yours: Slow Spirituality in a Fast-Moving World* (Milton
    Keynes and Colorado Springs: Paternoster, 2008), p. 27.

29 Culpepper, 'Luke', in *NIB*, vol. IX, p. 204.

30 Cicero, *Orator* XX.70.

31 David J. Schlafer, *Surviving the Sermon: A Guide to Preaching for Those Who Have to
    Listen* (Boston: Cowley Publications, 1992), p. 65.

32 Anna Carter Florence, *Preaching as Testimony* (Louisville, KY: Westminster John Knox
    Press, 2007).

Chapter 6: Struggling to obey God: Mark 14:32–42

1   See 'The Human Growth of Jesus', in Ch. 4 above: 'From Infant to Adolescent'.

2   'The Definition of Chalcedon, 451' in Henry Bettenson (ed.), *Documents of the Christ-
    ian Church* (Oxford: Oxford University Press, 2nd edn, 1963), p. 51.

3   D. Densil Morgan, *The Humble God: A Basic Course in Christian Doctrine* (London:
    SPCK, 2006), pp. 42–43.

4   Morgan, *The Humble God*, p. 42.

5   Morgan, *The Humble God*, p. 43.

6   J. D. G. Dunn, 'Prayer', in Joel B. Green, Scot McKnight and I. Howard Marshall
    (eds.), *Dictionary of Jesus and the Gospels* (Downers Grove, IL: InterVarsity Press, 2002),
    p. 619.

7   Dunn, 'Prayer', p. 619. Also see J. D. G. Dunn, *Christology in the Making: A New Testa-
    ment Inquiry into the Origins of the Doctrine of the Incarnation* (London: SCM Press, 2nd
    edn, 1989), pp. 22–33.

8   Morgan, *The Humble God*, p. 43.

9   R. T. France, *The Gospel of Mark: A Commentary on the Greek Text* (NIGTC; Grand
    Rapids, MI: Eerdmans, 2002), p. 582.

10 Joseph Ratzinger, Pope Benedict XVI, *Jesus of Nazareth: From the Baptism in the Jordan
    to the Transfiguration* (London and New York: Bloomsbury, 2007), p. 161.

11 J. Calvin, *Institutes of the Christian Religion* (ed. J. T. McNeill; Philadelphia: Westmin-
    ster Press, 1960), III.8.1.

12 Mk. 14.33–35.

13 France, *The Gospel of Mark*, pp. 582–83.

14 R. E. Brown, *Jesus: God and Man: Modern Biblical Reflections* (London: Geoffrey Chap-
    man, 1968), pp. 104–5.

15 Commentary on Mt. 26.37 in John Calvin, *A Harmony of the Gospels: Matthew, Mark and
    Luke; and James and Jude* (CNTC 3; Grand Rapids, MI: Eerdmans, 1972), p. 147.

16 Calvin, *A Harmony of the Gospels*, p. 147. Calvin's disturbing language about God dealing his Son 'a heavier blow' points to the horror which grips the incarnate Son as the awesome reality of divine judgement strikes home. Calvin bears witness to the profound struggle Christ faced as he was tempted to turn from such a costly mission; and seeks to show how this makes sense within the penal understanding of atonement which he advocates.

17 Morna D. Hooker, *The Gospel According to Saint Mark* (BNTC; Peabody, MA: Hendrickson, 1991), p. 346.

18 France, *The Gospel of Mark*, p. 586.

19 France, *The Gospel of Mark*, p. 585.

20 One early study pointing in this direction was Ralph P. Martin, *Mark: Evangelist and Theologian* (Exeter: Paternoster, 1972).

21 Janet Daley, *The Telegraph*, 6 March 2009, http://blogs.telegraph.co.uk/janet_daley/blog/2009/03/06/obama_was_no_ruder_to_brown_than_brown_was_to_bush.

22 Dr Peter Collett, *The Guardian* Wednesday, 4 March 2009.

23 Joel B. Green, 'Gethsemane', in Joel B. Green, Scot McKnight, I Howard Marshall (eds.), *Dictionary of Jesus and the Gospels* (Downers Grove, IL: InterVarsity Press, 2002), p. 268.

24 Heb. 5.7–9.

25 Brown, *Jesus: God and Man*, pp. 104–5.

26 Dorothy Frances Gurney (1858–1932), 'God's Garden', http://www.all-creatures.org/poetry/godsgarden-dfg.html.

27 See Lieutenant Colonel John McCrae, MD (1872–1918), 'In Flanders Fields' (May 1915), http://www.arlingtoncemetery.net/flanders.htm.

28 Royal Botanic Gardens, Kew, London, http://www.kew.org/.

29 David Buttrick, *Homiletic: Moves and Structures* (Philadelphia: Fortress Press, 1987), p. 23.

30 Buttrick, *Homiletic*, p. 153.

31 Kenton C. Anderson, *Choosing to Preach: A Comprehensive Introduction to Sermon Options and Structures* (Grand Rapids, MI: Zondervan, 2006), p. 123.

32 Anderson, *Choosing to Preach*, p. 124.

Chapter 7: In the likeness of sinful flesh: Romans 8:1–8

1 N. T. Wright, 'The Letter to the Romans', in Leander E. Keck (ed.), *NIB*, vol. X (Nashville: Abingdon Press, 2002), p. 574.

2 See, for example, N. T. Wright, *Jesus and the Victory of God*, Ch. 13, 'The Return of the King', pp. 612–53.

3 John Ziesler, *Paul's Letter to the Romans* (Valley Forge, PA: Trinity Press International, 1989), 201.

4 Phillips Brooks, 'O Little Town of Bethlehem' (1869), http://www.carols.org.uk/o_little_town_of_bethlehem.htm.

5 N. T. Wright, 'Romans', in *NIB*, vol. X, p. 588.

6 Ben Witherington, with Darlene Hyatt, *Paul's Letter to the Romans: A Socio-Rhetorical Commentary* (Grand Rapids, MI: Eerdmans, 2004), pp. 213–14.

7 C. E. B. Cranfield, *Romans: A Shorter Commentary* (Edinburgh: T&T Clark, 1985), p. 178.

8 Witherington, *Paul's Letter to the Romans*, p. 213.

[9] J. Calvin, *Institutes of the Christian Religion* (ed. McNeill), II.13.4. This traditional Reformed position is supported by Oliver Crisp, 'Did Christ Have *a Fallen* Human Nature?' *IJST* 6.3 (2004), pp. 270–88.

[10] Gregory of Nazianzus *Ep.* ci., 'If any one has put his trust in him as a man without a human mind, he is himself devoid of mind, and unworthy of salvation. For what he has not assumed he has not healed; it is what is united to his Deity that also saved': Bettenson (ed.), *Documents of the Christian Church* (1963), p. 45.

[11] T. F. Torrance, *Incarnation: The Person and Life of Christ*, p. 62.

[12] J. D. G. Dunn, 'Paul's Understanding of the Death of Jesus as Sacrifice', in S. W. Sykes (ed.), *Sacrifice and Redemption: Durham Essays in Theology* (Cambridge: Cambridge University Press, 1991), p. 37. Similar conclusions are reached by C. K. Barrett, *A Commentary on the Epistle to the Romans* (London: A & C Black, 1971), p. 156: 'We are probably justified . . . in deducing that Christ took precisely the same fallen nature that we ourselves have, and that he remained sinless because he constantly overcame a proclivity to sin'. See also John A. T. Robinson, *The Body: A Study in Pauline Theology* (London: SCM Press, 1952), pp. 37–38: 'The first act in the drama of redemption is the self-identification of the Son of God *to the limit*, yet without sin, with the body of the flesh in its fallen state'.

[13] Cranfield, *Romans: A Shorter Commentary*, p. 177.

[14] Geoffrey Wainwright, *For Our Salvation: Two Approaches to the Work of Christ* (Grand Rapids, MI: Eerdmans, 1997), pp. 150–51.

[15] 'For what was not assumed, was not healed'; see n. 10 above.

[16] K. Barth, *Church Dogmatics*, vol. IV, *The Doctrine of Reconciliation*, part 1 (Edinburgh: T&T Clark, 1956), pp. 258–59.

[17] Hans Urs von Balthasar, *Mysterium Paschale* (Edinburgh: T&T Clark, 1990), p. 22.

[18] Thomas G. Weinandy, *In the Likeness of Sinful Flesh: An Essay on the Humanity of Christ* (Edinburgh: T&T Clark, 1993), p. 70; see also Thomas G. Weinandy, *Does God Suffer?* (Edinburgh: T&T Clark, 2000), pp. 211ff.

[19] T. F. Torrance, *Incarnation: The Person and Life of Christ*, p. 62.

[20] Karl Barth, *Church Dogmatics*, vol. I, *The Doctrine of the Word of God*, part 2 (Edinburgh: T&T Clark, 1956), pp. 147–59.

[21] Colin Gunton provides a useful introduction to Irving's theology in the essay 'Christology: Two Dogmas revisited: Edward Irving's Christology', in Colin E. Gunton, *Theology Through the Theologians: Selected Essays 1972–1995* (Edinburgh: T&T Clark, 1996), Ch. 9, pp. 151–68.

[22] A useful survey of Campbell's theology can be found in Thomas F. Torrance, *Scottish Theology from John Knox to John McLeod Campbell* (Edinburgh: T&T Clark, 1996), Ch. 9. More detailed studies of his theology are provided by Peter K. Stevenson, *God in Our Nature: The Incarnational Theology of John McLeod Campbell* (Carlisle, UK, and Waynesboro, GA: Paternoster, 2004); and Leanne Van Dyk, *The Desire of Divine Love: John McLeod Campbell's Doctrine of the Atonement* (New York: P. Lang, 1995).

[23] James B. Torrance, 'The Contribution of McLeod Campbell to Scottish Theology', *SJT* 26 (1973), p. 296.

[24] A copy of 'Sermon on Titus 2.11–14' can be found as Appendix 5 in Stevenson, *God in Our Nature*, pp. 312–27, and the footnotes which follow refer to that source. Originally this sermon was published in *Notes of Sermons by the Rev. J. McL. Campbell, Taken in Short Hand*, 3 vols. (Paisley: J. Vallance, 1831–32).

[25] Stevenson, *God in Our Nature*, p. 284.

[26] Stevenson, *God in Our Nature*, p. 285.

27 Stevenson, *God in Our Nature*, p. 286.

28 Stevenson, *God in Our Nature*, p. 288.

29 Weinandy, *Does God Suffer?* p. 236: 'If it is not the Son of God as the risen man who makes present the eschatological Spirit, then it would mean that it was not as man that he obtained our salvation. If the Son of God, as the risen man, does not send forth the Spirit, then what he did as man, in his suffering and death, was not the means by which he obtained his risen lordship so as to be empowered and authorized to send forth the Spirit. As it was as man that the Son died on our behalf reconciling us to the Father, so it is now as the risen man that the Son makes available the fruit of his human suffering and death in the new life of the Holy Spirit'.

30 John McLeod Campbell, *Fragments of Expositions of Scripture* (London: J. Wright & Co, 1843), Ch. 18.

31 Campbell, *Fragments of Expositions*, p. 267.

32 Campbell, *Fragments of Expositions*, p. 269.

33 Campbell, *Fragments of Expositions*, p. 270.

34 Campbell, *Fragments of Expositions*, p. 274.

35 Campbell, *Fragments of Expositions*, p. 275.

36 Cf. Campbell, *Fragments of Expositions*, p. 270: 'The wells of salvation furnish a living spring of water, by which this evil fire of enmity may be quenched: the divine altar furnishes a fire by which this stubble may be consumed'. Cf. p. 273: 'It is by the infusion of this divine life, that we are delivered from the power of the flesh and its evil workings'.

37 Kelly M. Kapic, 'The Son's Assumption of a Human Nature: A Call for Clarity', *IJST* 3 (2001), p. 165.

38 Weinandy, *In the Likeness of Sinful Flesh*, pp. 18–19.

39 Weinandy, *In the Likeness of Sinful Flesh*, p. 49, refers to Aquinas, who claimed that 'the Son assumed a humanity that sin tainted, but did not assume original sin and he did not sin himself. Thus Jesus did not inherit interior moral concupiscence or the "fomes" of sin'. The Latin term *fomes* means 'touchwood' or 'tinder', likely implying a substance which absorbs disease or contagion and kindles it.

40 Campbell, *Fragments of Expositions*, pp. 270, 275.

41 Campbell, 'Sermon 30', in *Sermons and Lectures, Taken in Short Hand*, vol. II (Greenock: R. B. Lusk, 1832), p. 286.

42 N. T. Wright, 'Romans', in *NIB*, vol. X, p. 579.

43 James D. G. Dunn, *Romans 1–8* (WBC 38A; Dallas: Word, 2002), pp. 420–21.

44 The reflexive pronoun *heautou*, means 'his own'.

45 Witherington, *Paul's Letter to the Romans*, p. 213.

46 Richard Bauckham, *Jesus and the God of Israel: God Crucified and Other Studies on the New Testament's Christology of Divine Identity* (Milton Keynes and Colorado Springs: Paternoster, 2008), p. 26.

47 John McLeod Campbell, *The Nature of the Atonement*, with new Introduction by James B. Torrance (Carberry, UK: Handsel Press, 1996), p. 127.

48 Van Dyk's excellent study of Campbell's theology takes its title from this quotation: *The Desire of Divine Love*.

49 The secret working of the Holy Spirit in uniting believers to the ascended Christ is underlined by Calvin: 'But he unites himself to us by the Spirit alone. By the grace and power of the same Spirit we are made his members, to keep us under himself and in turn to possess him'. Calvin, *Institutes* (ed. McNeill), III.1.3.

50 James B. Torrance, *Worship, Community and the Triune God of Grace* (Carlisle: Paternoster, 1996), pp. 18–19.

51 Migliore, *Faith Seeking Understanding* (2004), p. 68.
52 N. T. Wright, 'Romans', in *NIB*, vol. X, p. 590.
53 Campbell, *Fragments of Expositions*, p. 275.
54 Joseph A. Fitzmyer, *Romans* (AB 33; Garden City, NY: Doubleday, 1993), p. 485.
55 James W. Thompson, *Preaching Like Paul: Homiletical Wisdom for Today* (Louisville, KY: Westminster John Knox Press, 2001).
56 J. Thompson, *Preaching Like Paul*, p. 124.
57 J. Thompson, *Preaching Like Paul*, p. 124.
58 N. T. Wright, 'Romans', in *NIB*, vol. X, p. 574.

Chapter 8: The self-emptying Christ: Philippians 2:1–11

1   Colwell, *Rhythm of Doctrine*, Ch. 2.
2   Mark I. Wegener, 'Philippians 2:6–11—Paul's (Revised) Hymn to Jesus', *CurTM* 25 (1998), p. 507.
3   Eugene L. Lowry, 'Surviving the Sermon Preparation Process', *Journal for Preachers* 24.3 (2001), p. 29.
4   Adela Yarbro Collins, 'Psalms, Philippians 2:6–11, and the Origins of Christology', *BibInt* 11 (2003), pp. 361–72, noting that at least since 1928 the majority of scholars have defined this passage as a hymn. However, she sees the passage as a 'brief speech in exalted prose honoring Jesus Christ' which had been composed by the apostle Paul.
5   Bauckham, *Jesus and the God of Israel*, p. 41.
6   G. B. Caird, *Paul's Letters from Prison* (New Clarendon Bible; Oxford: Oxford University Press, 1976), p. 104.
7   Charles Wesley, 1707–88, 'And Can It Be' (1739), http://gbgm-umc.org/umHistory/Wesley/hymns/umh363.stm.
8   Dunn, *Christology in the Making* (1980); Dunn's exposition of Phil. 2.6–11 appears on pp. 113–21. In the second edition of *Christology in the Making* (1989), the treatment of Philippians remains the same; but in the Foreword to that edition, Dunn notes some of the criticisms of his position.
9   Dunn, *Christology in the Making* (1980), p. 119.
10 Dunn, *Christology in the Making* (1980), p. 120.
11 James D. G. Dunn, *The Theology of Paul the Apostle* (Edinburgh: T&T Clark, 1998), pp. 281–88; cf. pp. 286–87.
12 Dunn, *The Theology of Paul*, p. 288.
13 Morna D. Hooker, 'Letter to the Philippians', in Leander E. Keck (ed.), *NIB*, vol. XI (Nashville: Abingdon Press, 2000), pp. 504–5.
14 Bauckham, *Jesus and the God of Israel*, p. 41.
15 Gerald F. Hawthorne, *Philippians* (WBC 43; Milton Keynes: Word [UK], 1983), pp. 83–84.
16 Ralph P. Martin, *Carmen Christi: Philippians 2:5–11 in Recent Interpretation and in the Setting of Early Christian Worship* (Cambridge: Cambridge University Press, 1967), p. 134.
17 Hooker, 'Philippians', in *NIB*, vol. XI, p. 507.
18 Hawthorne, *Philippians*, p. 86.
19 Barth, *Church Dogmatics*, vol. IV, part 1, pp. 179–80.
20 Barth, *Church Dogmatics*, vol. IV, part 1, p. 186.
21 Hooker, 'Philippians', in *NIB*, vol. XI, p. 508.

22 Colin E. Gunton, *Yesterday and Today: A Study of Continuities in Christology* (London: SPCK, 2nd edn, 1997), p. 172.

23 Brian K. Peterson, 'Philippians 2:5–11', *Int* 58 (2004), p. 180.

24 Daphne Hampson, *Theology and Feminism* (Oxford: Basil Blackwell, 1990), p. 155.

25 Sarah Coakley, 'Kenōsis and Subversion', in Daphne Hampson (ed.), *Swallowing a Fishbone? Feminist Theologians Debate Christianity* (London: SPCK, 1996), p. 107. See also Mark L. Yenson, 'Battered Hearts and the Trinity of Compassion: Women, the Cross and Kenōsis', *The Way*, January 2006, pp. 51–65.

26 Bauckham, *Jesus and the God of Israel*, pp. 200–201. The same point is made clearly by Christopher J. H. Wright, *The Mission of God: Unlocking the Bible's Grand Narrative* (Nottingham: Inter-Varsity Press, 2006), p. 109: 'The magnificent prophecies of Isaiah 40–55 assert again and again that YHWH is utterly unique as the only living God in his sovereign power over all nations and all history, and in his ability to save. Therefore Paul, or the composers of the early Christian hymn which he may be quoting in Philippians 2, by deliberately selecting a Scripture from such a context and applying it to Jesus, was affirming that Jesus shares the identity and uniqueness of YHWH in those same respects. So sure was this identification that he (they) did not hesitate to insert the name of Jesus where the name YHWH had occurred in the sacred text'.

27 Bauckham, *Jesus and the God of Israel*, p. 208.

28 Bauckham, *Jesus and the God of Israel*, p. 203.

29 D. J. Bosch, K. Kritzinger, W. Saayman and J. J. Kritzinger (eds.), *Mission in Bold Humility: David Bosch's Work Considered* (Maryknoll, NY: Orbis Books, 1996).

30 Lesslie Newbigin, 'A Sermon Preached at the Thanksgiving Service for the Fiftieth Anniversary of the Tambaram Conference of the International Missionary Council', *International Review of Mission* 77 (1988), p. 328.

31 Bauckham, *Jesus and the God of Israel*, pp. 197; cf. pp. 144–46.

32 See Ian M. Randall, *Communities of Conviction: Baptist Beginnings in Europe* (Schwarzenfeld: Neufeld Verlag, 2009), pp. 23–34.

33 Thomas Helwys, *A Short Declaration of the Mistery of Iniquity* ([Amsterdam?], 1612); extracts appear in H. Leon McBeth, *A Sourcebook for Baptist Heritage* (Nashville: Broadman Press, 1990), pp. 70–72.

34 Richard Dawkins, *The God Delusion* (London and Toronto: Bantam Press, 2006).

35 Ian Ramsey, *Models of Divine Activity* (London: SCM Press, 1973), p. 1.

36 Caroline Noel, 1817–77, 'At the name of Jesus' (1870), http://www.oremus.org/hymnal/a/a388.html.

37 Hans Urs von Balthasar, *Mysterium Paschale* (Edinburgh: T&T Clark, 1990), p. 26.

38 Wegener, 'Philippians 2:6–11—Paul's (Revised) Hymn to Jesus', p. 507.

39 Richard A. Jensen, *Thinking in Story: Preaching in a Post-Literate Age* (Lima, OH: CSS Publ., 1994).

40 Michael J. Quicke, *360-Degree Preaching: Hearing, Speaking, and Living the Word* (Grand Rapids, MI: Baker Academic, 2003), p. 112.

41 Long, *The Witness of Preaching* (2005), Ch. 4.

42 See http://michaelquicke.blogspot.com/2008/04/preaching-incarnation-2.html.

Chapter 9: God's true image: Colossians 1:15–20

1 I use 'Paul' as a convenient cipher for the author of this letter, acknowledging the continuing debate about whether it is indeed from his hand, but not regarding it as

relevant for our purposes. Another complication we cannot discuss here is the frequent claim that Col. 1.15–20 is an early Christian hymn from which the letter's author is quoting.

2   Marianne Meye Thompson, *Colossians and Philemon* (Two Horizons New Testament Commentary; Grand Rapids, MI: Eerdmans, 2005), p. 28.

3   A powerful case for the existence of such a belief is made by Bauckham, *Jesus and the God of Israel*. Note the comment of R. McL. Wilson on this passage: 'Later debates . . . as to whether such passages refer to the pre-existent eternal Christ or to the Christ incarnate in Jesus only introduce confusion: the Christ of faith is both': *Colossians and Philemon* (ICC; London and New York: T&T Clark International, 2005), p. 134.

4   Caird, *Paul's Letters from Prison*, p. 179.

5   See Stephen I. Wright, 'The Phrase "Image of God" in the New Testament', in Jean Mayland (ed.), *Growing into God: Exploring our Call to Grow into God's Image and Likeness* (London: Churches Together in Britain and Ireland, 2003), pp. 31–44, here pp. 32–34, with literature cited there.

6   Cf. M. Thompson, *Colossians and Philemon*, 29. On the politically subversive nature of the claim in Gen. 1 that *all humanity* was created in God's image, not just kings or priests, see J. Richard Middleton, *The Liberating Image: The 'Imago Dei' in Genesis 1* (Grand Rapids, MI: Brazos Press, 2005), p. 231.

7   *Contra* James D. G. Dunn, *The Epistles to the Colossians and to Philemon: A Commentary on the Greek Text* (NIGTC; Grand Rapids, MI: Eerdmans; Carlisle, UK: Paternoster, 1996), p. 88, who does not think the author has Gen. 1.27–28 in mind here. Yet I argue that the associations with Genesis via the phrase 'image of God' remain important here, not least because of the theme of rulership in the preceding verses, and the way Paul returns to the phrase, with clear reference to humans, in Col. 3.10.

8   Cf. John W. Rogerson's argument that the *imago Dei* in the OT is seen as destiny rather than reality: 'Made in the Image and Likeness of God', in Mayland (ed.), *Growing into God*, pp. 25–30.

9   E.g. Wisd. 7.26; see Dunn, *Colossians and Philemon*, p. 88; Wilson, *Colossians and Philemon*, pp. 134–38.

10   Dunn, *Colossians and Philemon*, p. 88.

11   Cf. Dunn, *Colossians and Philemon*, pp. 87–88.

12   Dunn draws out the significance of this for the claim being made in Col. 1.15. 'The effect is the same: not to predicate the actual (pre)existence of either Torah or Christ prior to and in creation itself, but to affirm that Torah and Christ are to be understood as the climactic manifestations of the preexistent divine wisdom, by which the world was created': *Colossians and Philemon*, p. 89. Dunn's denial that Colossians speaks of a 'preexistent' Christ remains controversial, but much ambiguity inevitably attends any notion of 'preexistence', stretching as it does our normal human categories of time, language and being. Suffice it to say here that maybe those on different sides of this debate are closer than may sometimes appear. It is important also to affirm the validity of Dunn's project of outlining a 'christology in the making' from the NT evidence. It is surely a violation of the text and of historical sensibility to approach every passage that has been or might be taken to support a notion such as the 'preexistence' of Christ with the presupposition that it *has* to do so. Scriptural authority is not respected when later formulations of doctrine are automatically read back into Scripture.

13   In support of this view, see Caird, *Paul's Letters from Prison*, pp. 176–79. Hanson, on the other hand, argues that 'image' (*eikōn*) here refers to the pre-existent Christ: *Image*, p. 88.

14   Dunn thinks this background is 'less relevant' than that of Wisdom as 'firstborn' (Prov. 8.22, 25) (*Colossians and Philemon*, p. 90), but see my discussion above of Col. 1.12–14. N. T. Wright points out that in Rom. 8.29 'first-born' seems to have a clearly temporal sense ('. . . that he might be the first-born among many brethren'): *Colossians and Philemon* (TNTC; Leicester: Inter-Varsity Press; Grand Rapids, MI: Eerdmans, 1986), p. 71. But one might argue that even here the sense of authority dominates over the sense of temporality. In the Arian controversy, Arius took the temporality of 'firstborn' as placing Christ firmly *within* the creation, whereas Athanasius took the statement that 'all things were created in him' as affirming that Christ is *not* a 'creature': Athanasius, *Contra Arianos* 2.62; cited in M. Thompson, *Colossians and Philemon*, p. 32.

15   Caird is once more clear and convincing here: 'Wisdom is a personified attribute of God, but an attribute which God always intended to communicate to men (Prov. 8.4, 31; Ecclus. [Sir.] 24.8; Wisd. 7.27). In her most exalted guise, she never ceases to be a way of life. The ideal man, therefore, was bound to be one in whom Wisdom made her home, and whose life had thus become a perfect mirror *of the invisible God*; and this is precisely the justification which Paul offers in [Col. 1] v. 19 for the claims he has made for Christ' (*Paul's Letters from Prison*, pp. 177–88).

16   Though compare Irenaeus' famous image of the Word and Spirit as the 'hands of the Father' (e.g. *Adv. Haer.* IV.20.1); see discussion in M. Thompson, *Colossians and Philemon*, p. 31.

17   The difference is seen in the NRSV but not the NIV.

18   Caird, *Paul's Letters from Prison*, p. 172.

19   Caird, *Paul's Letters from Prison*, p. 178.

20   Dunn, *Colossians and Philemon*, p. 93.

21   Dunn, *Colossians and Philemon*, p. 94.

22   'Beginning' (*archē*) is also language used of Wisdom (Prov. 8.22 LXX), as well as echoing Gen. 1.1; a tight connection is thus here being drawn between creation and new creation in Christ (cf. Dunn, *Colossians and Philemon*, p. 97; Wilson, *Colossians and Philemon*, p. 148).

23   Cf. Caird, *Paul's Letters from Prison*, p. 180; Wilson, *Colossians and Philemon*, pp. 152–53.

24   Paul's truest heirs in subsequent centuries were therefore those who refused to countenance an artificial separation between two 'natures' of Christ.

25   N. T. Wright, *Colossians and Philemon*, p. 68.

26   N. T. Wright points out that the parallelism between the two halves of Col. 1.15–20, when analyzed as lines of a poem, itself makes the point that the Creator is also the Redeemer: 'He is the image of the invisible God, the firstborn of creation. . . . He is the beginning, the firstborn from the dead': 'Poetry and Theology in Colossians 1:15–20', in *The Climax of the Covenant: Christ and the Law in Pauline Theology* (Edinburgh: T&T Clark, 1992), pp. 99–119, here p. 107.

27   *Adv. Haer.* III.xviii; in Henry Bettenson (ed.), *Documents of the Christian Church* (1963), p. 30.

28   Cf. M. Thompson's comments on Irenaeus' strong affirmation of God's creation and incarnation: 'If the Son of God, the agent of God's creation of the world, took to himself human flesh, it follows that nothing created or material can be deemed evil by virtue of simply being material' (*Colossians and Philemon*, p. 167).

29   N. T. Wright points out how the passage has a double cutting edge: both against Judaism, which had identified Wisdom with Torah, and against the dualism and polytheism of paganism, for 'there is one creator/redeemer God', revealed in Christ: 'Poetry and

Theology', p. 118.

30 Handley C. G. Moule, *Colossian Studies* (London: Hodder, 1898), p. 15.

31 Moule, *Colossian Studies*, pp. 80-82.

32 Moule, *Colossian Studies*, p. 73.

33 Moule, *Colossian Studies*, pp. 74-75.

34 George Orwell, *Nineteen Eighty-Four* (Harmondsworth: Penguin Books, 1949), p. 16. I ran the risk here of distracting people with thoughts of the infamous 'Big Brother' TV programme and its relatives—no doubt a much more immediate association for most than Orwell's book.

35 David J. Schlafer, *Surviving the Sermon: A Guide to Preaching for Those Who Have to Listen* (Cambridge, MA: Cowley Publications, 1992), pp. 63–76.

36 Brian J. Walsh and Sylvia C. Keesmaat, *Colossians Remixed: Subverting the Empire* (Milton Keynes: Paternoster, 2005), p. 63.

37 See e.g. Jean Baudrillard, *Simulations* (trans. Paul Foss, Paul Patton and Philip Bleitchman; New York: Semiotext, 1983).

38 Schlafer, *Surviving the Sermon*, p. 67.

39 Cf. David J. Schlafer, *Playing with Fire: Preaching Work as Kindling Art* (Cambridge, MA: Cowley Publications, 2004), p. 148.

Chapter 10: Able to help: Hebrews 2:5–18

1 Heb. 13.8.

2 Craddock argues that Heb. 13.8 'echoes the affirmation of Christ's eternal sameness in chap. 1 (1.8, 10–12)': Fred B. Craddock, 'The Letter to the Hebrews', in Leander E. Keck (ed.), *NIB*, vol. XII (Nashville: Abingdon Press, 1998), p. 165.

3 Bauckham, *Jesus and the God of Israel*, pp. 243–44.

4 So we find Lane arguing that 'v 8 is not to be interpreted as an acclamation of Jesus' timeless ontological immutability, corresponding to the assertion that the Son remains ὁ αὐτὸς, 'the same', in 1:10–12. . . . The reference is rather to the immutability of the gospel message proclaimed by the deceased leaders in the recent past': William L. Lane, *Hebrews 9–13* (WBC 47B; Dallas: Word, 1991), p. 528.

5 Bauckham, *Jesus and the God of Israel*, pp. 252–53.

6 Bauckham, *Jesus and the God of Israel*; see, for example, Chs. 1 and 6.

7 Bauckham, *Jesus and the God of Israel*, p. 239.

8 Bauckham, *Jesus and the God of Israel*, p. 235.

9 'The Definition of Chalcedon, 451', in Bettenson (ed.), *Documents of the Christian Church* (1963), p. 51.

10 T. F. Torrance, *Incarnation: The Person and Life of Christ*, p. 186.

11 'If any one has put his trust in him as a man without a human mind, he is himself devoid of mind and unworthy of salvation. For what he has not assumed he has not healed; it is what is united to his Deity that is saved': Gregory of Nazianzus, Archbishop of Constantinople, 390/1, 'An Examination of Apollinarianism', in Bettenson (ed.), *Documents of the Christian Church* (1963), p. 45.

12 G. B. Caird, *New Testament Theology* (ed. L. D. Hurst; Oxford: Clarendon Press, 1994), p. 285.

13 C. J. H. Wright, *The Mission of God*, p. 425.

14 Heb. 2.8.

15 William L. Lane, *Hebrews 1–8* (WBC 47A; Dallas: Word, 1991), p. 48.

[16] Stevenson, *God in Our Nature*, Ch. 1; and Van Dyk, *The Desire of Divine Love*, Ch. 1.

[17] Reflections on Jesus' cry of dereliction can be found in 'The Crucified God: Mark 15:25–39', in P. K. Stevenson and S. I. Wright, *Preaching the Atonement*, Ch. 4.

[18] Hugh Montefiore, *A Commentary on the Epistle to the Hebrews* (London: A & C Black, 1964), p. 59.

[19] Lane, *Hebrews 1–8*, p. 43.

[20] This priestly understanding of atonement is explored in P. K. Stevenson and S. I. Wright, *Preaching the Atonement*, Ch. 10.

[21] This connection is highlighted in Steven R. Harmon, 'Hebrews 2:10–18', *Int* 59 (2005), pp. 404–6.

[22] Craddock, 'Hebrews', in *NIB*, vol. XII, p. 39.

[23] Montefiore, *Hebrews*, pp. 59–60: 'Since God had created man, it was fitting that God should take steps to enable man to reach the goal for which he had been created, for the route to this goal had become blocked by sin. The suffering of Christ was not fortuitous, but part of God's providence (cf. Mark viii. 31). It was appropriate that the action taken to help man should include suffering, since suffering is mankind's common lot. God's action is appropriate too at a profounder level. In as much as God is the Creator, he is the final and efficient cause of the universe, for whom and through whom all things exist. . . . The costly self-offering of a suffering Saviour is, in a mysterious way, congruous with the generosity of a self-effacing Creator. The very idea of creation suggests self-emptying, self-effacement, self-denial by him in whom lies all the fullness of infinite being'.

[24] Commentary on Heb. 2.17 in John Calvin, *The Epistle of Paul the Apostle to the Hebrews and the First and Second Epistles of St. Peter* (Grand Rapids, MI: Eerdmans, 1963), p. 33.

[25] *Who Do You Think You Are?* is the title of a popular British TV programme exploring the family histories of various celebrities. For further information see http://www.bbc .co.uk/whodoyouthinkyouare/.

[26] Caird, *New Testament Theology*, p. 285.

[27] Pope Benedict XVI, *Jesus of Nazareth*, p. 26.

[28] Ivor J. Davidson, 'Pondering the Sinlessness of Jesus Christ: Moral Christologies and the Witness of Scripture', *IJST* 10.4 (2008), pp. 385–86.

[29] Colin E. Gunton, *The Christian Faith: An Introduction to Christian Doctrine* (Oxford: Blackwell Publishing, 2002), pp. 105–6.

[30] Diane B. Stinton, *Jesus of Africa: Voices of Contemporary African Christology* (Maryknoll, NY: Orbis Books, 2004), pp. 146–52. See also J. Levison and P. Pope-Levison, 'The New Contextual Christologies: Liberation and Inculturation', in William A. Dyrness and Veli-Matti Kärkkäinen (eds.), *Global Dictionary of Theology* (Downers Grove, IL: InterVarsity Press; Nottingham: Inter-Varsity Press, 2008), p. 181: 'One of the more popular interpretations of Jesus in the African context, both in song and academic theology, is that of an elder brother. This portrait of Jesus flows out of certain kinship responsibilities of the elder brother: defending younger siblings in quarrels; mediating between younger siblings and parents in matters of importance such as marriage; even bearing responsibility for younger siblings' actions. These responsibilities resonate with those of Jesus, who also is defender and mediator. Further the elder brother is not unlike the high priestly figure in Hebrews 2:11, 17–18—a firstborn brother whose solidarity with his family leads [them] to salvation'.

[31] Tony Campolo, 'Preaching to the Culture of Narcissism', in Michael P. Knowles (ed.), *The Folly of Preaching: Models and Methods* (Grand Rapids, MI: Eerdmans, 2007),

p. 32.

[32] A stimulating attempt to combat this confusion can be found in N. T. Wright, *Surprised by Hope* (London: SPCK, 2007).

[33] Theos calls itself "The Public Theology Think Tank" and presents news at http://www .theosthinktank.co.uk/mainnav/theos-news.aspx. The "Headline findings" of this survey are given at http://campaigndirector.moodia.com/Client/Theos/Files/TheosDeath Pollheadlines.pdf.

[34] Brief reflections on the *Christus Victor* model of atonement can be found in P. K. Stevenson and S. I. Wright, *Preaching the Atonement*, Ch. 9.

[35] Richard Bauckham and Trevor Hart, *Hope Against Hope: Christian Eschatology in Contemporary Context* (London: Darton, Longman & Todd, 1999), pp. 201–10.

[36] N. T. Wright, *Surprised by Hope*, Ch. 13, 'Building for the Kingdom'.

[37] Thomas G. Long, *Hebrews* (IBC; Louisville, KY: John Knox Press, 1997), p. 3.

[38] Martin Luther, *Sermons on the Gospel of St John*, 7th sermon on John 1, in J. Pelikan (ed.), *Luther's Works*, vol. XXII (St. Louis: Concordia Publishing House, 1957), p. 113.

[39] Vinoth Ramachandra, *The Scandal of Jesus* (Downers Grove, IL: InterVarsity Press, 2001), 23, http://www.ivpress.com/title/exc/51-X.pdf; as adapted ('But the cross speaks' changed to 'The incarnation speaks') in H. Peskett and V. Ramachrandra, *The Message of Mission* (Leicester: Inter-Varsity Press, 2003), p. 86.

[40] Ewen MacAskill, *The Guardian*, 15 November 2008.

[41] Linda Slaughter, *The Guardian*, 15 November 2008.

[42] Long, *Hebrews*, p. 45

[43] Thomas G. Long, 'Preaching with Ordered Passion', *Leadership* 12.2 (1991), pp. 137–38: '[The] best preachers may never become known beyond their own congregations. If you were on a . . . church conference committee responsible for selecting a speaker a generation ago, you could come up with lots of names of nationally known preachers. You can't do that anymore. You'd be hard pressed to come up with more than a handful of nationally known preachers today. Some people think that's evidence of preaching's decline. I think it's evidence that good preaching is now much more local. It's being done by this preacher, standing in front of these people, whom he or she loves, speaking this text to their mission in this place on this day. That doesn't travel; it doesn't print. That's local and specific. And that's good preaching'.

[44] Kenton C. Anderson, *Choosing to Preach*, esp. Chs. 5–9.

Conclusion

[1] Robert Backhouse (ed.), *The Autobiography of C. H. Spurgeon: Compiled by His Wife and Private Secretary* (London: Hodder & Stoughton, 1993), p. 186.

Subject and Name Index

Adam Christology. *See* Christology
Anderson, Kenton C., 104, 185
anthropomorphic language, 3
anti-imperial rhetoric, 138
Arius, 28
Athanasian Creed, 204n6
atonement, 76–78
    Christus Victor, 176
    incarnation, connection with,
        111–112
    soteriology, connection with,
        171
Augustus, Emperor, 46

Barth, Karl, 57, 56, 57, 111, 112,
    133–134
Bartholomew, Craig, 28
Bauckham, Richard, 117–118,
    128, 130–131, 137–138,
    166, 176–177
Benedict XVI. *See* Pope Benedict
    XVI
birth narratives
    Luke's Gospel, 44–46
    Matthew's Gospel, 39–43
Bloom, Harold, 9
Boethius, 33, 36
Bonhoeffer, Dietrich, 82

Borg, Marcus, 46
Brooks, Phillips, 64
Brown, Raymond E., 92, 98–99
Browning, Elizabeth Barrett, 13
Buttrick, David, 103

Caird, George B., 59, 129, 150,
    215n15
Calvin, John, 92–93, 110, 172,
    209n16, 211n49
Campbell, John McLeod, 112–
    119, 169–170
Campolo, Tony, 175
Canterbury, Archbishop of. *See*
    Williams, Rowan
Carmody, John, 18
Celsus, refuted by Origen, 41
Chalcedon, Chaledonian
    Definition, 55–56
cheap grace, 82
Christ. *See* Jesus Christ. *See also*
    Christology
    assumes fallen humanity, 105–
        125, 173–174
Christmas, 37
Christology
    Adam Christology, 129–131,
        156–157

Christology (*continued*)
　African Christology, 80–81
　Christology of divine identity,
　　117–118, 137–138, 165–
　　167
　docetism, 55, 89, 168
　kenōsis, 132–136
　pioneer of salvation, 172, 181–
　　184
　wisdom Christology, 152–156
Cicero, 87
Coakley, Sarah, 136
Colwell, John E., xiii, 8, 127
Cotes, Mary, 37–38
Craddock, Fred, 18
Cranfield, C. E. B., 109, 110
Crashaw, Richard, 57, 206n11
Creation, doctrine of, 5
Crossan, Dominic, 46
Culpepper, Alan, 72, 75, 82

Davidson, Ivor, 173
Dawkins, Richard, 51, 53, 77–79,
　139
death
　defeat of, 175–177
　fear of, 175–177
docetism. *See* Christology
Donne, John, 57–58
Dunn, James D. G., 22, 57, 91,
　110, 117, 130, 153–154,
　166, 214n7, 214n12,
　215n14

fallen humanity, assumed by
　Christ, 105–125, 165–185,
　210n12
Florence, Anna Carter, 83–88
France, Richard T., 91–93

Fraser, Giles, 38
Fretheim, Terence, 4, 9, 17

genealogy, Matthew's Gospel,
　39–41
Gethsemane, 89–104
Green, Joel, 59–60, 97
Gregory of Nazianzus, 110–111,
　122, 210n10, 216n11
Gregory Thaumaturgus, 55,
　205n1
Gunton, Colin E., 134, 174

Hampson, Daphne, 135–136
Hanson, Anthony, 14, 56–57,
　201n25, 201n26
Hart, Trevor, 176–177
Hawthorne, Gerald F., 131, 133
Helwys, Thomas, 138–139
Hooker, Morna, 93, 130
Holy Spirit, xv–xvi, 44–45,
　114–120

image of God, 149–164, 168–
　169
Irenaeus, 64, 157
Irving, Edward, 112

Jensen, Richard A, 146
Jesus Christ
　ancestor, 81
　birth narratives, 37–48
　chief, 81
　circumcision of, 58
　consciousness, 79–80
　elder brother, 174–175,
　　217n30

humanity, 60–65, 91–93, 95–
102, 104, 106–112, 127,
165–185
identified with Yahweh, 137–
138, 149
image of God, 149–164
life-giver or healer, 81
Messiah, 18, 40–43, 45, 71,
74–75, 106, 108, 153–154,
156
name above all names, given to
Jesus, 137–138
prayer, 89–102
pre-existence, 117–118, 129–
131, 149–151, 200n6
presentation at the Temple,
58–60
prophet, 73–74
redeemer, 8, 215nn26, 29
Son of God, 90–91, 110
Son of Man, 75–78, 89
temptations, 173–174
virgin birth, 40, 48
virginal conception, 37, 39,
41–42, 44
Wisdom, 30
John of the Cross, 48–53

Kapic, Kelly, 115
kenōsis. See Christology
Kuyper, Abraham, 139

Lane, William, 216n4
Lewis, C. S., xiii, xviii, 76, 78,
199n2, 200n2, 207n10
Logos, 23, 32, 152, 202n5
Long, Thomas G., 14–19, 69,
178, 182, 184, 218n43
Lowry, Eugene, 128

Luther, Martin, 179
Lyotard, Jean-François, xvi

Marshall, I. Howard, 76,
Martin, Ralph P., 131
Mary, 61–63
messianic secret, 75
Migliore, Daniel L., 78, 80, 119
Montefiore, Hugh, W., 172,
217n23
Morgan, D. Densil, 90–91
Moses, 2–14, 17, 19
Moule, Handley, 158–159
Muslims, xiii, 21, 79

Newbigin, Lesslie, 138
Nicene Creed, xiv, 10
Nietzsche, Friedrich, 33, 35–36

Obama, Barack, 96, 181, 183,
184
Origen, 41

Pannenberg, Wolfhart, 204n7
Peterson, Brian, 135
Plato, xiii, 2
Pope Benedict XVI, 92, 173
preaching
definition, 86
'embodying the word', 35
episodic preaching, 103–104
as testimony, 87–88
moves, 103–104
New Homiletic, 123, 146–147
theological preaching, 123–125

Quicke, Michael J., 141–148

Rahner, Karl, 14, 218n1
Ramachandra, Vinoth, 180
Ramsey, Ian, 139
Ratzinger, Joseph. *See* Pope
    Benedict XVI,
recapitulation. *See* Christology:
    Adam Christology

Samuel, Calvin T., 120–125
Schlafer, David, 87, 163
Sermon
    Focus and Function, 69, 147
    inductive, 18–19
    integrating principle, 87m 163
    integrative sermon, 185
    moves, 103
    upsetting the equilibrium, 35
sinful flesh, assumed by Christ,
    105–125, 165–185, 210n12
Son of God, 1, 11, 44–45, 47, 63,
    79–80, 90–91, 94, 98, 100,
    102, 109–111, 133–134,
    137, 142, 157, 166–167,
    171–172, 179
Son of Man, 75–78, 80, 83–86,
    89, 102, 142
soteriology. *See* atonement
Spurgeon, Charles Haddon, 104,
    187
Stackhouse, Ian, 82
Stinton, Diane B., 81, 174–175

Tennent, Timothy C., 80–81
theological method
    a priori, 133
    a posteriori, 133–134
Thompson, James W., 123–125
Thompson, Marianne Meye, 149,
    215n28

Torrance, James B., 119
Torrance, Thomas F., 48, 110,
    112, 168
Trinity, 21, 22, 32, 78, 117,
    119–120
truth, 32–33

virgin birth, 42–43
virginal conception, 40–45
von Balthasar, Hans Urs, 140

Wainwright, Geoffrey, 111
Waruta, Douglas, 81
Wegener, Mark I., 128, 140
Weinandy, Thomas, 111, 115–
    116, 211nn29, 39
Wesley, Charles, 122, 129, 142
Williams, Rowan. Archbishop
    of Canterbury, xvii–xviii,
    48–53
Willimon, William, 31–36
Witherington, Ben, 108, 109,
    117
Wisdom, 21–36
Word of God, xvi, 36, 62, 147
    See also Logos
Wright, Christopher, J. H.,
    213n26
Wright, N. T., 57, 73–74, 76, 79,
    107, 117, 119–120, 157,
    215n26

Yahweh, 1–19
    name above all names, 137–138

Ziesler, John, 106

Scripture and Ancient Source Index

OLD TESTAMENT

Genesis

1	152, 214n6
1.1	215n22
1.2	42
1.26–27	153, 156, 157
1.26–28	149, 168, 169
1.27–28	152, 214n7
11.5	7
18.1–15	4
18.13	4
18.22–23	4
19.1	4
19.5	4
19.10–22	4
21.1–2	44
22.18	40

Exodus

2	3
2.10	3
2.11	3
2.13	3
2.15	3
2.22	3
2.23b–35	3
2.25	4
3	12, 17, 200n8
3.1	4
3.1–6	4–7
3.1–15	1–19, 11, 12, 13, 14, 157
3.2	4
3.4	5, 6
3.5	6, 9
3.7–10	7–8
3.10	7
3.11	8
3.11–15	8–10
3.11–4.17	8
3.12	8
3.13	9
3.15	9
4.14	8
4.22–23	62
10.21	206n21
13.2, 12	58
13.21	5
14.19	5
20.4–6	17
29.9	172

Leviticus

5.6–7, 11	108
12.1–8	58
12.8	59
16.32	172

Numbers
3.3   172
6.16   108

Deuteronomy 26
6.4   1
22.23–27   204n13

Judges
21.25   105

1 Samuel
2.1–10   47

1 Kings
10.1–9   61

2 Kings
2.16   42

1 Chronicles
29.11   142

Job   26
23.1–5, 8–9 183

Psalms
2   80
5.12   61
8   169
8.6–8   169
42–43   92
65.7   90
73   26
74   26
74.18–21   26
89.9   90
89.27   153
89.36   40
102   165, 166
102.25–27   166

107.28   90
107.29   90
111.10   5
115.3–8   3
147.15   23

Proverbs
1.7   24
1.20–33   202n6
3.3–4   61
4.5   28
7.6   35
8   xvii, 21–36, 23,
             29, 30, 31, 157
8.1–3   31
8.1–4, 20–31 203n16
8.1–11, 32–36 24
8.4   215n15
8.4–5   24
8.6–9   24
8.10–11   24
8.12   25
8.12–21   25–27, 30
8.12–31   30
8.13   25
8.14   25
8.15–16   25
8.17   25, 28
8.18   26
8.18–21   26
8.19   26
8.20–21   26
8.21   26
8.22   28, 203n8,
             215nn14, 22
8.22–31   22, 27–29,
             202n7
8.23   27
8.25   215n14
8.30   27, 29, 203n8
8.31   27, 30, 215n15

8.32–36	24
8.35	61
10–31	24

Isaiah
6.8	6
7.14	42, 206n18
8.14	60
10.17	206n21
40–55	28, 200n2, 213n26
40–66	27, 60
42.6	60
43.19	45
45.23	136, 137
49.6	60
51.4	206n21
55.11	23

Ezekiel
34.11–31	10
36.26	42
40–48	27
42.13	108

Daniel
3.25	5
7.9–14	76
7.13	75
7.13–14	76

Malachi
3.1–2	67, 207n30
3.1–5	69
3.2–5	207n31

APOCRYPHA

Wisdom of Solomon 152
7.26	214n9
7.27	215n15

Ecclesiasticus (Sirach)
24.8	215n15
40.1–5a	176
40.2	176

NEW TESTAMENT

Matthew
1	43
1.1	40
1.1–17	40
1.1–25	39–43
1.18	41, 45
1.20	41, 45
1.21	45
1.21–23	45
1.23	8
2	46
2.13–23	171
3.16	8
4.1	92
4.1–11	201n14
4.11	8
16.13–15	83
26.36–46	201n14
26.37	208n15
28.17	202n1
28.19	119
28.20	8

Mark
1.1	90
1.11	90
3.31–35	62

Mark (*continued*)

4	90
6.3	41
8.29	75
8.31	75, 217n23
9.7	90
10.45	8
14.27–31	101
14.32–36	96
14.32–42	89–104
14.33–35	208n12
14.34–36	97
14.36	90
14.37–38	101
14.38	94
14.41–42	102
15.25–39	217n17
15.34	170, 180
15.39	90

Luke

1	44, 58
1.26–2.21	44–46
1.31	58
1.32–35	47
1.38	6, 58
1.46–55	47
1.52	48
2.1–14	53
2.8–15	4
2.10	46
2.14	46, 53, 61
2.16	58
2.19	62
2.21	55, 58, 61
2.21–40	62
2.21–52	55–70
2.22–40	58–60, 65
2.28	55
2.32	62
2.35	60, 62

2.40	58, 60
2.41–50	62
2.41–52	60–63, 64
2.46–47	61
2.48	55
2.49	61
2.50	62
2.51	62
2.52	58, 60
4.18	14
4.24	207n3
5.8	6
5.21	72
6.17–49	73
6.20–21	26
7.49	72
8.19–21	61, 62
8.25	72
9.1–11	72
9.9	72
9.18	71, 72
9.18–27	71–88
9.19	73
9.20	71, 74
9.21–22	75
9.23	63, 82
9.23–26	82
9.51–19.40	63
10.38–42	61
12.4–7	61
12.22–34	61
19.41–44	73
22.15–20	8
22.28	63
23.32–43	162

John | 39, 47, 154

1	199n6, 218n38
1.4	30
1.1–5	30
1.1–14	29, 150

1.1–18	202n5	3.24	8
1.4	30	3.25	108
1.5	30	5	108
1.6–8	30	5.12–21	110, 157
1.9	30	5–8	105, 125
1.12–13	31	6.23	108
1.14	23, 30, 98, 109,	7	113, 122
	167, 179	7.6	106
3.21	31	7.12	107
4.24	13	8	106, 112, 117,
6.15	75		118, 119, 120
6.38	7	8.1	105, 106
8.41	41	8.1–11	105–25
8.58	142	8.2	107
8.59	142	8.3	108, 109, 110,
10.10	7		112, 113, 117,
10.7	10		121, 124
10.9	10	8.3–4	105, 125
10.11	10	8.14–17	118
10.14	10	8.29	215n14
10.20	10	9.8	43
10.34–36	200n2		
19.7	1	**1 Corinthians**	
20.19–23	4.24	15.57	170
20.28	202n1	15.42–50	157
20.31	31	15.45	114
Acts		**2 Corinthians**	
1.11	38	4.5	140
1.14	63	8.9	133
2.23–24	48		
2.33	48	**Galatians**	
3.13–16	48	5.14–18	114
3.15	206n23		
4.10–12	48	**Ephesians**	
5.30–31	48	1.23	133
5.31	206n23	4.10	133
Romans	94, 107	**Philippians**	128
1.3–4	47	2	117, 130, 139,
1.1–6	21		140, 213n26

Philippians (*continued*)
2.1–11	127–148
2.3–4	144
2.5–7	129
2.6	131, 132, 143
2.6–11	128, 129, 130, 133, 142, 201n22, 212n8
2.8	134
2.9	166
2.9–11	136, 137, 138
4.8	25

Colossians 150
1.3–12	151
1.11–20	162
1.12	151
1.12–14	151-2, 215n14
1.13	151, 155
1.14	155
1.15	149, 152–153, 163, 214n12
1.15–16	203n11
1.15–20	29, 149–164, 214n1, 215n26
1.16	154
1.16a	153
1.17–18	154
1.18	155
1.19	215n15
1.19–20	155
1.21–23	155–156
3.5–9	150
3.10	214n7

Titus
2.11–14	112

Hebrews 47, 154, 166, 173, 178, 185
1	167
1.1–3	178
1.4	166
1.10–12	166
2	173, 175, 182, 208n23
2.5–9	168–169
2.5–18	165
2.8	170, 216n14
2.9	169, 171
2.10	171, 172, 180, 206n23
2.10–18	171
2.11	217n30
2.13	173
2.14	179
2.14–15	176, 181
2.14–18	184
2.17	171, 172, 179, 217n24
2.17–18	217n30
2.18	183
4.14–16	102
4.15	173
5.7–9	209n24
5.7–10	173
5.8	62
5.8–9	6
7.26	171
9.12	171
9.14	174
9.26	171
9.28	171
10.5–10	6
10.10	171
12.2	206n23
12.4	176
13.8	165–166, 216nn1, 2

James
1.1–3   116
1.17   205n20

1 John
3.16   133

GRECO-ROMAN LITERATURE

Cicero
Orator
XX.70   208n30

EARLY CHRISTIAN LITERATURE

Ambrose
De Fide
I.13   93, 201n23

Athanasius
Contra Arianos
2.62   215n14

Eusebius
Praep. Ev.
XI 9ff.   201n23

Gregory Nazianzus
Ep.
ci   110, 122, 168,
               210nn10, 15;
               216n11

Gregory Thaumaturgus
Twelve Topics on the Faith
Topic XII   205n1

Irenaeus
Adv. Haer.
II.22.4   64, 206n24
III.6   201n23
III.18   157, 215n27
IV.10   201n23
IV.20.1   215n16
V.16.2   206n14

Justin
Trypho, 59–60   201n23